Transnational TV Crime

Transnational TV Crime

From Scandinavia to the Outback

Sue Turnbull and Marion McCutcheon

EDINBURGH
University Press

Edinburgh University Press is one of the leading university presses in the UK. We publish academic books and journals in our selected subject areas across the humanities and social sciences, combining cutting-edge scholarship with high editorial and production values to produce academic works of lasting importance. For more information visit our website: edinburghuniversitypress.com

© Sue Turnbull and Marion McCutcheon, 2024

Grateful acknowledgement is made to the sources listed in the List of Illustrations for permission to reproduce material previously published elsewhere. Every effort has been made to trace the copyright holders, but if any have been inadvertently overlooked, the publisher will be pleased to make the necessary arrangements at the first opportunity.

Edinburgh University Press Ltd
13 Infirmary Street
Edinburgh EH1 1LT

Typeset in 12/14pt Arno Pro by
Cheshire Typesetting Ltd, Cuddington, Cheshire, and
printed and bound in Great Britain

A CIP record for this book is available from the British Library

ISBN 978 1 4744 9681 0 (hardback)
ISBN 978 1 4744 9683 4 (webready PDF)
ISBN 978 1 4744 9684 1 (epub)

The right of Sue Turnbull and Marion McCutcheon to be identified as the authors of this work has been asserted in accordance with the Copyright, Designs and Patents Act 1988, and the Copyright and Related Rights Regulations 2003 (SI No. 2498).

Contents

List of Illustrations		vi
Acknowledgements		viii
Chapter 1	Transnational TV Crime	1
Chapter 2	The Total Value Proposition	21
Chapter 3	Valuing Miss Fisher	48
Chapter 4	*The Kettering Incident*	75
Chapter 5	*Secret City*	96
Chapter 6	*Mystery Road*	117
Chapter 7	Valuing the TV Crime Drama	141
Notes		154
Bibliography		156
Index		175

Illustrations

Figures

1.1	Proportional budget breakdown of a mid-size Australian drama series. Source: Olsberg.SPI (2023)	14
1.2	Number of Australian titles on streaming services, 2017–2021. Source: Ampere Analysis – SVOD Analytics dataset, published in Bureau of Communications Arts and Regional Research (2022)	19
1.3	Number of Australian shows on foreign streaming services, Top 10 countries, 2021. Source: Ampere Analysis – SVOD Analytics dataset, published in Bureau of Communications Arts and Regional Research (2022)	20
2.1	Total Economic Value of Culture. Source: Allan et al. (2013, p. 13)	28
2.2	The independent film production value chain. Source: Bloore (2009, p. 8)	35
2.3	The television global value chain. Source: Chalaby (2019)	36
2.4	The total value of a television crime drama	37
3.1	Audience demand multiplier for *Miss Fisher's Murder Mysteries*. Source: Parrot Analytics (2021)	74
4.1	Audience demand multiplier for *The Kettering Incident*. Source: Parrot Analytics (2021)	95
5.1	Audience demand multiplier for *Secret City*. Source: Parrot Analytics (2021)	116
6.1	Audience demand multiplier for *Mystery Road*. Source: Parrot Analytics (2021)	140

Tables

3.1	*Miss Fisher's Murder Mysteries* (2012–2015)	73
4.1	*The Kettering Incident* (2016)	94
5.1	*Secret City* (2016–2019)	115
6.1	Overview of *Mystery Road* series	137
6.2	*Mystery Road* (2018–)	137

Acknowledgements

There many people to thank who have helped this little book along its way, not least the Australian Research Council, who initially awarded a Discovery Grant for the project *Border Crossings: The Transnational Career of the Television Crime Drama* (DP160102510), which helped launch this investigation. Subsequent contact with the research team engaged in the project *What Makes Danish TV Travel* funded by the Danish Council for Independent Research proved invaluable. In particular we'd like to thank project leader Anne Marit Waade, Pia Majbritt Jensen, Kim Toft Hansen and Ushma Chauhan Jacobsen for exciting scholarly collaborations and much valued friendship. Thanks also to Robert Saunders for opening up the geo-political dimensions of transnational TV crime. In Australia, we'd like to thank Fiona Eagger and Deb Cox from Every Cloud Productions for so generously sharing their *Miss Fisher* archive with us; as well as our interviewees at Foxtel including Ross Crowley, Tony Pollitt and Penny Win. Alex Sangston and Alex McPhail from Screen Tasmania provided valuable insights into the production environment in that state, while Penny Chapman of Matchbox Pictures shared her illuminating thoughts on production development and Canberra as a setting for crime. Special thanks also to Anousha Arkesh for her vivid account of the casting process and introductions. The authors would like to thank Guesswork, Amazon and Kates McCartney, McLennan and Box for their permission to use a production still from *Deadloch* by photographer Sarah Enticknap as a cover image. We'd also like to thank the patient production team at Edinburgh University Press as we navigated the trials of meeting deadlines in unfortunate and unforeseen circumstances. Last but by no means least, there are our beloved families, who have tolerated our crime watching as well as our frequent disappearances on research trips for days at a time. Thank you team Thompson.

Thank you team Lahtinen. And thank you to the dearly missed Maureen, whose voice and values echo in these pages.

Chapter 1

Transnational TV Crime

As anyone watching television over the last twenty years might agree, what you can watch and how has changed dramatically since the turn of the millennium. Largely as an effect of digitisation, the increasing availability of video on demand (VOD) and streaming platforms such as Netflix, Amazon, and Disney+, people across the globe can now watch – if they can afford the subscription fees and have a reasonable internet service – a much more extensive range of content than ever before on a variety of devices. As a media technology, television has evolved from a broadcast mass medium consumed primarily in the home to an internet-connected experience that can be watched on a smartphone (Johnson, 2019, p. 2). However, while the technology itself may have evolved, what people are watching in terms of the types of content available has remained relatively stable. Television, however it might be defined, is still a site for the consumption of news, sport and entertainment, even though content may come from a much wider range of sources.

For example, in 2020, the Australian Communication and Media Authority reported that 77 per cent of all television households subscribed to a pay-per-view service (ACMA, 2020). Inevitably, increased access to streaming services facilitates access to more content from places other than Australia, a development that points not only to changes in what people can watch, but also to some significant changes in global production strategies, particularly as they apply to specific genres such as the television crime drama. No longer are crime series being produced that speak only to their national audiences, although American and British shows have long travelled beyond their original shores (Weissmann, 2012). In the new global market for content, crime drama series are now more likely to be produced in different locations through international co-production deals that not only enable the creators to meet the increasing costs of production, but that also guarantee a much bigger audience in other territories through distribution deals (Steemers, 2004, p. 9).

A turning point for the crime drama, as one of the most popular and enduring genres of television, was the year 2000, when the newly launched American series *Crime Scenes Investigations*, better known as *CSI* (2000–2015), was claimed to be the 'most watched television drama series in the world' (Andreeva, 2016). Produced for American television network CBS, the original *CSI* set in Las Vegas spawned three spin-off series (*CSI: Miami* in 2002 and *CSI: NY* in 2004, not forgetting the short-lived *CSI: Cyber* in 2015), becoming something of a global phenomenon in the process, with much attention being devoted to the ways in which it slickly represented the game-changing significance of forensic evidence (Allen, 2007; Turnbull, 2007). While the success of *CSI* might appear to encapsulate the on-going domination of the global television industry by popular American series at the time, the industry was about to undergo a dramatic transformation over the following twenty years, with the dominance of American, and the ever-popular British crime dramas, being increasingly challenged by new players from what Cunningham and Jacka (1996, p. 7) identified as 'the peripheries' of the global TV market. As Jeanette Steemers has demonstrated, this challenge was also being pushed by transnational media corporations eager for the removal of the trade barriers and legislative constraints that might hinder their global ambitions (Steemers, 2004, p. 8). As evidence of this globalising ambition, in April 2023, the streaming service Amazon Prime Video launched the six-part spy thriller series *Citadel*. With a budget of US$300 million, and projected spin-off series to be made in Italy, India, Spain and Mexico, *Citadel* nevertheless failed to excite the critics despite its record-breaking budget (Petski, 2020). As the website *Rotten Tomatoes* (2023) concluded, '*Citadel* spares no expense but still feels underdeveloped, yielding a fairly fun spy caper that nonetheless creaks under the weight of its own exorbitance'. When it comes to the television crime drama series, big isn't necessarily better.

A significant feature of the story we will tell here about the evolution of the TV crime drama has to do with what McCulloch and Proctor (2023) characterise as the 'Scandinavian Invasion' that arguably began with the global success of the Danish series *Forbrydelsen/The Killing* (DR 2007–2012). Produced for the Danish public service broadcaster DR, in a co-production with Germany's second public service broadcaster Zweites Deutsches Fernsehen (ZDF), *The Killing* was in the vanguard of a wave of productions from Scandinavia and Northern Europe that would impact TV production and markets across the world. While the American, somewhat predictable response (Turnbull, 2015) was to remake *The Killing* and subsequently the Danish/Swedish co-production *Bron/Boren/The Bridge* (SVT & DR 2011–2018) in the belief that American audiences would not, or could not, read subtitles and had no taste for crime dramas from somewhere else, this proved not to be the case. American niche audiences, alongside niche audiences for innovative crime drama across the globe, were to embrace these Scandinavian series in ways that would have a significant impact on the development of the genre (McCulloch & Proctor, 2023).

In Australia, *The Killing* first appeared in 2010 on Australia's second public service broadcaster, the Special Broadcasting Service (SBS), with its remit to 'provide multilingual and multicultural radio and television services that inform, educate and entertain all Australians' (Ang et al., 2008, p. xiii). SBS had been showing earlier crime series from Denmark including *Rejseholdet/Unit 1* (DR 2000–2004) and *Ørnen/The Eagle* (DR 2004–2006) prior to the arrival of *The Killing*, with audiences increasing as both *The Killing* and *The Bridge* attracted international attention (Jensen & McCutcheon, 2020). While the SBS audience was initially quite small, following the success of *The Killing* on British television's Channel 4, the international buzz about these shows became impossible to ignore, although as Jensen and Jacobsen (2020) have pointed out, while these series may have enjoyed big audiences in Scandinavia, they tended to appeal to a niche cosmopolitan audience when shown in other countries. In Australia, this niche audience would appear to have encompassed a range of programmers, television producers and other creatives within the screen industry, given the number of times these series were mentioned in the press and in the interviews we conducted for this book. One of the more significant effects of this Scandinavian invasion was the ways in which subsequent Australian television crime dramas sought to emulate the tropes, aesthetics and global success even when the setting might be the Australian outback, as we shall argue here.

This book therefore takes up a story about the evolution of the TV crime drama that was initiated in an earlier monograph, *The TV Crime Drama* (Turnbull, 2014), with renewed focus on how Australia, as a relatively small player in the global television market, responded to the challenge of producing television crime dramas that would appeal to a global audience while retaining their Australianness. Australian television producers, like their counterparts in film, have routinely faced the dilemma of making content that speaks directly to a relatively small national audience with limited potential for a financial return and/or producing content that will sell overseas. The 'and/or' here is significant, since the ultimate goal would be to achieve both. It might be noted that Australia's 'first' multi-reel feature length film, *The Story of the Kelly Gang* (1906), often claimed to be the first feature film ever produced, was shown in New Zealand and in England only one year after it was made (National Museum of Australia, 2023).

While Australian soap operas such as *Neighbours* (Seven Network & Network Ten 1985–) and *Home and Away* (Seven Network 1988–) enjoyed international success in the 80s and 90s, to the extent that concerns were raised about the possibility that they were 'dulling the senses' of British school children (Cunningham & Jacka, 1996, p. 139), there have been relatively few Australian crime dramas that have enjoyed such international success. Australia's first ever crime drama, the long-running police procedural *Homicide* (Seven Network 1964–1977), while much appreciated by Australian audiences who warmed to the local accents and the Melbourne landscapes, was never destined to travel. Created by Crawford Productions for the commercial Seven Network, *Homicide* was a curious amalgam of British and American police procedural tropes that exemplified how Australian television has always, in the words of the late Australian scholar Tom O'Regan, faced 'two ways' (O'Regan, 1993). As Cunningham and Jacka (1996, p. 54) observed in their ground-breaking study of Australia's transnational trade in television, while Australia had neither the deep commitment to a public service ethos of the UK nor the universalist appeal and talent pool of the US commercial television industry, what it did have was the ability to recombine the best of both systems in the development of its own product.

One example of this recombinative skill is the controversial soap opera *Prisoner* a.k.a *Prisoner: Cell Block H* (Network Ten 1979–1986), which might be loosely described as a crime drama. The series was created by Reg Watson, an Australian who had enjoyed a successful television career in the UK, where he created the long running soap opera, *Crossroads* (ITV 1964–2003), and who would later go on to create *Neighbours*. After first appearing on the KTLA channel in Los Angeles, *Prisoner: Cell Block H* found a niche American audience in the 1980s and has since become a cult classic (O'Meara et al., 2022). While the global success of Australian soap operas during the 1980s is now legendary, during the 1990s a number of Australian crime dramas did enjoy success overseas, including *Bony* (Seven Network 1992), which was sold to ZDF in Germany (Cunningham & Jacka, 1996, p. 157). Based on the Indigenous detective Napoleon Bonaparte created by Arthur Upfield in his crime novels, Bony was reimagined as a white man brought up by an Aboriginal family and, as in the first television adaptation (*Boney*, ATV7 1971–1972), once again played by a non-Indigenous actor, a controversial casting choice even at the time. Other overseas success stories include the telemovie series *Halifax fp* (Nine Network 1994–2002), featuring a forensic psychiatrist, which was sold into more than 100 countries (Fidgeon, 2001), and the police procedural *Water Rats* (Nine Network 1996–2001), with its touristic gaze firmly on Sydney Harbour, which was apparently shown in Asia, Europe and parts of the Middle East (TV Tropes, 2022).

Our story, however, begins in the new millennium and is set against the backdrop of a rather different television landscape, one dominated not by the old mix of public service broadcasters and commercial networks, but by the advent of the streaming services. For example, while Australia's most recent foray into the period crime drama, *Miss Fisher's Murder Mysteries* (ABC 2012–2015), first appeared on the public service network the Australian Broadcasting Corporation, it has gone on to enjoy global success on a number of different platforms including a Chinese franchise deal with Netflix. Although *Miss Fisher* might be seen to sit comfortably within a tradition of British period crime drama that has been popular the world over, since she first appeared in 2012, new forces have come to play in the development of the Australian crime drama, in particular the impact of Nordic Noir.

While Nordic Noir may be a somewhat problematic term (Hansen & Waade, 2017, p. 4), it has been associated with a raft of television crime dramas such as *Forbrydelsen/The Killing* and the Danish/Swedish co-production *Bron/Broen/The Bridge* as well as the political drama *Borgen* and the genre-bending Swedish series *Jordskott* (SVT & DR 2015–2017), all of which have had a significant impact on the subsequent development of Australian TV crime drama. As we shall argue, this influence can be seen in Australian series as diverse as the eco-sci-fi mystery *The Kettering Incident* (Showcase 2016), the political thriller *Secret City* (Showcase & Netflix 2016–19) and the 'outback noir' *Mystery Road* (ABC 2018–), all of which demonstrate how Australian producers have sought to incorporate some of the features associated with Nordic Noir in the development of crime dramas intended to have local, national and international relevance and appeal. Our study concludes with the timely appearance of the Nordic Noir spoof, *Deadloch* (Amazon Prime Video 2023–), set in Tasmania, which is so uncompromising in its portrayal of the Australian vernacular that at the time of writing we are waiting with bated breath to see how it will fare overseas.

In tracing the inspiration for these Australian crime dramas and their subsequent national and international careers, we found ourselves continually asking questions about the value they might have for everyone involved in their production as well as their reception both nationally and internationally, and to the Australian screen industry in general. While there have been a number of reports that have attempted to measure cultural value, including one commissioned by the government-funded body Screen Australia in 2016 entitled *Measuring the Cultural Value of Australia's Screen Sector*, it was our perception that such approaches continued to miss the big picture. In order to grasp the complexity of what is at stake, in Chapter 2 we tease out the concept of the 'total value' of a television crime drama that underpins our analysis before applying this to a series of case studies. Our approach here is therefore informed by critical industry and policy studies while our concept of total value draws on ideas from philosophy, sociology and economics. It is this approach that we will employ to perform a meta review of recent screen production research and policy papers before applying these to the crime dramas under consideration. But first we will set the scene by describing the context in which this discussion is taking place: a context that includes a battered car on a dusty road travelling through an anonymous desert, which is in fact outback Australia about 400 kilometres North of Adelaide. So begins the television crime drama *The Tourist* (BBC One, Stan, HBO Max & ZDF 2022), which appeared on the Australian streaming service Stan in 2022.

Gone Missing

At the wheel of the car is a man who, as the prepublicity has already informed us, is played by the instantly recognisable Jamie Dornan, an Irish actor whose international reputation had already been established in another controversial crime drama series, *The Fall* (BBC Two & RTÉ1 2013–2016). There, Dornan played a menacing serial killer, before going on to his memorable turn as Grey in the film adaptation of the controversial erotic romance *Fifty Shades of Grey* (2015) and its two sequels. The choice of Dornan for this 'Australian' thriller thus immediately signals the show's off-kilter appeal and international ambition. This is hardly surprising given that the companies backing the project include the BBC, HBO Max and the German public broadcaster ZDF. Clearly *The Tourist* was a television show intended to travel internationally and to sit alongside what television critic Michael Idato described as the 'blue chip' productions that characterise the high end of television drama production in the new millennium (Idato, 2016).

In terms of its 'blue chip' status, the amount of money required to get this series onto the screen is immediately apparent in the first eight-minute pre-title sequence as a huge semi-trailer bears down on the man's little car to engage in a car chase that is never going to end well. Echoing Steven Spielberg's remarkable debut film *Duel* (1971), what we witness is a breathless cat and mouse chase that in reality took over eight days, seven clapped-out cars and five locations to shoot (Aird, 2022). It ends with the man upside down in his broken vehicle, with a serious head injury and no memory of who or where he is. This befuddlement is somewhat justified given the driver of the truck is played by Icelandic actor Ólafur Darri Ólafsson, star of the Icelandic crime drama *Ófærð/Trapped* (RÚV 2015–). Just to confuse the issue Ólafsson is sporting cowboy boots, a Stetson and a convincing American accent, which recalls his cameo appearance in the first season of HBO's *True Detective* (2014–19), in which he played a paedophile. While the hospital in which our man in the car subsequently wakes up might be located in outback Australia, there are once again very few markers of Australianness to be found, except for the accents of the bit players and the presence of some well-known Australian acting talent, including Alex Dimitriades (speaking Greek), Damon Herriman and Geneviève Lemon. This could be a remote desert location almost anywhere. Even the flies, those persistent predators of the Australian bush, were apparently screen-shot out of the final cut (Aird, 2022).

With its focus on a man's existential struggle to figure out who he is, and why he is where he is, enacted against a backdrop of international crime in which he is somehow involved, *The Tourist* could be a metonym for the ambiguous state of the Australian television industry in the new millennium as it struggles to survive the transition from producing drama for a national broadcast audience to producing drama with international appeal. As Amanda Lotz and Anna Potter argued in 2021, it would seem that 'the harsh truth is that most Australian television is not particularly

Australian' (Lotz & Potter, 2022, p. 684). In their opinion, policy frameworks since the early 1990s have set the bar too low for Australian scripted television, with a drama deemed 'Australian' if it employs sufficient numbers of Australians in creative roles. As a result, the cultural objectives of representing Australian identity, character and cultural diversity have simply been sacrificed to what Chalaby (2016) describes as the multinational logics of the global television economy. This is hardly a new phenomenon in Australia, where cultural debates about the need to ensure the Australianness of what appears on Australian screens are as 'old as cinema itself' (Cunningham & Jacka, 1996, p. 63).

In terms of the operations of the global television economy, the international orientation of *The Tourist* is hardly surprising. While it might appear on first glance to be Australian, it was written by Harry and Jack Williams, who launched their London-based production company Two Brothers in 2014. Prior credits include the award-winning British comedy series *Fleabag* (BBC Three & BBC One 2016–19) and the Netherlands-based crime drama *Baptiste* (BBC One 2019–21). According to Two Brothers head of drama Chris Aird (2022), they chose Australia as a location for *The Tourist* because they wanted to shoot in a 'unique environment'. As it happened, this choice of location was judicious, enabling them not only to beat the safety measures instated in response to the COVID-19 pandemic in 2020 since South Australia was still COVID-free, but also to secure funding from the South Australian Film Corporation eager to bring work and opportunities to the region. And then there was the contribution of the Australian streaming service Stan, equally keen for high-end content with an Australian look and feel. Indeed, as many commentators have noted, the Australian government and screen industry have become increasingly interested in attracting 'footloose' high-end film and television production to the region, even extending the taxation offsets available to international productions to shore up the industry against a COVID-driven downturn (Ausfilm, 2020).

As Network Ten's Head of Drama Rick Maier suggested in an interview with C21 (Maier, 2021), this confluence of factors produced something of a bottleneck in 2021, with local productions finding it hard to find a crew since they had already been snaffled by the international players. There was, it would appear, just too much work available. Maier, however, was inclined to put a positive spin on this challenge by suggesting that this production boom should be seen as an opportunity to create new training platforms for Australian creatives that would outlast the current surge in overseas productions and provide a firm basis for the future health of the industry. In other words, Maier was keen to signal the potential value of the increase in overseas productions in Australia, not so much in cultural terms as in the industrial and economic value that they might have. Such an argument is very familiar in Australia and has been well rehearsed over the years in relation to Australian film (Dermody & Jacka, 1988) as well as television (Cunningham & Jacka, 1996, p. 3).

Policy Matters

While Maier's point is well taken, the cultural value argument was once again brought to the fore in January 2023, when the new Labor government in Australia released its cultural policy statement, *Revive*, with the significant sub-title *A Place for Every Story, a Story for Every Place*. Inspired by the arts initiatives of former Labor prime ministers Gough Whitlam in the 1970s and Paul Keating in the 1990s, with a nod towards the Labor government's tax incentives in 2007, the Albanese Labor government's vision for Australia's cultural life included commitments of direct relevance to the future of the screen industry. The first of these reaffirmed the economic incentives that made choosing Australia as a location for *The Tourist* an attractive proposition by promising to 'Continue support for investment in large-scale screen productions in Australia through film tax offsets and location-based production incentives' (Commonwealth of Australia, 2023, p. 108). This was delivered in Labor's 2023 budget through an increase to the incentives available to international drama productions to match those for Australian drama series (Australian Government, 2023).

The second, and potentially more significant commitment, suggested that there would be ongoing government intervention to ensure the presence of Australian content on the streaming platforms. This policy stated that the government intended to:

> Introduce requirements for Australian screen content on streaming platforms to ensure continued access to local stories and content in the third quarter of 2023 and to commence no later than 1 July 2024, with the Minister for the Arts and the Minister for Communication to undertake further consultation with industry in the first half of 2023 on the details of actions to be taken and implementation as part of the Commonwealth broader reforms to media legislation (Commonwealth of Australia, 2023, p. 105).

Moving on this commitment, at the time of writing the Australian government had canvassed two local content quotas for streamers. These included levies of 10 per cent of their revenue, which in 2021–22 totalled approximately $1.7 billion, and a minimum expenditure guarantee (similar to the subscription television model) with the proportion of drama spend to be directed to Australian content pegged to the number of subscribers. With regulation to be in place by mid-2024, the operating environment for streaming services delivering Australian drama may be about to change significantly (Quinn, 2023a).

The imperative to regulate local content on streaming services is growing as the business model for traditional television broadcasters crumbles. With Australian audiences increasingly turning to streaming services to watch drama series and feature films and away from the traditional television platforms that are still regulated to provide local content, a shrinking audience share provides commercial broadcasters with a diminishing incentive to invest in drama. With drama hours on commercial television services halving from 1999 to 2019, it is little wonder that Australian audiences now prefer to get their drama from the deep catalogues of the streaming services (Lotz & McCutcheon, 2023a; Lotz et al., 2021).

Australia's efforts to shore up the future of its screen stories thus follows that of other nations in negotiating with the streamers to establish local content quotas. For example, the European Union currently has a catalogue quota of 30 per cent for European works on international streaming platforms, although not all countries have managed to achieve this. In Denmark, somewhat ironically given the global popularity of its crime dramas, negotiations in 2022 led to Netflix, Viaplay, TV2, HBO Max, Disney+ and Amazon Prime Video stopping orders for local Danish content, with streamers objecting to high costs and Create Denmark seeking ground on the terms around creative rights (Eklund, 2022; Goldbart, 2022).

Underpinning the debate about the need to ensure that Australian content is available on the streaming platforms is the tenuous but persistent argument about the need to preserve the Australianness of Australian drama, a case forcefully made by screen journalist Sandy George in her essay, 'Nobody Talks about Australianness on our Screens' (2022b). Directed primarily at the government-funded body, Screen Australia, George argued that 'only when drama is recognisably Australian, that is, when it has on-screen Australianness, is there any chance of it deeply connecting with Australians'. In her attempt to define a notion of Australianness George went on:

'Australianness' might reflect a sense of place. If creatures as peculiar as kangaroos are in our lives why not flaunt them (though be prepared for some eyerolling). ... There are so many things that on-screen 'Australianness' can be – one size does not fit all and ideally there is enough homegrown drama to cater for every taste and sensibility – but it has an underlying unity of soul, and above all, is *recognisable* (George, 2022b, p. 8).

While George's intention may be admirable, there have always been significant challenges in defining a notion of 'on-screen' Australianness. As the first respondent to George's subsequent article in *IF Magazine* sensibly pointed out:

Australianness means different things to each and every Australian you speak to, and each generation has a very different view of what it is. How do you pin down a definition for Australianness? Is it because we live here? Where we live? The Indigenous custodians? The commonwealth descendants? The migrants? The refugees? (Fromez response to George, 2022a).

As revealed by a recent Screen Australia report on diversity, while 53 per cent of the Australian population identify as being of Anglo-Celtic origin, 25 per cent are of Asian heritage (Screen Australia, 2023). Australia's most recent census figures reveal that 29.1 per cent of the Australian population in 2021 were born overseas and while the majority of migrants still hail from the UK (3.8 per cent), immigration from India (2.8 per cent) and China (2.3 per cent) are evidently on the rise (Australian Bureau of Statistics, 2022). These statistics beg the question, just what kind of Australianness matters to the culturally diverse Australian population? Perhaps it doesn't matter equally for everyone – in a 2022 survey, Lotz and McCutcheon (2023b) found that for 62 per cent of Australians, a story being set in Australia is not at all important. So, if an Australian backdrop isn't essential for all Australian viewers, what does this diverse audience actually want to watch?

As Stephen Harrington and Oliver Eklund point out, echoing the familiar mantra about film, debates about the need to ensure that there is Australian content on Australian screens are as old as television itself in this country (Harrington & Eklund, 2024, p. 207). Indeed, even before television arrived in Australia, there was concern about the possible effect of imported programming on a nation under construction as well as a debate about whether Australia should follow the American commercial network system or the British public service model. The compromise solution was to do both, with ABC television commencing broadcasting in 1956 alongside two commercial networks (subsequently the Seven Network and Network Nine). While all of these networks included local news, current affairs and drama, they also included a great deal of imported and therefore cheaper content in order to fill up their schedules. While the ABC tended (and still does to this day) to re-broadcast many British shows, the commercial channels were more inclined to import American programming.

In 1970, a third commercial network (Network Ten) was introduced despite arguments that the Australian television market might not be able to support it, and in 1980 a second public service network launched – the Special Broadcasting Commission (SBS) – with a specific remit to reflect the multicultural composition of the Australian population (O'Regan, 1993, p. 121). The introduction of the latter was not without controversy in that it was also seen to undermine the mission to promote a unified Australian national identity (Ang et al., 2008). As Tom O'Regan observed, cultural and broadcasting policy in Australia was always endeavouring to maximise the Australian component of television in order to give television's common culture 'a national cultural shape' (O'Regan, 1993, p. 81). While this included measures such as quotas for the commercial channels to ensure that the production of local drama would be ensured, as O'Regan observes, this might not have been what people actually wanted to watch. For example, British migrants in the 1990s might prefer the soap opera *Eastenders* over *Neighbours*, Italian migrants might prefer watching Italian movies on SBS, and Asian migrants preferred Hong Kong films on video (O'Regan, 1993, p. 82).

The current argument about the need to return to a notion of 'on screen Australianness' is, as Mark Ryan suggests, a 'recycling and a return to anachronistic arguments about the representation of national identity that raged during the 1980s in the screen industry and in academia' (Ryan, 2014, p. 170). Furthermore, the acquisition of nationalistic cultural value inevitably depends on whether or not people actually watch or seek out Australian content. This is a moot point in terms of Australian film production, as box office figures continue to demonstrate. In the period 2019–2021, Australian films counted for only 6.9 per cent of the total box office share, with American films still dominating the market with a 69.9 per cent share (Screen Australia, 2023a). This would suggest that Australians are not preferring Australian content at the cinema, begging the question, what does this mean for Australian television drama?

Despite the poor showing of Australian films at the box office, a recent Olsberg.SPI report (2023) seeking to evaluate the impact of film and television production incentives in Australia estimated that across all states and territories these measures had attracted productions that contributed a staggering total of A$16.5 billion to the economy over four years as reported in the financial year 2021–2022. While this success was attributed to the 'increasingly footloose nature of global production' attracting such large international productions as *Thor: Love and Thunder* (2022), *Godzilla vs Kong* (2021), *Nautilus* (Disney+ unreleased) and *Shantaram* (Apple TV+ 2022), it was noted that both local and international streamers were also expanding their production slates in Australia (Olsberg. SPI, 2023, p. 15). In 2021–2022, there were apparently twenty-nine productions underway for subscription TV and SVOD services, a 222 per cent increase on the previous year (ibid). This upsurge is then attributed to what the report describes as a 'boom in film and television production' with a record expenditure on Australian titles alone of $A1.5 billion (ibid).

What enabled this boom, the report went on to suggest, is the Producer Offset incentive, a tax rebate first introduced in 2007 as part of the then Labor government's strategy to boost the screen sector in Australia. In order to qualify for the Producer Offset, a film or television production has to meet the Significant Australian Content (SAC) test as administered by Screen Australia. According to Screen Australia's guidelines for applicants, to meet the SAC test, Australians need to be key contributors, 'responsible for the project's core origination' and that there is a need for 'significant involvement by Australians in the creative development of the project' (Screen Australia, 2022b). Additional factors to be considered are subject matter, location, production expenditure details and 'any other matters [considered] relevant'. The Production Offset was bolstered by a Location Offset and in 2018 by an additional Location Incentive, specifically designed to attract international productions to Australia. In Labor's May 2023 budget, the Location Offset was raised to match the Producer Offset at 30 per cent, a clear indication of the government's ongoing support for the production industry even if most beneficiaries were immediately identified as being big international productions (Frater, 2023).

While 'film' is the medium specified here, the Producer Offset also applies to 'television and other projects', although there is a clear hierarchy at work. While a film may attract a 40 per cent rebate, domestic TV drama production only attracts 30 per cent. Furthermore, productions made in Australia need not meet the SAC test in order to access the Location Offset, which clearly helps explain the lack of overt Australianness identified earlier in the drama series *The Tourist*, as well as the upswing in international productions that found a COVID-safe haven in Australia in 2020 and 2021. However, as the Olsberg.SPI report suggests, the value of a drama series such as *The Tourist* lies not just in the work it provides for the screen sector, but in what they identify as 'the ripple effect', impacting on a whole range of ancillary services (Figure 1.1). Although economic benefit is usually the trump card in debates about the value of the screen industry, as we will argue in Chapter 2, there are many other benefits that may accrue from a screen production that also need to be acknowledged.

Culture vs Economics

When it comes to Australia's response to the changing dynamics of global screen production, it is clear that Australia is not alone in its anxiety about the possible effects of footloose productions commandeering the screen sector. The current ongoing tension between the cultural call for more Australianness on our screens as opposed to the economic argument touting the benefits that may accrue from attracting the big, often American,

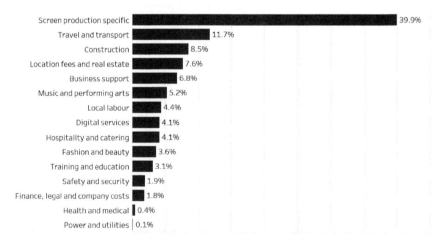

Figure 1.1 Proportional budget breakdown of a mid-size Australian drama series
Source: Olsberg.SPI (2023).

productions to our shores, closely follows (with some significant differences) that of Canada at the turn of the millennium, as described by Sara Tinic (2005). With a population of around 30 million at that time, dispersed in vastly different regional contexts across a large land mass, like Australia, Canada has long turned to the media, and in particularly the public service media, as a means of maintaining what Sara Tinic identifies as a 'sense of national self-consciousness' (Tinic, 2005, p. viii). Following Benedict Anderson, Tinic argues that if a sense of nationhood is imagined, then clearly the media inevitably plays a significant role in that self-imagining (Tinic, 2005, p. 16). The problem being, just whose idea of a nation gets to be imagined on screen.

Like Australia, Canada has experienced ongoing cultural tension about whose version of the nation is realised. While there have long been calls for more regional productions in Canada, history reveals a gradual centralisation of services that do not speak directly to their more remote communities. As Tinic points out, in the late 1990s independent television producers found that stories that were 'overly particular to place' became more difficult to pitch, since it was believed that in order to reach a larger market, the 'more homogenous or universal' the program needed to be (Tinic, 2005, p. 13), with the resulting loss in value that was termed a 'cultural discount' (Hoskins & McFadyen, 1993). As we will argue in the case studies that follow, this is clearly no longer the case. Following the example of the Nordic crime dramas that revelled in the cultural specificity of their cities and regional landscapes, becoming in the process a primary attraction for viewers keen to engage in armchair, or even real, tourism (Hansen & Waade, 2017; Reijnders, 2009; Waade, 2016), the Australian crime dramas we discuss here also celebrate their diverse settings.

According to Tinic, as a result of Canada's generous tax provisions and shelters, by the end of the 1990s, Vancouver in British Columbia had become the largest production centre for American television series outside the United States, earning Canada the title of 'Hollywood North' (Tinic, 2005, p. ix). Somewhat ironically, this led to actors and producers in Los Angeles calling for federal government intervention to provide similar tax incentives in the US to stop the exodus. Meanwhile in Australia (Hollywood South?), the fact that during the early COVID-19 pandemic years of 2020 and 2021, Australian productions were finding it difficult to get access to sound stages, production services and crews because they were commandeered by the big American productions, led to a resurgence of demands for more federal and state assistance in the creation of new production hubs and sound stages outside the state capitals.

For example, the relatively small regional industry body, Screen Illawarra, located just south of Sydney, is currently lobbying local governments and state agencies to support the establishment of the Illawarra as a new centre for screen production. As their website ambitiously states, they seek to make 'the Illawarra a screen content production region of global significance' (Screen Illawarra, 2023). This would involve repurposing the buildings of a former steel producing precinct at Port Kembla as a sound stage and related production offices in order to attract both Australian and international productions to the region. For the members of Screen Illawarra, while local jobs may be a priority, the possibility of creating opportunities for more regional stories comes a very close second. The Screen Illawarra initiative also highlights the shifts that are taking place in the economy more generally as heavy industry gives way to new centres of creative production. Encouraged by the current Labor government's commitment to a cultural policy that will require the streamers to meet a quota in Australian-based productions, initiatives like that of Screen Illawarra appear to be prescient.

As Vilde Schanke Sundet (2021) reveals in her account of how the new streaming environment impacted on the Norwegian production industry, increasing competition from emerging streaming series has led to the co-production of more crime drama series. As evidence of this, Sundet describes how NRK partnered with Netflix to produce Norway's own response to the Nordic Noir genre, *Lilyhammer* (2012–2014), a crime drama that has also been identified as Netflix's own first original series. Furthermore, not only was *Lilyhammer* made available on Netflix almost immediately after its launch on NRK, but as a result of a distribution deal with the Red Arrow company the series was shown in 130 different countries (Sundet, 2021, p. 8). As a crime drama with comedic elements with a nod to Nordic Noir, *Lilyhammer* was something of a genre mash-up following the adventures of a US mafia boss, Frank Tagliano, played by Steven Van Zandt, who had a starring role as a gangster in HBO's much lauded series *The Sopranos* (HBO 1999–2007). After being placed in a witness protection company, Tagliano finds himself in the regional town of Lilyhammer where he has to deal with, among other challenges, the machinations of the Norwegian welfare state, observed from a somewhat stereotypical American perspective (Sundet, 2021, p. 8). This begs the question about what kind of influence a streamer like Netflix might have on a co-production set somewhere other than the US, a question that came up in the exploration of another production context – Iceland.

With a population of just over 350,000, similar to that of the Illawarra in Australia, Iceland has a very small viewing audience, but has enjoyed considerable success in producing crime dramas that have found a global audience (Hansen & Waade, 2017, pp. 247–267). The breakthrough series in this regard being *Ófærð/Trapped* starring Ólafur Darri Ólafsson, who popped up in *True Detective* and *The Tourist*. Produced for the Icelandic public service broadcaster RÚV, *Trapped* enjoyed a worldwide premier at the 2015 Toronto International Film festival, following which rights were sold to a number of different countries, including Australia, where the series screened on the channel SBS's streaming platform in 2016. As Icelandic television producer David Oska Olafsson (2019) reported, the international success of *Trapped* 'kind of opened a door for Icelandic crime drama' with the result that 'we were able to do shows for a higher budget' although they were 'very, very dependent on foreign financing'. Having had Netflix pick up an earlier crime drama production, *Fangar* (YLE 2017), Olaffson was emboldened to approach the streamer with a new project, *The Valhalla Murders* (RÚV, BBC Four & Netflix 2019–2020), which was subsequently branded Iceland's first Netflix original. When asked if Netflix was involved in the production in terms of providing 'notes', about content or style, Olaffson reported that having negotiated on the pitch and received a financial commitment from Netflix, his production team was left to its own devices. Like it did with *Lilyhammer*, Netflix agreed to a first release on the Icelandic public service station, RÚV, which was also invested in the series. This latter agreement enabled access to the Nordicom public service network covering Scandinavia, as well as the BBC in the UK, before the series went 'global' on Netflix in March 2020 (Olafsson, 2019).

As these Norwegian and Icelandic examples suggest, the earlier Canadian experience of the 1990s that required dramas to eschew a specific sense of place is no longer an expected outcome of an international co-production. As the crime dramas we will explore in the following chapters demonstrate, and most particularly in the case of the outback noir series *Mystery Road*, being compelled to find an international co-producer in order to finance an expensive project does not have to mean compromising on the local, regional or national specificity of the drama. As we will reveal, cultural and economic imperatives can be balanced and a production can speak directly to its national audience while also being of interest and value to an audience from somewhere else. And this is particularly so in a crime drama, where the crime may be universal (for example, murder), even though the specific cultural context may vary considerably. What motivates that crime is then the work of the drama itself to explain to audiences already familiar with the genre and its tropes.

Australian Content

The emergence of streaming services as a significant and influential force in the production and distribution of drama series has forced gargantuan change on the established dynamics of the traditional television broadcasting sector. As audiences are watching more drama on streamers and less on the commercial terrestrial services that were previously relied upon to fund local content in return for privileged access to spectrum, commercial services are funding decreasing amounts of Australian drama: between 1999 and 2019, total hours of first-release adult and children's Australian drama broadcast on commercial services more than halved (Lotz et al., 2021). In Australia, the Federal Government is paying particular attention to local content offered by streamers, which at the time of writing continue to be unregulated. Their different business models mean that streamers have a strong incentive to invest in the types of content that will sweeten their subscription offerings, and therefore may be more likely to invest in local drama than commercial terrestrial services, but streaming services are still new and are competing vigorously for market space, and the production sector, being vocal and well-organised, has been quick to sell the idea that they and the Australian stories that they create may be at risk.

With the possibility of creating productions that speak directly to the Australian experience in mind and with the added incentive of a cultural policy that invites 'a place for every story' and 'a story for every place', the availability of Australian content on streaming platforms in Australia has been very uneven. As reported by the Australian Government's Bureau of Communications Arts and Regional Research (2022), in June 2021 Foxtel Now was carrying the greatest number of Australian titles, with over 300. Close behind were Stan, Amazon Prime and Netflix, with just over 200. By way of contrast, the relatively new entrants in the Australian SVOD landscape, Acorn TV, Hayu and Disney+, had little or no Australian content available (Figure 1.2).

But streaming services are not a one-way street: by June 2021 a total of 1611 Australian titles were available on overseas streaming services. These included over 600 titles available in the USA, closely followed by other English-speaking countries such as the UK, New Zealand, Ireland and Canada, and – of particular interest for our study – Sweden and Finland (Figure 1.3). And, by mid-2023, Australian series were popular hits on streaming platforms across the world. The ABC-commissioned legal comedy *Fisk* (ABC 2021–) was a Top 10 show on Netflix in countries as diverse as Kenya, Sri Lanka, South Africa, Argentina, Canada and Uruguay, as well as the US, UK, Ireland, New Zealand and Australia. Amazon Prime Video's *The Lost Flowers of Alice Hart* (2023) reached the top five in seventy-eight countries and the top three in forty-two countries on its first weekend, and its Nordic Noir spoof *Deadloch* (2023–) held the number one position in Australia and New Zealand for weeks as well as the Top 10 in the US, UK, Canada, South Africa, Ireland, Spain and France. Disney+'s first Australian drama commission, *The Clearing* (2023), also appears to have been a hit, attracting intense online interest (Quinn, 2023b).

The appearance of Sweden and Finland in Australia's top ten export markets suggest that the flow of European content to Australia, including

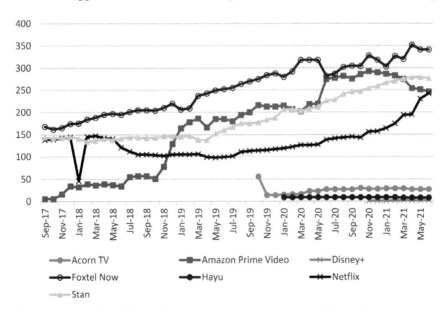

Figure 1.2 Number of Australian titles on streaming services, 2017–2021
Source: Ampere Analysis – SVOD Analytics dataset, published in Bureau of Communications Arts and Regional Research (2022).

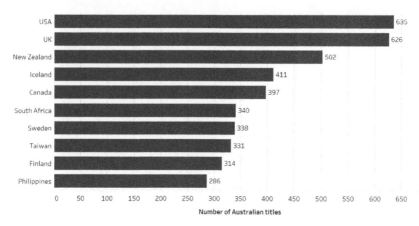

Figure 1.3 Number of Australian shows on foreign streaming services, Top 10 countries, 2021

Source: Ampere Analysis – SVOD Analytics dataset, published in Bureau of Communications Arts and Regional Research (2022).

The Bridge from Sweden and Denmark as well as Finnish crime drama series such as *Bordertown* (Yle TV1 2016–2019) and *Deadwind* (Yle TV2 2018–2021), is being reciprocated by a contra-flow of Australian content into European territories. In other words, Australian crime drama series are indeed travelling and finding new audiences overseas, as the case of *Miss Fisher's Murder Mysteries* clearly demonstrates. Just how *Miss Fisher* found its international audience is part of the story we shall tell in Chapter 3. However, before we embark on this, in the next chapter we will explore the core concept of 'total value' that underpins this study as a whole. Here we identify approaches to understanding the value of culture that have evolved within different disciplines and how they have been applied in policy and research contexts, with a focus on those relating to screen production.

Chapter 2

The Total Value Proposition

At the outset of this project, we wanted to find a way to write about Australian television crime drama in terms of its production and reception, and what it can tell us about the contemporary issues that surface in its narratives. We wanted to explore how Australian crime drama has evolved during an era characterised by major shifts in the ways in which people consume screen content. Digitisation has had a revolutionary impact on the consumption and distribution of traditional cultural artefacts. It has led to the emergence of new cultural forms, and new ways of creating value, as perfect, infinitely re-usable (durable) digital copies can potentially generate endless revenue streams (Caves, 2000). Streaming services and their online catalogues, museums and libraries have opened new markets for rights holders. This has driven internationalisation and vertical integration in the television industry as businesses shift the focus of their core competencies from technology investments and media delivery to intellectual property investment and management (Chalaby, 2019, p. 170 & 185). We wanted to find out what impact streaming networks such as Netflix and Amazon Prime have had on Australia's screen industries and the careers of those who work in them and how they have affected the people who enjoy Australian and international crime drama. Our desire to answer these questions meant we needed to find a way to articulate how television crime drama series generate value for society through their entire ecosystem, through production and reception as well as all the kinds of spin-off effects they may have. But where to start?

Television drama series – indeed all screen productions – are multifaceted cultural artefacts that draw on multiple skill sets. They might be sold into multiple markets, or to a single streamer. In an era characterised by the exponential growth of video on demand, television drama series potentially can reach diverse audiences all over the world who consume them in unique ways. They have the capacity to carry significant local stories internationally, bringing new perspectives and understandings, sharing history, changing minds and inspiring travel, real and virtual. The popularity of the television crime drama – a near-universal component of a good life in the twenty-first century – is evidence that the genre delivers value, not only as entertainment for the people who watch and a living for the people who make it, but also for the communities associated with the stories that are being told.

Central to our exploration of the value of the television crime drama within this national and global ecosystem is the concept of culture, defined here broadly to encompass artefacts such as paintings, theatre, or literature and digital media including movies and computer games. In this particular context, we are talking about a television crime drama as a cultural artefact that carries with it a whole set of intrinsic and extrinsic values. The discussion that follows draws on the extensive literature addressing cultural and economic value, developing our approach to considering the 'total value' of recent television crime drama production in Australia. In our endeavour to understand just what might be at stake, we found ourselves turning to philosophy.

Phronesis and the Greater Good

The desire for a good life, a life imbued with meaning, has a long tradition in western thinking. The Ancient Greeks sought *eudaimonia*, a good life cultivated through moral virtue, personal behaviour and political choices made to benefit the community as a whole. In his writing, the philosopher Aristotle (384–322 BC) encouraged his son to distinguish means from ends and to be guided by *phronesis*, practical wisdom for the greater good. Before economics was swept away by the complex modelling made possible by computational science, its luminaries such as Adam Smith and Maynard Keynes argued that economic policy must be managed for the common good, also guided by *phronesis*. However, while the concept of maximising welfare in favour of the common good is now an established core concept in public decision making (even if it is sometimes overlooked), bureaucracies striving for objectivity have come to rely on instrumental processes that model the intangible as monetary flows.

Culture, however, does not comfortably lend itself to decision-making processes couched only in dollar terms. As Doyle (2010, p. 245) points out, 'Culture seems to both attract and resist economic analysis'. While cultural artefacts and services are bought and sold every day through ordinary financial transactions, they are also imbued with meaning that extends beyond their price. While this might seem intuitive – and this intangibility has been a compelling motivator for cultural economists who have created a body of theory and applied research that delves into the question of where culture fits in economic systems – cultural economics has never become part of mainstream economic study. There are, for example, no research codes for cultural economics and it is rarely offered as a subject at any university. Given these difficulties, why bother with attempting to pinpoint the value of culture? What is at stake?

It is generally accepted that the value of a cultural product cannot be judged purely in economic, or rather financial, terms, and that a cultural artefact can deliver benefits that extend well beyond its initial costs. We see recognition of this in the ubiquity of government support programs for artists and cultural programs. In Australia, as well as funding public broadcasting services and subsidising content production, federal government mandates local content quotas for expensive television genres that are at risk of market failure, a real risk in a country with a small population and similarly small production sector. In Europe, appellation rules extend beyond the traditional cultural industries to protect highly desirable agricultural products connected with the cultures and histories of specific regions. And international intellectual property regimes protect creators' rights to control use of their ideas to ensure they continue to benefit from their work and can continue to produce new and innovative knowledge and content.

These kinds of intervention are not cheap and require ongoing expenditure of public funds, which inexorably draws public policy decision makers back to the instrumental tools of economics. As a result, a considerable body of grey literature has emerged over the last twenty years as governments engage consultants and academics to tackle the question of how to value culture. Examples include the two reports commissioned by Screen Australia in 2016, each aiming to capture different aspects of the value of Australia's screen industry: one from an economic consultant to estimate economic benefits and the second from social researchers to identify cultural benefits (Deloitte Access Economics, 2016; Olsberg. SPI, 2016; Screen Australia, 2016).

So, What is Cultural Value?

Cultural value is indeed a slippery concept. While it is not testable in a market, it is nevertheless intrinsically connected to economic value. Perception of cultural value can influence the monetary value of an artefact and can attract people to performances and institutions: the perceived cultural value of a film or television drama that has won many awards may be a key factor in ensuring its success at the box office or in terms of ratings. Drawing on the work of Swiss economist Bruno Frey, Hasan Bakhshi (2012) differentiates between the 'economics of culture' and an 'economic approach to culture'. For example, an economics of culture would encompass the metrics of employment, output and productivity, and is essential for understanding how culture contributes to economic development. An economic approach to culture, on the other hand, allows for other kinds of value, including the comparison of individual works or productions, an evaluation of the work of an institution against its goals, or the return on investment from a publicly funded art program.

In 2012, Bakhshi lamented the dearth of valuation studies, pointing to a 'lack of engagement by economics in the cultural and creative area', and the 'unwillingness of cultural institutions to engage with the tools of economics as a theory of value'. As a result, he argued, no one has 'the long-term aim of systematically building a rigorous body of evidence which can be used to understand the value of cultural activity in its various forms'. Bakhshi exhorted cultural economists to undertake valuation studies that draw on established economic valuation tools. His central point was that we need a *holistic view of cultural value* to understand how culture is made and consumed across sectors of society in the UK (Neelands et al., 2015). It is such a holistic approach that we are advocating here.

In attempting to do this, we would argue that there has been very little traction in cultural valuation studies because there is no consensus on the relationship between economic value and cultural value. Separately, their meanings are uncontroversial. Economic value is generally agreed to encompass the exchange value or monetary value, plus the value placed on non-market use (Throsby, 2003a). Cultural value, on the other hand, is more nebulous. We see it in the creativity, the intellectual property, the source of inspiration for the symbols employed in a cultural output. Bring them together, however, and a plethora of divergent views and theories emerge.

David Throsby (2003a, pp. 279–280), for example, describes cultural value as 'multi-dimensional, unstable, contested, lack[ing] a common unit of account, and … [not] easily expressed according to any quantitative or qualitative scale'. Rather than propose one measure, Throsby identifies several component values, with the most important including the aesthetic, spiritual, social, historical, symbolic and authentic. John Holden (2004, 2006), on the other hand, takes a broader view, proposing that the value of culture should be considered in terms of its *instrumental value* (direct social or economic impact), *institutional value* (gaining trust and esteem of the public) and *intrinsic value* (giving people a way to engage with ideas and aesthetic experiences).

While Throsby's approach is broadly accepted in the cultural economic literature and Holden's appears in government policy grey literature, new ways of understanding the relationship between cultural and economic value continue to emerge (Angelini & Castellini, 2018). These include the propositions of Arjo Klamer (2004, 2008), who argues that 'being a symbol of something' does not equate with cultural value and that there are three mutually exclusive components: economic value (or exchange value), social value (in the context of interpersonal relationship and the community) and cultural value (everything else). Also cited is Terry Smith (2008), who recognises that value accrues through production as well as consumption, while Elisa Hernando and Sara Campo's (2017) analysis of the art market draws on multiple disciplines to distinguish four components: hedonistic value (including aesthetic, emotional, ownership and cognitive values), economic value (investment, legacy and scientific values) and social, symbolic and status values. According to Velthuis (2007), it is not possible to evaluate artistic merit without considering economic value, while for Hutter and Frey (2010), cultural value inevitably affects economic value.

A large part of the difficulty here, and part of what makes cultural value such a slippery concept, is that much of the value associated with culture is intangible. It is unquantifiable using numerical metrics and therefore not fully reflected in the exchange value or monetary value of cultural goods. This has led to cultural theorists from both the economics and humanities disciplines introducing such a plethora of categories to help characterise intangible cultural value and to, where possible, quantify it.

Klamer (2016a) helpfully cuts a pathway through this literature, by demonstrating that culture has three distinct meanings and that there is more than one 'conversation' to be had about the relationship between economics and culture. He identifies three distinct types of culture:

(C1) Anthropological culture that derives from the distinct culture of a family, region, nation or ethnic group and its shared stories, symbols and artefacts, that can bond a society, but may also exclude outsiders.
(C2) The culture of a civilisation that is accumulated in a particular place over a period of time as best practice and ensuring the best ideas prevail.
(C3) Distinct practices such as architecture, design, arts practice and screen production that connect with (C2).

Each of these matter, as decisions made both in business and in society derive from and are influenced by culture (p. 10). In surveying the debate concerning the nature of the relationships between economics and these three forms of culture, Klamer identifies 'six conversations on the relationship between culture, economy, economics and the arts' (p. 13). These conversations are highly nuanced and demonstrate the complexities inherent in the relationship between cultural and economic value:

1. Culture does not matter in economic processes. This is how economics is generally taught and as such is the prevailing view. Culture of any kind (C1, C2, C3) is rarely factored into economic modelling.
2. The economy does not matter to culture. Arts and culture (C2 and C3) are not concerned with economic conditions. Cultural activities may even exist on a separate plane to commercial activity.
3. Economics matters to culture. Cultural economists apply the standard tools of economics (markets, rational choice, consumer surplus etc.) to cultural activities and outputs (C3).
4. The arts matter to the economy. The arts (C3) have economic impact that can be measured in the national accounts. Artists transform struggling cities, leading to stronger economic growth, and thriving creative and tourism industries.
5. Culture matters to the economy. Cultural values (both C1 and C3) affect economic processes and were, for example, implicit in the rise of capitalism, the Dutch Golden Age and growth in post-WWII Japan.
6. The economy is embedded in culture. 'Economic phenomena [are] manifestations of culture.' For Klamer, 'culture is what life is about and the ordinary business of mankind – including the trading,

consuming and working that people do – are part of that phenomenon' (p. 18).

Angelini and Castellini (2018) provide an alternative overview that considers whether economic value and cultural value are interconnected, identifying through a meta-analysis three ways of defining the relationship. The first is that economic value incorporates cultural value, the second that cultural value affects economic value but they are separate, and the third that they are indeed separate. This suggests that economic value can be assessed without taking into account cultural value and that since economic value makes sense only in the market, cultural value can be assessed outside of it. This analysis forces a choice: do we accept that economic and cultural value are inexorably intertwined and must be considered in tandem, or that they should be considered as being independent of each other?

How Can We Observe Cultural Value?

In their report for the Warwick Commission, Eleonora Belfiore, Catriona Firth and Dom Holiday (2014, p. 3) identify the challenge of locating a methodological approach to the valuation of culture and ask:

> … how can we develop a methodological approach to measurement and evaluation that can reflect, account for and respect these 'varieties of value' without falling into the trap of either collapsing all notions of value into a narrow focus on economic value or the equally dangerous trap of focussing on the cultural dimension of value whilst ignoring its connection to the economic sphere. Either of these scenarios would be reductionist and problematic.

In light of this, it is clear that what we need is an analytical framework that will help us avoid overlapping conceptual categories such as economic value, public value, instrumental value and cultural value (Crossick & Kaszynska, 2014, p. 123), and that does not force us to express cultural value simply in monetary terms (Crossick & Kaszynska, 2014; Donovan, 2013). We also need to bear in mind the advice of Donovan (2013), who found through consultation with industry stakeholders in the UK that for smaller organisations the best way to observe cultural value in practice was to employ holistic valuation methodologies using consistent economic frameworks that recognise both monetary and non-monetary outcomes. This begs the question, what could such a framework look like?

In attempting to answer this question, Belfiore et al. point to a study by consultants Corey Allen, Arthur Grimes and Suzi Kerr (2013) for New Zealand's Manatū Taonga Ministry for Culture and Heritage, which reviews methods for measuring and quantifying value in environmental economics. Building on Dave O'Brien's (2010) work for the UK Department for Culture, Media and Sport, this approach employs the concept of 'total economic value', which aims to capture the entirety of the value that accrues through both market transactions and non-market uses. Total economic value encompasses both the economic and cultural forms of value generated by a cultural artefact as it is enjoyed by many interrelated stakeholders, including the producers, the consumers and society as a whole (Figure 2.1).

Allan et al. comprehensively define these categories as:

- The non-monetary return to producers: 'The non-monetary satisfaction derived from the production of cultural goods and services.' This includes the pleasure a cultural worker takes in producing within their

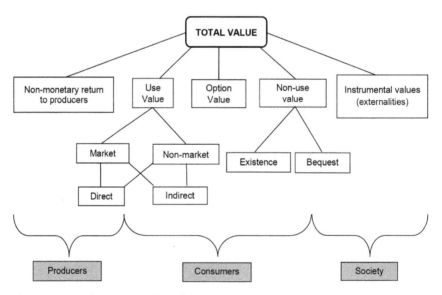

Figure 2.1 Total Economic Value of Culture

Note: The use of 'instrumental value' here is not identical to that used by Holden, which he defined as measurable economic or social benefits. Here, Holden's instrumental value would be categorised as a 'use value' (Belfiore et al., 2014).

Source: Allan et al. (2013, p. 13).

profession and the value derived from positive reviews and awards. It can build as a reputational effect, as involvement in one project leads to opportunities to work in others and as colleagues are benefitted by and learn from others' skill sets. These are forms of value that might accrue through a production value chain.
- Market use value: 'The value derived from the consumption of cultural goods and services purchased on the market.' The difference between consumers' willingness-to-pay and the market price, this is the enjoyment *directly* experienced in excess of a ticket price and the benefits *indirectly* gained later in life from purchased experiences or training.
- Non-market use value: 'The value derived from consumption of cultural goods and services NOT purchased on the market.' The enjoyment *directly* experienced from public artworks or public broadcasting, and the knowledge *indirectly* gained and fostering of life-long learning from visiting museums or watching television programs produced specifically for children.
- Option value: 'The value an individual places on themselves or others having the option to consume and enjoy a cultural good at some point in the future, if the future provision depends on continued provision in the present.' The value derived from retaining the choice to attend a theatre performance, visit a museum or catch up on a television program on a streaming service.
- Existence value: 'The value an individual derives from knowing that a good exists, even if they will not consume the good.' The enjoyment experienced, for example, from knowing that Indigenous sacred sites are preserved or that television content is produced in accordance with children's development needs, even though neither will be consumed.
- Bequest value: 'The value an individual derives from knowing that a good will be preserved for future generations to enjoy.' The enjoyment derived from knowing that Indigenous sacred sites or local feature films are preserved for future generations.
- Instrumental value, or externalities: 'Benefits that accrue to people other than the producer or consumer as an indirect benefit from provision of the cultural service.' This can encompass increased community understanding through multicultural communication, reduced crime as disadvantaged groups are engaged in cultural activities, the attraction of the 'creative class' to vibrant places, and economic growth by virtue of cultural tourism.

The virtue of this approach is that it provides both an objective and practical guide to identifying distinct types of value that might accrue from the production, distribution, consumption and non-consumption of a cultural artefact. It acknowledges both an industry view of cultural industries (its ability to generate monetary value and jobs) and a public value approach, acknowledging the special non-monetary aspects of culture that differentiate it from other sectors. By distinguishing between monetary value, the types of intangible value that might contribute to monetary value (artist reputation, material inputs, brand) and the many qualities that are not reflected in exchange values, but undoubtedly confer considerable benefits to society as a whole, the total economic value approach side-steps the challenge of settling on an appropriate system of cultural component values, such as those proposed by Throsby (2003a). This does not mean that cultural components are irrelevant, however. Here, they contribute to the total economic value categories for different users and different communities. Spiritual value, for example, might contribute to market value for people belonging to a particular religious group, while for others it might have existence and bequest value, as they value an artwork in terms of the satisfaction they feel from the fact it is available to that religious community, now and in the future.

Given this, how to go about using these categories to identify the total value of a cultural artefact such as a television crime drama? Economics has already developed a suite of tools to assist in estimating the value of intangibles and adoption varies across institutions, as none 'can be identified as "the best" or "the most suitable for arts and culture". They all have their distinctive strengths and weaknesses in relation to cultural value…' (Belfiore et al., 2014, p. 9). One example is stated preference modelling (O'Brien, 2010). The two most common approaches to stated preference modelling are contingent valuation (determines maximum willingness to pay for a good through a structured survey) and choice modelling (compares attributes of different goods to estimate willingness to pay). Unlike cost-benefit analysis, these techniques allow, at least to some extent, the non-market and non-use values of cultural goods to be captured. They are not, however, simple to implement, being complex and time consuming and heavily reliant on the assumptions that individuals have full knowledge of their preferences, that these preferences are stable over time and that all goods are comparable in terms of value. Because of these challenges, there have been few attempts to apply them to empirically estimate cultural value. One is Franco Papandrea's (1997) contingent valuation willingness to pay for Australian television programs compared with international programming, which found that the benefits of Australian programs were at least commensurate to their cost, with the most substantial effects flowing from drama requirements for adults and children.

Another approach for inferring the value of a non-market good is the concept of the 'revealed preference', which uses the choices that people actually make in markets. Techniques include hedonic pricing, which infers value based on how a market prices a good with particular characteristics (for example, the effect of proximity of a theatre on property prices) and travel costs, which estimates value based on the value of the time spent to travel to the cultural experience in question. While these methods are based on real-life data, they are also problematic. It is difficult to accurately capture all the elements that drive property markets, and travel time is not necessarily an accurate indication of the value of the activity being travelled to (Belfiore et al., 2014; O'Brien, 2010).

A third approach is assessing the 'social return on investment', which involves using a selection of qualitative and quantitative metrics that represent cultural value alongside monetary and other measures. An example is the Triple Bottom Line, which was designed to encourage businesses and governments to make sustainable investment decisions, and which Jon Hawkes (2001) extended to include culture, arguing that it had an essential role in public planning. An example of applied work in this area is Flinders University's project Laboratory Adelaide: The Value of Culture, which experimented with applying innovative reporting frameworks to determine the assessment of culture (Meyrick, 2016). These approaches nevertheless struggle with their goal of capturing the ephemerality and even the purpose of culture (Doyle, 2010).

Arjo Klamer (2016b, p. 369) pushes all this vacillation to the side, arguing that people in the arts world do not take to economic concepts such as rational choice, and they are likely to recoil from them. Instead, he advocates for a 'value-based approach' that recognises the values and qualities that people regard as important, which might be artistic qualities, or social cohesion or justice. Here Klamer places the recognition of an artwork within a cultural context that, in addition to the possibilities of monetisation through market-based sales or subsidisation through government supports, provides space for artistic status and reputation. Klamer's values-based approach thus relies on valorisation, the recognition of the achievements of people, organisations and governments through 'the weighing of values, conditions, interests and findings in order to do the right thing'. It is, he notes, 'often a chaotic process with a lot of talk, a going back and forth, the making of mistakes, and more talk and deliberation' (p. 372). The focus is on the *qualitative* outcomes – not the number of visitors who might have attended a museum, but rather the contribution of the experience to the cultural and social qualities of a jurisdiction. Thus, Klamer exhorts us to return to the process of *phronesis* in economic and policy decision making, in order to 'do the right thing' and to make choices about the arts that benefit communities, rather than focussing only on instrumental, profit-focussed criteria (Klamer, 2016a).

Thus, having traversed the complexity of the debates that have ensued about cultural value, we propose that in this study we will employ the concept of *phronesis* informed by the fine-grained approach to total economic framework of Allan et al. (2013). This will enable us to bring together the economic and social science disciplines, using normative economic and media industry studies frameworks to shape empirical observation. It will also allow us to employ a mixed-methods study, as suggested by Flew (2019, p. 61), which includes qualitative research methods such as 'mapping, ethnography, attitudinal analysis, content analysis and aesthetic critique', as well as quantitative insights where available. There are rich insights to be found in working in this cross-disciplinary space, as demonstrated by Shiller (2017) and Sacco (2020) in their adoption of textual analysis techniques from literary theory to understand how shared stories – narratives – affect human behaviours.

The Total Value of a Television Drama Series

And so we return to our central theme: how does value accumulate through the production, distribution and reception of a television drama series? Here we examine each of the elements of a total economic value framework for television drama and identify the ways in which each element enables us to perceive how value might accrue. Before we start, it is helpful to consider Michael Porter's widely-adopted 1985 concept of the 'value chain', which represents the activities and processes that culminate in a single company making money, and the broader concept of a 'global value chain', which recognises that value can be generated by multiple agents and across borders – and what a television drama value chain might look like.

The value chain for television content encompasses the generation of an original story idea, development and production, distribution to broadcasters and streamers, and its eventual reception via a variety of platforms and over time. The television content value chain is unique, beyond the differences that might be seen between tradable goods. According to (Caves, 2000, p. 2), 'creative goods and services, the processes of their production, and the preferences or tastes of creative artists differ in substantial and systematic (if not universal) ways from their counterparts in the rest of the economy where creativity plays a lesser (if seldom negligible) role'. According to Caves, not only are the economic characteristics of creative goods and services different to other activities in an economy, they can also differentiate creative activities as well. For example, while some outputs may be produced by only one creative, *many require diverse skill sets*. Television content brings together expertise from many creatives and support workers, and all team members must work at the same minimum level of proficiency – if one contribution fails, then the entire output will be valueless. Another characteristic is that there is an *infinite variety* of creative products. Any similar type of creative product can be horizontally differentiated by many different dimensions: paintings may be differentiated by size, colour and material, and television series by country of origin, genre, starring actors, writers and directors. Creative products can also be differentiated vertically by quality, achieved through the skills of the workers involved. Attracting star creatives to a project is an important way of signalling quality, especially early in project development, and producers lure talent with high fees in order to line up financing. Time, *temporal coordination*, is also important for complex creative products, with the availability of performers, musicians and writers a crucial determinant. For example, a less well-known performer may be contracted if she is the best option available to minimise the costs of delaying a production.

All this suggests that identifying the layers of value for a screen production is a very complicated task, and it is not always clear where each stage of the value chain begins and ends, nor how that value should be attributed. Approaches to developing a value chain for screen production include Bloore's (2009, 2013) value chain model for independent film, which recognises that many differently skilled creative and business professionals contribute to each stage of a production from development to consumption and that their relative value changes as a project moves through the value chain from development to consumption (Figure 2.2).

Bloore's value chain also illustrates how producers consolidate value through horizontal integration and media businesses extend the potential for value generation through vertical integration.

Looking specifically at television, Chalaby (2016, 2019) locates the global value chain for television content within a global value chain for television (Figure 2.3), segmenting it into production, facilities, distribution and aggregation. *Production* commences with the conception of the initial idea, and ends with the approval of a final production master (Chalaby, 2019, p. 174). Once focussed on the needs of a single broadcaster, globalisation and digitisation have led to the transnationalisation of production. Businesses connect through television's global value chain, coordinating across international borders with the aim of delivering content to multiple markets (Chalaby, 2016, p. 35).

While both of these approaches illustrate the complexity of value generated through the creation of television content, neither capture the entirety of the value that might be generated by a television drama. The television value chain is shaped by the particular economic characteristics of television content, some of which is shared with other cultural products. Cultural creators, for example, face *uncertain demand*, with little knowledge of how consumers will value their products until all costs are incurred and the product is in the market. A cultural product is an 'experience good', with consumers' satisfaction being a subjective response (Caves, 2000, pp. 2–10). As knowledge accumulates as the original concept for a drama series transitions through the value chain, so does knowledge about its potential success, increasing the incentive for participants to invest and hold rights in the series, thereby increasing its monetary value. In addition to this potential accumulation of financial value through the production process, non-monetary value directly benefiting creators also accumulates, potentially creating a virtuous circle further enhancing monetary value. As our research will demonstrate, however, not all forms of value are fully realised in the sales generated by a series. Value can accumulate to creators in ways that do not necessarily translate in financial terms, and benefits also can accrue to audiences and society in ways that reflect the social and cultural contexts in which a television series is made and consumed.

The Total Value Proposition 35

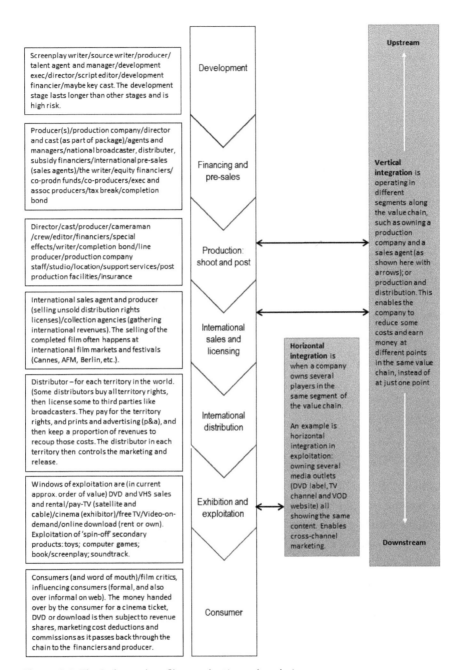

Figure 2.2 The independent film production value chain
Source: Bloore (2009, p. 8).

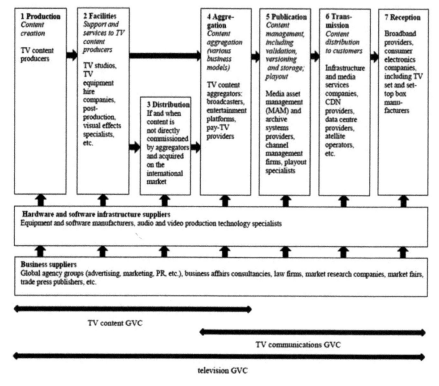

Figure 2.3 The television global value chain
Source: Chalaby (2019).

Accounting for Total Value

Building on our discussion of cultural value and how to observe it, here we outline how we will explore the total value generated by the production, distribution and reception of television crime drama series. The core of our approach is the Total Economic Value of Culture (Figure 2.1), as it articulates so well how value accumulates through the life of a cultural artefact. In applying this framework to our case study series, however, we found the value generated by a television drama can overlap across production and consumption, and consumption and externalities. Figure 2.4 maps out the elements of value that we observed as most significant for the evolution of the television crime drama series we selected as case studies, and how they accumulate for different types of creator and community.

By laying out the different ways in which we can observe the value of a television drama series, we can see the centrality of cultural value, how it permeates the value chain, that it is central to audience engagement and core to the ways in which dramas can affect people who choose not to watch them. In Jane Roscoe's words, it is 'embedded within the decision-making process' (Corner & Roscoe, 2016, p. 157). The discussion that follows explores each of the elements outlined in Figure 2.4, providing background and context from relevant literature and considering how it might be possible to observe each through the process of *phronesis*.

Making: The idea and development

Initiating this entire process, is the idea. Although Chalaby (2019) includes the idea as part of the production stage of the global value chain for television, our study participants saw the identification of the idea, and to some extent its development, as a distinct and defining stage of successfully imagining and creating a drama series. It is, after all, the idea

The making – the value chain	The using	The flow-ons
The idea and development • A new idea • The genre • Book adaption • Influence from another TV series, story, the look, the location • Cultural and national representation	Audiences • Direct vs indirect benefits • Market vs non-market • Ratings and engagement metrics • Indirect use: Fans, knowledge • Critical reviews	Externalities • Economic stimulation from production activity • Economic stimulation from activities inspired by a series – tourism, festivals
Development, production and post-production • Development – the writers' room • Facilities • Jobs, jobs, jobs		
Financing, distribution and aggregation • Commissioning broadcasters • International sales • Other funding sources • Where does it go / role in catalogue offerings	Cultural impact • Education and information, drawing attention to an issue • Showcasing a nation / culture • Mirror on / revision of societal and political histories • Influence on other creators – inspiration for other TV series (or other artefacts) • Changing cultural outlook • Archives – recording a society, a point in time	
Non-monetary benefits to creators • Critical recognition and awards • Pride and satisfaction • Cultural impact – making a difference / diversity-aware employment practices		

Figure 2.4 The total value of a television crime drama

that writers and would-be producers pitch to broadcasters, it is the idea that attracts star talent and it is the idea that sparks interest and engagement in viewers. Bloore's description of the creative process illustrates how the generation of an idea has a value chain all of its own, requiring preparation, conscious work, incubation, illumination and verification (2013, p. 147). An idea might come from any of many places. It might be something new, an original concept for screen, it might be an adaptation of a book, a retelling of a legend or a remake of a story already told on screen. An idea is shaped by genre choices, and influenced by choices of location, style and even colour palette. Designers and directors create 'look books' and 'sizzle reels' that imagine the possibilities of the visual story, to hook in crucial interest from commissioning broadcasters and distributors. However, it is a rare idea that goes straight to screen. Invariably, much development – Bloore's creative process – occurs in the writers' room with the creative team working together and taking into account feedback from commissioning broadcasters as well as each other (Awad, 2018).

Culture has a key role in the genesis of an idea and its development, in the stories that are told, in the people the drama series will potentially represent and the country on which it is located. Without creators inspired and supported to tell the stories of their nations and local communities, there would be little local storytelling on our screens – globalisation encourages creators to make content that appeals to an extremely broad audience base to ensure it can sell to SVODs and other aggregators with international reach. Long-held assumptions about cultural relevance – for example, cost disease (Baumol & Bowen, 1966), cultural discounts (Hoskins & McFadyen, 1993) and cultural proximity (Straubhaar, 2007) – are being disproven as international distribution and streamer platforms globalise television markets.

Making: Development, production and post-production

This is the engine room of value creation. It is where the script is refined and the acting talent practices its craft. Costume and set designers and composers contribute to the look and feel of the production, and the administrative, legal and financial teams keep the whole production machine in control and within budget. Star actors and star directors may be attached to a production early, bringing cachet and international recognition, and signalling the intention of producers that they are creating 'quality' content with potential for international reach. While the investment in a star is generally likely to be costly, it increases the potential for larger audiences and subscriber interest – although this may come with the risk of diluting culture and local relevance for domestic viewers.

All parties contribute to the final value of the production – all with the intention of creating outstanding television that will be attractive to audiences and broadcasting services with the ultimate aim of maximising monetary value – and perhaps also making a cultural impact on society. These phases are also highly dynamic, with economic cycles and the ongoing aftermath of digital disruption continually impacting on workflows (PricewaterhouseCoopers, 2013), evidenced at the time of writing by the SAG and AFTRA strikes in the US.

Facilities provide services to the production sector and include film and television studios and sound stages, and post-production services (Chalaby, 2016, p. 40). Large independent studios are important infrastructure investments that attract footloose productions as well as providing facilities for local productions. They support employment for specialist creative professionals, as well as for support staff, generating flow-on benefits (or externalities, discussed below). Post-production or elements of post-production are readily outsourced and the sector is highly competitive, reliant on rapidly evolving technologies and talented creative practitioners.

Making: Financing, distribution and aggregation

Financing, distribution and aggregation are inextricably interwoven, as broadcasters and distributors often take key roles in funding and greenlighting drama series. The central aim of all these roles is to maximise financial value, that is, maximise profits. Distributors generally get involved when aggregators do not produce or commission content themselves and acquire it from a third party. Their role is to 'wring every last drop from the [intellectual property] they represent', creating value by coordinating production and content aggregation and disaggregating intellectual property rights, generally by maximising sales to multiple buyers and in multiple markets (Chalaby, 2016, pp. 42, 174). The intellectual property rights attached to television content are complex. They include interactive, adaption and VOD broadcasting rights, defined for different regions and for different periods of time, and may extend to ancillary rights for licencing and merchandising.

Now near-ubiquitous, government subsidisation schemes provide financial incentives to attract productions, with the dual aims of industry development and, particularly in small countries where local content is vulnerable to market failure, to ensure availability of local cultural content. Successful international production attraction can mean production expenditure inflows, jobs and experience working with the world's best, generating economic externalities, but it can also mean that crews are not available for domestic production and escalated costs (George, 2022b).

Content aggregation is the process of bringing together content as a branded package to be marketed to audiences and/or advertisers (Chalaby, 2016, p. 43). Internet-distributed television has disrupted the ways in which television services traditionally reach their audiences and the content they buy. With television content now accessible and consumed across time and geographical boundaries, the relationship between economic value and cultural value is changing as content finds audiences in new markets (Corner & Roscoe, 2016, p. 161). Previously, linear broadcaster services were the arbiters of what was available on television screens. Streaming services now give people more autonomy, with choices of services and content, paid and free to watch. This means we now have parallel distribution systems, with traditional broadcasters adapting their business models to also offer VOD services. For an aggregator, value creation strategies are influenced by its broadcasting (or VOD) business model. Commercial, advertising-funded television services aim to maximise viewers in order to maximise advertising revenues, and they will be willing to pay more for content that attracts large target audiences. The core aim of subscription television services (cable and SVOD) is to attract and retain paying subscribers – they may not be looking to maximise viewership at a particular point of time or for a particular genre, but are focused on offering a consistently-attractive content package. Public service broadcasters have different goals to profit-maximising television services, instead aiming to deliver entertainment, education and information.

Although the part of the television global value chain that includes equipment and communications service providers (Figure 2.3) is not strictly part of our analysis, it needs to be acknowledged here that aggregators use their internet-based infrastructure to create program catalogues and deliver algorithm-driven recommendations. These functions push audiences to discover content they may not otherwise have encountered, further increasing the value of the content to their host aggregators. Examples include the viral interest in the Korean Netflix Original *Squid Game* (2021–), which would not initially have been discovered by English-speaking audiences without being led to it by an algorithm, and SBS OnDemand's playfully curated drama listings Nordic Noir, Nordic not Noir and Noir not Nordic.

Making: Non-monetary returns to creators

In a competitive labour market, creative workers in the television production industry earn incomes that reflect the value of their contribution to content sold in international markets. Film and television workers have among some of the highest and most rapidly growing creative incomes, in Australia at least (McCutcheon & Cunningham, 2023). But monetary income does not capture everything that creators gain from working on television productions. Value is retained by individuals and by the industry more broadly in building skills and reputational gains through peer and audience recognition. In this way, value is accumulated through the efforts of the highly skilled individuals who are crucial to the creation of a cultural product and to the distribution services that help it get to market (Caves, 2000; Throsby, 2003b).

Phronesis allows us to examine holistically and in detail exactly what motivates creatives beyond monetary income. Cultural producers care about their work in ways that may elude consumers and not be reflected in market prices (Caves, 2000). They value highly the time they spend pursuing their craft, and the 'psychic income' they derive from their work keeps them creating and enabling the production of what might be otherwise unfeasible projects (Cameron & Verhoeven, 2010; Papandrea & Albon, 2004; Throsby & Zednik, 2010). This is despite the reality that creative careers can be highly precarious (Curtin & Sanson, 2016; Ross, 2009; Sullivan & McKee, 2015). The benefits that arise from the satisfaction derived from getting one's message across, from critical praise, from working with brilliant peers and from 'making a difference' can counter the disheartening effect of the highly variable incomes usually associated with what we now recognize as precarious professions.

Screen production typically requires a mixture of individual work and team collaboration, with creatives and contractors all benefiting from their association with successful projects and from their association with good talent. Satisfaction is also gleaned through the contributions that creative producers make to other people's lives. Producers provide work to emerging talent, mentoring them through internships and entry-level jobs and connecting them with the networks that will help them establish their careers. Similarly, broadcasters are hungry for the new talent that will differentiate them from other services and will provide opportunities for new and established producers to reach new audiences.

Creative people are motivated intrinsically, through personal growth and achievement, and work best when driven by genuine interest and passion and supported by producers who invest in and champion their vision. They do not want to be bought – they want to be valued and recognised for what they bring to their role, especially by their peers (Amabile, 1983; Amabile & Khaire, 2008; Bloore, 2013; Csikszentmihalyi, 1990). In this regard, the television industry in Australia as elsewhere provides its creators with opportunities for their work to be recognised through awards and critical reviews, and by audiences through ratings, viewing data and social media. Success builds on success, with recognition of achievements enhancing reputations and lowering hurdles to financing and selling future projects.

Telling stories that reflect people's diverse lives and open debates about social issues are a key source of satisfaction and professional pride for television producers. The ABC's Head of Scripted Production Sally Riley articulated this speaking about *Wakefield* (2016):

> I was really proud of [*Wakefield*] for the diversity it had, for the storytelling and a really difficult kind of structure. It had tap dancing, it had music ... It was a really challenging show, because we're talking about mental health, we're talking about something really important. But it's really fun and funny. And I thought for me, that was a real achievement, and a really successful show (Riley, 2022).

Using: audiences

Ultimately, drama series are entertainment (McKee, 2017), made for audiences to enjoy, to expand their horizons and debate, perhaps even becoming part of a society's cultural fabric. As television content travels globally, so does its impact on audiences: flows of television across international borders 'widen the range of our imaginative geography, multiply our symbolic life worlds, familiarize ourselves with "the other" and "the distant" and construct a sense of imagined places' (Buonanno, 2008, p. 2).

Drama series are thus a significant contributor to what might be regarded as a twenty-first century 'good life'. Despite their everyday nature, however, television drama series are an exceedingly complicated product to study. While the value of a 'normal' good can simply be estimated as its users' accumulated willingness to pay, television programs are public goods, created and consumed within potentially different cultural contexts, conveying messages that have potential to influence ideas and actions. Their broadcast rights can be sold and resold indefinitely, generating revenues for rights holders for as long as they have value to their audiences. Audiences themselves, however, rarely acquire drama series through a direct transaction. Although it is possible to purchase a drama series as a DVD box set or a digital download, drama series are generally commissioned or acquired by broadcasting services, who make them available through linear broadcast and SVOD catalogues. To deal with this complexity, the total economic value framework sets out four overlapping concepts. *Market value* and *non-market value* differentiate whether a cultural good or service is purchased or is free of charge, while *direct benefits* and *indirect benefits* differentiate the immediate benefit of a cultural experience and those that might emerge over time as the experience is synthesized.

Market value is at first glance a monetary measure, the sum of what a rights holder earns by selling the various associated broadcasting, streaming and DVD rights associated with a drama series. Taking this view, however, tells us very little about how audiences value what they are watching, because most revenue here comes from aggregators, not audiences, and the amount an aggregator is willing to pay is specific to its business model. For example, the price that a commercial terrestrial broadcaster is willing to pay depends on how much advertisers will pay to access its audience, while the price a subscription service will pay depends on what it believes it needs to invest to attract and retain its subscribers. Because it is so tightly bound to business strategy and planning, any information that helps us understand the market value of drama is commercially sensitive, but the high cost of collecting data has meant that the television industry itself and third-party providers have developed audience size and attention metrics to track viewership and engagement with television content. Because they reveal the relative appeal of content to audiences, these can be used as indicators of relative market value.

Drama series are also available to audiences free of cost, whether that be paid in monetary terms or through time and attention. Audiences accrue *non-market value* through accessing television drama series through cost-free public broadcasting services and libraries, and through content available on social media entertainment services and peer-to-peer sites (although pirated peer-to-peer consumption opens a gap in the value chain, side-stepping the mechanisms that ensure rights holders are paid for their work). In markets such as Australia and the UK, public service broadcasters are an important source of non-market value for audiences consuming drama series, delivering culturally-significant programming that might be vulnerable to 'market failure', that is, unlikely to be supplied by a for-profit broadcaster as their costs are too high, or potential revenue too low. The founding legislation and mission statements of public service broadcasters provide insights into the non-market social and cultural values they deliver for their citizen viewers. The BBC, for example, is required under its charter 'to act in the public interest, serving all audiences through the provision of impartial, high-quality and distinctive output and services which inform, educate and entertain' (UK Government, 2016), and the ABC's charter requires it to provide innovative and comprehensive broadcasting services of a high standard to all Australians that inform, educate and entertain as well as share Australian culture and perspectives with the world (Australian Government, 1983). Thus, while BBC and ABC viewers can expect to be entertained, they are also likely to experience programming that has been designed to deliver social value – educating, informing, shining a light on an important issue, holding a mirror to a diverse community – and to exemplify quality and innovation, through which local producers benefit through the opportunity to do outstanding work that they might sell internationally.

Streaming services, on the other hand, monetise *option value*, leveraging their extensive catalogues of television and movie content (Lobato & Lotz, 2020). The emergence of internet-delivered television brought about the 'creative destruction' of video hire shops, outcompeting them by offering the options of a greater range of video content for less inconvenience and for (often) a lower price. Government archiving services and libraries, on the other hand, generate option value as non-monetary returns through making content available for future audiences free of charge to future users.

Both market value and non-market value mechanisms have *direct and indirect* components, reflecting the enjoyment and engagement at the time of consumption, and the value that continues and might be reflected upon over time. The experience of the direct benefits of television content is highly variable: 'viewers attest in different ways to the value for them of what they choose to watch across the spectrum from strong enthusiasm to cooler responses, even at the level of material they find silly being a pleasurable diversion' (Corner & Roscoe, 2016, p. 164). Audience experience can vary by platform and setting, with viewers of different kinds of services preferring different kinds of content: paying audiences, for example, 'tend to be the most critical' (Corner & Roscoe, 2016, p. 164). The value in the sheer entertainment provided by a television program can be enhanced by audience reactions and critical reviews – which can in turn have a reinforcing circular effect on monetary and non-monetary value, affecting the monetary value of a production to its rights holders and the non-monetary benefits that flow to producers. Textual analysis, usually the purvey of academic researchers, can also 'add subtlety and penetration to understanding the social character of television as well as offering critical appreciation' (Corner & Roscoe, 2016, p. 166).

Television drama has the potential to be richly symbolic, reflecting a society's values and aspirations, culture and beliefs, thereby directly connecting with viewers but also potentially creating indirect influence that extends beyond its immediate audience, also accrued as *non-use* and *option value*. 'Television's vast generic range and expanding modes of engagement still seem to suggest quite strong kinds of "social" accountability' (Corner & Roscoe, 2016, p. 162). For Australian public broadcaster SBS, whose charter requires it to promote inclusion and reflect its multicultural nation, it is important for its commissioned content to 'get people talking about the issues, and not just audiences but those within the broader sphere of politicians and stakeholders' (Corner & Roscoe, 2016, p. 159), resulting in series such as the crime drama *True Colours* (SBS & NITV 2022), which explores the tensions between the law and Indigenous lore in central Australia.

Notions such as national identity, pride in local culture and stories cannot be valued in a monetary sense. In Australia, where its small population and competition from large English-speaking countries make drama, documentary and children's content vulnerable to market failure, local content quotas and production subsidies are crucial drivers of television production activity and essential for ensuring a local look and feel. And access to locally-relevant content is not something only valued by viewers – people also value programs that they may not choose to watch (Papandrea & Albon, 2004).

The industry itself also responds to changes in societal values and culture. Funding agencies and broadcasters are making deliberate efforts to ensure that the content they commission reflects their potential audiences, in recognition of the value that diverse communities place on seeing themselves on screen and distinctive local storytelling and its educative role, particularly in relation to Indigenous Australia (Ipsos Australia, 2013, p. 1; Screen Australia, 2023b). 'Intelligence' about the complexities of a changing pattern of tastes and taste-combinations 'has become a necessity for television planning' (Corner & Roscoe, 2016, p. 165). The benefits of inclusivity and diversity on screen do not only accrue to audiences: drama that connects with national conversations can 'really take off ... getting off the entertainment pages and onto the news pages' (Eckersley & Ryan, 2022).

Flow-ons: Externalities

The final type of value we are going to explore here is what economists call externalities – benefits or costs that accrue as a by-product of the television content value chain. Externalities can occur at any point along the value chain, from production to years after its initial release. Externalities even have a role in the budgeting and financing stage, as the anticipation of future externalities incentivises governments to compete for international footloose productions, and domestic productions from interstate.

While footloose projects inevitably import at least some creative talent, they do offer employment opportunities for local creatives and other production specialists, and for the many professionals that provide support services and skills to the production industry. The economic benefits that flow from this employment expenditure are often cited by advocates of international production attraction schemes as generating significant value for local economies – not only do these productions inject money into local businesses, the money stays there and circulates, helping grow regional economies. However, empirical evidence of ongoing benefits following footloose production activity (particularly in remote filming locations) is hard to come by, and it appears more likely that production industry supports are more likely to grow and consolidate the existing industry in existing locations.

The social impact of the stories told in drama series can also be interpreted as an externality. Stories can change the ways in which people understand the world around them and the ways in which they behave, potentially generating externalities that benefit society through community building as well as in economic terms (Sacco, 2020; Shiller, 2017). This connects with the satisfaction of producers – the same aspects of storytelling that provide a psychic income for creators can ricochet through society, creating ongoing positive change. We see this in the appetite for Indigenous stories by Australian audiences, and in the shift towards ensuring that Australian screen stories reflect the diversity of Australian society.

Another externality with both social and economic outcomes is cultural and landscape tourism. Nationally and internationally, cultural tourism is one of the fastest-growing parts of the tourism market, at least prior to the COVID-19 pandemic (Australia Council for the Arts, 2020; Richards, 2018; World Tourism Organization, 2018). Viewers actively seek out the places they see on screen, visit exhibitions and partake in activities that draw on drama series. Fan communities come together at filming locations, sharing their enthusiasm for a series and its characters, staying in the same locations and dressing in theme.

In conclusion, from the perspective of a total value of culture, cultural value cuts through and is part of everything. It is an instrumental contributor to economic value, and cannot be considered as something separate. Using the words of Arjo Klamer (Klamer, 2016a), culture matters to the economy and the economy is embedded in culture. Since the value of culture and economic value are so inexorably intertwined, they do not lend themselves to neat and tidy metrics. Rather, in order to observe the multifaceted and finely nuanced value of culture and to compare the different ways in which we experience its value, we found ourselves turning to phronesis. And that is what we do here, applying phronesis to the total value of the television crime drama in order to identify what the crime drama brings to society and how it makes our lives better.

Chapter 3

Valuing Miss Fisher

As a period crime series with a feisty female protagonist, *Miss Fisher's Murder Mysteries* (ABC, 2012–2015) (MFMM) is one of Australia's most successful television drama productions both at home and abroad. While *Miss Fisher* may have more in common with British 'cosy' crime series such as *Midsomer Murders* (ITV 1997–) and *Agatha Raisin* (Sky One & Acorn TV 2014–) than the 'gritty' crime dramas which excite the critics (Turnbull, 2014, p. 10), the series has been sold to an unprecedented 247 territories in 179 countries and is available on a range of different networks and platforms, thereby illustrating the potential reach of a TV crime drama in an era of multi-platform streaming.[1] The original three-season show has also generated a number of spin-offs, including a computer game *Miss Fisher and the Deathly Maze*, two seasons of *Ms Fisher's Modern Murder Mysteries* (Seven Network & Acorn TV 2019–2021) set in the 1960s featuring Phryne's niece Peregrine, as well as a Chinese franchise version, *Miss S* (Tencent 2020–) set in Shanghai: the latter marking the first time an Australian drama has been remade in mainland China. Also appearing in 2020 was the film *Miss Fisher and the Crypt of Tears*, funded in addition to a $620,000 investment from Film Victoria by fans through a Kickstarter campaign that proved to be the most successful Australian crowdfunding campaign at that time, with half of the funders being located overseas (Every Cloud Productions, 2022; Film Victoria, 2019, 2020).

As this chapter will reveal, *Miss Fisher's Murder Mysteries* has been an outstanding success in both popularity and reach, while in terms of genre, no other Australian crime drama series to date has attracted either the same enthusiastic fan base or international currency.[2] *Miss Fisher's* success therefore highlights the significance and value of the audience experience, the direct and indirect benefits, the cultural impact and economic flow-ons that may be produced by a television crime drama, as well as the financial and career benefits to the creators and the creative team. In the discussion that follows, we will be drawing on our concept of 'total value' in order to demonstrate the complexity and multi-layered nature of this value system.

Making *Miss Fisher*

The *Miss Fisher* story begins in 1989 when Melbourne author Kerry Greenwood published her first book, *Cocaine Blues*, in what would become her long-running series of crime novels featuring the wealthy and glamorous Miss Phryne Fisher. At the time of writing this series includes twenty-two novels, as well as two collections of short stories. In an interesting reverse move, the first novelisation of *Ms Fisher's Modern Murder Mysteries* by Australian crime writer Katherine Kovacic appeared in 2021, based on an original screenplay by Deb Cox. A former barrister from the suburb of Footscray in Melbourne, Greenwood's writing career began after entering a historical novel about a highwayman for the Vogel prize. She didn't win, but judge and publisher Hilary McPhee offered Greenwood a contract to write two crime novels as a result (Schmidt, 2008). With an opening chapter describing a society dinner, and a line borrowed directly from the Tintin graphic novel, *The Castafiore Emerald* (1963),[3] *Cocaine Blues* introduced the crime-solving Miss Phryne Fisher to an international readership, which has subsequently embraced a character Greenwood herself has described as 'a female hero'. While Miss Fisher, the charming action hero, might bear some similarity to James Bond, as Greenwood subsequently quipped, she has 'fewer product endorsements and a better class of lovers' (Allen & Unwin, 2022). Set in Melbourne in 1928 and 1929, the series has followed the intrepid Miss Fisher's adventures in detection across the state of Victoria in books that have seen her solve a mystery on a train, fly a light plane and perform circus tricks on a horse, while also entertaining a number of exotic lovers and acquiring an ever-expanding household of loyal waifs and strays. While the books deliver both entertainment and fun, they also combine an attention to social issues with a post-feminist critique of the treatment of women (Taddeo, 2016). This critical edge is one of the reasons that producers Fiona Eagger and Deb Cox were attracted to Greenwood's books when they were initially planning a TV series that would be 'female-based' but would also deliberately buck the 'gritty' noir trend. As Eagger explained, 'because Kerry was a legal aid solicitor in Sunshine, she brought a great sense of social justice to the work, looking at such subjects as abortion and the sexual exploitation of women' (Eagger, 2016).

Eagger and Cox co-founded Every Cloud Productions in 2009, with the specific aim of 'fostering Australian talent' while supporting 'co-operative alliances with creative producers across various media formats' taking advantage of then current development opportunities within the industry (Every Cloud Productions, 2015). What Cox and Eagger brought to this endeavour was their own different career experiences and expertise. Cox was a seasoned screenwriter who had contributed to such successful Australian productions as *Simone De Beauvoir's Babies* (ABC 1997), the popular romantic comedy *Sea Change* (ABC 1998–2000) and *East of Everything* (ABC 2008–2009), on which she was already collaborating with Eagger (Blatchford, 2015). Eagger herself was an experienced producer who had recently worked on the TV true crime movie *The Society Murders* (2006) and the development of the popular *Underbelly* series (2008), portraying Australia's criminal underworld for Screentime. As a result of this latter endeavour, Eagger was aware of the fact that 'crime was hugely popular domestically' (Eagger 2016). After a conversation with Miranda Dear, then Head of Programming at the ABC, the pair were alerted to the possibility that there was a 'little bit of a thirst out there in the marketplace' for an Australian murder mystery with a period setting (Sdraulig, 2014, p. 48).

Having decided they wanted to produce a TV drama series in a 'recognisable genre that we knew there was an audience for', and after reading a lot of Australian crime fiction which they found 'a bit nasty', Cox and Eagger eventually discovered Greenwood's *Cocaine Blues* and realised that this would give them opportunity to base their TV show on a successful book series that people 'already loved' (Blatchford, 2015). As they realised at the time:

> This is it, she's got everything. She's got the period happening, she's got the murder mysteries happening, but she's also a formidable, joyous woman who's a great example for younger women and a feminist without being strident (Sdraulig, 2014, p. 48).

There was, however, another hurdle to overcome, since *Cocaine Blues* had already been optioned by a UK company that was still undecided whether or not to produce an adaptation (Eagger, 2016). After an anxious few weeks, Eagger and Cox were at last successful in acquiring the rites and determined to put 'a spin on' the series that would be unique 'and definitely not Miss Marple' and that would enable them to say 'this is how Australian women do murder mysteries' (Blatchford, 2015). As Eagger observed, the two were totally clear about their vision for the series: 'We wanted Phryne Fisher to be a great role model for women and we wanted it to be fun' (Eagger, 2016).

Greenwood herself was reportedly delighted by the fact that two women would be bringing her character and her world to life in a production intended for the ABC. For Greenwood, having trust in her production partners was a key factor in her decision to accept their offer, given that she was 'very careful who I was going to sell the rights to Phryne to. I wasn't very interested in handing over my life's work for a pound of tea' (Knight, 2013). Although she was aware that an ABC production would probably not involve a 'great deal of money', Greenwood was reassured by the fact that this gave her an opportunity to 'meddle' in the production. With encouragement from Cox and Eagger, she was subsequently involved in the choice of the lead actress and script development and given a cameo role as a fortune teller in the episode set in a circus (Clark, 2011). Greenwood also provided a guided tour of the set for the subsequent DVD release of the first series, where her glee in the faithful recreation of the period details is vividly apparent:

> It's almost exactly as I wrote it. It's a very peculiar feeling... The costumes are fantastic. The set is perfect. There's nothing in it that is not 1928 or before. And it's not only accuracy, it's the chemistry between the actors: the voltage of that unresolved relationship [between Phryne and Jack]. It's fast, it's funny, and I just don't remember writing it that well (Every Cloud Productions, 2011).

While the success of the three *Miss Fisher* series, the Chinese adaptation, the spin-off *Modern Murder Mysteries* and the film may well have garnered both Greenwood and the producers considerable monetary returns over the last ten years,[4] what is evident from Greenwood's involvement is that the non-monetary benefits of participating in the construction of her characters and fictional world on screen, and subsequently enjoying the results, were of considerable value to her as a writer and a creator.

According to Cox and Eagger, acquiring *Miss Fisher* also gave them an opportunity to say something important about the lives of women during the 1920s in the shadow of the First World War. While this had resulted in the tragic loss of so many young men, it also opened up new possibilities for women. Indeed Phryne Fisher herself is described as having been a member of the all-women ambulance brigade attached to the French army during the war. As Deb Cox told journalist Graeme Blundell:

> Many women missed out on partners and marriage and the conventional choices because there just weren't the men around, but then there were women like our Phryne Fisher who embraced the opportunity (Blundell, 2012).

In adapting Greenwood's crime novels for television, there were some strategic decisions to be made. To begin with, Eagger and Cox's initial pitch for an adaptation included a range of possible formats including three telemovies, a miniseries, or an episodic series, with the latter being the option that was eventually agreed upon (Sdraulig, 2014, p. 48). Once they knew that each of the books had to be fitted into a one-hour slot, the next challenge was to consider which would be 'production friendly' given that one book is set on a ship and another largely in underground caves (Sdraulig, 2014, p. 48). In the first series, Cox also introduced the character of Murdoch Foyle and a season-length storyline featuring Phryne's sister, in order to shed light on Phryne's working-class origins and sense of injustice (Sdraulig, 2014, p. 48).

Development, Production and Post-Production

With Eagger as producer and Cox as head writer, the pair subsequently assembled a predominantly female production team with women in key creative roles. Of the twelve directors employed over the three seasons of *MFMM*, five were women. This included Emma Freeman, who would go on to direct another of the case studies in this book, *Secret City* in 2016 (see Chapter 4), and Daina Reid, who would go on to direct four episodes of the second season of the internationally successful Hulu production, *The Handmaid's Tale*, in 2018. Thirteen of the nineteen writers on the original series were also female, including Deb Cox as Head Writer, and Greenwood herself, who is also given a writing credit (IMDb, 2017). Film Victoria funded three internships attached to the first season of MFMM, two of which were given to women (Film Victoria, 2011, 2012). These figures compare very favourably with then current estimates that women constituted only 16 per cent of directors employed in feature film production in Australia, and 21 per cent of writers (Screen Australia, 2015b).

In bringing Miss Fisher's world to the screen, the production design, art and set direction were vital to recreate the 1920s, providing work for many talented creative professionals who proved their ingenuity time and again when it came to what appeared on screen. As Eagger noted, while *Miss Fisher* only cost A$1.1 million to A$1.2 million per hour to produce – a shoestring budget when compared with the US$11.2 million per first-season episode for the British drama *Downton Abbey* – it managed to look as though it cost a lot more despite what she described as some very 'ambitious episodes' (Eagger, 2016). As Eagger subsequently noted, there was some pride on behalf of the production team given the level of their budget and what they managed to achieve in the look of the series (Sdraulig, 2014, p. 54).

In bringing the 1920s to the screen, Eagger was keen to only use buildings dating from 1928 or earlier, and as a result the production formed a significant partnership with the Victorian branch of the National Trust of Australia. This gave them access to a number of historic houses and buildings in Melbourne and across the state, including Rippon Lea House and Gardens in Elsternwick, Luna Park in St Kilda, the Windsor Hotel and the Comedy Theatre in Melbourne's CBD (Neill, 2016). This partnership subsequently led to a travelling exhibition of *Miss Fisher*'s costumes hosted by the National Trust in 2015 and 2016 as part of a Festival of Phryne, which included over fifty branded events from afternoon teas and walking tours of Melbourne to Miss Fisher Murder Mystery Dinners at Como House and Rippon Lea, such was the enthusiasm generated by the production design's attention to detail. As the success of the travelling exhibition suggested, one of the most significant aspects of the production design was clearly the costumes, in particular the glorious outfits created for *Miss Fisher* by costume designer Marion Boyce, a specialist in 1920s fashion, who would go on to win an AACTA|AFI Award for her work on the show (Table 3.1). While Boyce herself has a collection of 1920s fashion, it was revealed that she sourced most of her materials on a buying trip in China and everything was made 'pretty much from scratch' with a 'huge team of people making hats' (Sdraulig, 2014, p. 50).

Production designer, Robert Perkins, has characterised the process of designing the sets for *MFMM* as both 'a pleasure and a challenge' describing how objects were sourced from antique dealers who gave the production team 'quite good deals: otherwise [we] probably couldn't have afforded them' (Neill, 2016). However, as the series went on and gained a 'reputation', antique collectors began to take note and to offer both props and advice. As Perkins noted, these contributions proved 'invaluable' as they provided first-hand insight and the kind of knowledge that would normally take hours of research to acquire (Neill, 2016). Significant attention was also paid to the music for the series, with Greg Walker sourcing different music of the time for each of the end credits, which was another delightful period detail (Neill, 2016, p. 48).

When it came to shooting the series, Eagger was keen to draw attention to the period details, the costumes and location by investing in two cameras, two operators and a Director of Photography who could light the sets, rather than both operate and light. This she regarded as a point of difference in the way in which the series was shot (Sdraulig, 2014, p. 54), one that yielded a NSW/ACT Award for Cinematography for Cinematographer Roger Lanser (Table 3.1). With thirteen episodes to the first and second series, they routinely filmed two episodes in a block. This gave the team eight days per episode in order to produce what Eagger described as an ABC hour, noting that this is slightly longer than an hour produced for commercial TV, which has to allow for advertising breaks (Sdraulig, 2014, p. 54).

Financing, Distribution and Aggregation

Produced by Every Cloud Productions for the ABC in association with Screen Australia and Film Victoria – together investing $3.6 million in the first two seasons – the series was initially distributed by All3Media International after something of a bidding war at MIPCOM, the annual trade show for TV content held in Cannes (Blatchford, 2015). Well aware that they could not compete with the huge budgets and the lavish casts of British period crime drama, Cox and Eagger decided to push the line that while people might be familiar with the Miss Marples and the Poirots, no other series has such a 'young, unconventional, daring heroine who is part James Bond and more swashbuckling' (Sdraulig, 2014, pp. 49–50). Their flyer and poster for the series in Cannes featured a shapely leg in a lace top stocking with a dagger in the garter, high heels, blood and a pearl-handled pistol. Apparently, it 'worked like a charm' (Sdraulig, 2014, p. 50).

According to All3Media's head of acquisitions, Maarjtje Horchner, this pitch was particularly timely because her company was already looking for a long-running detective series to sit alongside other successful British crime shows in their catalogue, such as *Inspector George Gently*

(BBC 2007–2017) and *Midsomer Murders* (ITV 1997–) (Akyuz, 2012). As Horchner observed, '*The Miss Fisher Murder Mysteries* leapt out – it's so distinctively stylish, sumptuous even, and full of charm' (Akyuz, 2012). Presale buyers for *Miss Fisher* subsequently included Russia's Mauris Corp, Danish public service broadcaster DR and ProSiebenSat.1's Kanal 9 in Sweden and Globosat in Brazil (Akyuz, 2012). As was later revealed, initially the Scandinavian countries were not keen on *Miss Fisher* but were persuaded to take the show as a condition for acquiring a show they did want. However, when *Miss Fisher's Murder Mysteries* aired, they were apparently 'surprised and delighted' to discover that it was extremely popular with Scandinavian viewers and immediately ordered a second series (Lazarus, 2013).

Other deals for the first season included those to Alibi in the UK as well as Netflix and Acorn in the USA, Canal Plus for Poland, DR Denmark, Globosat, Knowledge Canada, Kanal 5 Sweden, HRT Croatia and Viasat for Estonia, Latvia, Lithuania and Norway – as well as a clutch of deals with local broadcasters in Hungary, Ukraine, Azerbaijan, Georgia, Russia and Turkmenistan. While France 3 was also an initial buyer, in 2014 All3Media International announced that major terrestrial broadcaster Channel 5 was now on board in the UK, and Singapore's MediaCorp had also taken the series (Ling, 2014). As Louise Pedersen, Managing Director at All3Media International, observed:

> *Miss Fisher's Murder Mysteries* has gone from strength to strength on the global stage and we're delighted to see the second season promising equal success. From the moment we became involved with this series we could see its great international potential. The meticulous and opulent recreation of the 1920s combined with outstanding performances and lively stories from award-winning author Kerry Greenwood creates fantastic primetime viewing, which holds strong appeal for a wide audience demographic (Ling, 2014).

While the first two seasons of *Miss Fisher* were supported by Screen Australia and the ABC, there was also a substantial advance from All3Media for season 3 that helped make up for a financing shortfall. Although it was clear to Eagger and Cox that *Miss Fisher* was growing in value with each new season (Eagger, 2016), in considering the possibility of a fourth, they were also aware that previous seasons would be repurchased to play again – especially by subscription television and streaming services, because they generally bought much shorter repeat windows than terrestrial broadcasters. Eagger was also of the opinion that there was still a need for a domestic broadcaster, otherwise there would be a big budgeting hole. With this in mind, she noted that at one point they were looking at doing the fourth series as a co-production with Ireland (Eagger, 2016).

In terms of international sales, *Miss Fisher* appeared to be doing very well. Reporting on the returns for Australian television in 2017 for Screen Australia, Sandy George and Rakel Tansley noted that while the Tasmanian-based supernatural crime drama *The Kettering Incident* (see Chapter 4) had come out on top, *MFMM* Series 1 and 2 had come in at numbers two and three respectively. Other crime dramas in the top 10 included the first season of the Jane Campion-directed series *Top of the Lake* (2013), shot in New Zealand, at number 5, and the first season of *The Code* (2014), a thriller set in Canberra and the outback, at number 8. Also reported was the fact that as a group, these top 10 Australian dramas had notched up a total of 340 rest of world (ROW) sales valued at nearly $70 million, an amount that delivered a net return of $20 million for investors (George & Tansley, 2018). In 2020, Every Cloud Productions announced *MFMM* alone had accumulated sales of $20 million, reaching 179 countries and 247 territories (Every Cloud Productions, 2020b).

There was, however, another set of international possibilities opening up for *Miss Fisher's Murder Mysteries*. According to David Tiley, while Fiona Eagger was busily producing what would be the final third season, the ABC was already talking to the Chinese government journalist Jin Weiyi, who had requested Mandarin translations of the *Miss Fisher* scripts. This subsequently led to a format deal with Shanghai 99 Visual Company in partnership with Tencent Penguin Film and Easy Entertainment, a management company. As Eagger observed, this partnership was something of a struggle to achieve 'as there was no template for a format deal based on a drama' (Tiley, 2020). Nevertheless production of the Mandarin adaptation of *Miss Fisher's Murder Mysteries* was soon underway in what Tiley likens to an industrial-scale production process. Thirty episodes were shot in 100 days, with some content carefully modified to satisfy the Chinese authorities (Tiley, 2020). Apparently, this effort was well worth it. When the series, titled *Miss S*, appeared on Tencent in China, it cleared over a billion views, before then appearing on HBOAsia, HBO Go and regular subscription television. Tiley completes his account of this triumph with the observation that Spanish, Indian and Korean versions had also been flagged (Tiley, 2020).

Non-Monetary Benefits to Creators

When it comes to the non-monetary benefits of *Miss Fisher* to its creators, the series was recognised both by the audience and the industry in terms of its excellence, although as Eagger noted somewhat ruefully in 2016, 'The domestic industry has not celebrated Miss Fisher's success as much as it could have' (Eagger, 2016). Nevertheless, Eagger and Cox were nominated in the 2015 TV Week Logie Awards in the category Most Popular TV Program as judged by the audience, as well as an Australian Academy of Cinema and Television/Australian Film Institute Award (AACTA/AFI) for Best Television Drama series as judged by the industry. Costume Designer Marion Boyce was an industry winner in the third Annual AACTA/AFI Awards, as was Roger Lanser for Cinematography (Table 3.1). Actor Essie Davis, who played Miss Fisher, was nominated in two audience categories in the 2014 and 2016 TV Week Logie Awards for Most Popular Actress as well as the Gold Logie for most Popular TV Personality. In 2016 she was also nominated in the industry-judged category Most Outstanding Actress. Meanwhile, Davis's career blossomed with the critical and international success of the Australian art-horror film *The Babadook* (2014), which had its global premiere at the Sundance Festival in the US (Howell, 2017), as well as her appearance as Lady Crane in the sixth season of *Game of Thrones* in 2016.

Intangible Returns to Creators

While industry and audience awards may represent the tangible benefits of a successful television drama, ultimately enhancing the monetary value of the creative talent involved, there were clearly many intangible benefits too. As suggested above, for Kerry Greenwood there was the sheer joy in seeing her character brought to life by a team that respected and admired her work. For Cox and Eagger, *Miss Fisher* was also the realisation of their ambition to make an entertaining crime drama with a strong female role model, created largely by women. In her interview with Sandra Sdraulig (2014, p. 46), Deb Cox spoke passionately about being a writer with 'things I wanted to say about the world'. Cox also referred to the 'certain values' that she communicates as a writer in the hope that 'people might treat each other better and contribute something to society' (Sdraulig, 2014, p. 46). While these are worthy goals, Cox also talked about the 'fun part' of being involved in production with Eagger and the fact that they came together with 'a shared sensibility' (Sdraulig, 2014, p. 46). Clearly this was a working relationship that was of considerable personal value to them both.

There were also other non-monetary values involved in the venture. As Eagger observed, when it came to shooting the film spin-off in Morocco, *Miss Fisher and the Crypt of Tears*, they had the opportunity to film on the Ridley Scott set for *Kingdom of Heaven*, which she described as a 'big thrill'. They also filmed in an 'amazing crater' near the edge of the Sahara, where *The Mummy* (Stephen Sommers, 1999) was filmed, and at 'amazing sand dunes' near Merzouga, where films such as Herzog's *Queen of the Desert* (2015) were made (Every Cloud Productions, 2020b). As Eagger's enthusiasm attests, these were significant moments for her and the crew that clearly surpassed any financial returns.

For Essie Davis, playing Miss Fisher was also an enjoyable experience, especially given that it provided her with the opportunity to play an action hero (Fenton 2015). Describing these sequences as her favourite parts of the show, Davis described how she was required to scale the Victorian Parliament House, perform underwater escape tricks and race motorcycles while being filmed by drone helicopters. Somewhat regretfully Davis observed that they often had to curtail such sequences as they 'take quite a bit of time' (Fenton, 2015). Given each episode had to be completed in eight days, this was a luxury the production could not always afford: 'I'm always pushing for more action, but you know there's all kinds of risks they don't want me to take and there's budget issues,' said Davis (Fenton, 2015). It might be noted that Davis herself came on board as a producer for season 2 – giving her greater creative control over her character (Meares, 2015).

According to one report, while Davis was highly praised for her roles in other ABC-produced dramas, including adaptations of Tim Winton's novel, *Cloud Street*, and *The Slap* by Christos Tsiolkas, it was her 'star turn' as Miss Fisher that made Davis an instantly recognisable face (Meares, 2015). Whether or not this was true, it is clear that following the international success of the art-horror film, *The Babadook* (which enjoyed only moderate success in Australia), *Time* magazine named Davis one of 2014's ten best actors, male or female, anywhere in the world. In the opinion of Meares, in 2014 Davis was poised for international success and had already acquired a 'wonderful new American agent' to answer the phone (Meares, 2015). While it's hard to say how much *MFMM*, *The Babadook* or *Game of Thrones* contributed to Davis's international career, there is no doubt that her turn as Phryne Fisher highlighted her range as both a glamorous heroine and an action hero.

Reception: Watching *Miss Fisher*

The first episode of *Miss Fisher's Murder Mysteries* appeared on the ABC at 8.30 p.m. on 24 February 2012 in its niche 'Friday night crime' spot. As a whole, the first series was considered a success for the ABC, attracting an average of 1.1 million per episode across the run (Every Cloud Productions, 2020a). By way of comparison, when this series appeared on the France3 channel, it ranked second for the night with an average of 3.28 million viewers. Series 2, also of thirteen episodes, appeared on the ABC on 6 September 2013, to be followed by a Christmas Special aired in the family friendly timeslot of 7.30pm on Sunday, 22 December. While this second series attracted an average of 1.7 million viewers per week, the TV Special garnered an audience of 1.56 million viewers and was one of the ABC's Top 4 programs for 2013 (Every Cloud Productions, 2020a). A third series of eight episodes returned on Friday, 8 May 2015, again in the 8.30pm time slot on the ABC with a sold-out finale screened at the Australian Centre for the Moving Image in Melbourne. Although in general the audience for *Miss Fisher* (and for the ABC as a whole) tends to skew older, series 3 also proved to be increasingly popular with a younger audience, up 43 per cent in the 0–24 demographic. By 2015, it was reported that *Miss Fisher's Murder Mysteries* was amongst the most popular programs on both the ABC's free-to-air broadcast service and its catch-up streaming service iView, with a broadcast audience of 1.4 million and 600,000 total iView plays (Inside Film, 2015). Parrot Analytics' online metric shows that audience demand for *MFMM* has been consistently around twice that for the average TV show in the Australian market, peaking at nearly five times average demand with the launch of the third series and with the release of the *Crypt of Tears* movie (Figure 3.1).[5]

One of the more surprising aspects of *Miss Fisher*'s success was its popularity with the American audience, as reported by Lilit Marcus in *The Guardian*, who wrote:

> Move over, *Orange is the New Black*. There's another female-led Netflix show that's winning over a growing, devoted fan base: the Australian TV

series *Miss Fisher's Murder Mysteries*. Based on a popular book series by Kerry Greenwood, the show follows Phryne Fisher, an heiress in 1920s Melbourne, as she fights crime and the status quo – all while impeccably dressed in flapper chic kimonos, beaded dresses, jewelled brooches, and cloche hats (Marcus, 2015).

According to Marcus, many American fans first discovered the show through mentions on style blogs. However, she goes on to point out that 'Beyond the sumptuous interiors and beautiful clothes, though, there are major feminist messages' (Marcus, 2015). These include the observation that one of Phryne's close friends, Mac, is 'an out lesbian doctor', and that various episodes have touched on everything from women getting clandestine abortions to unsafe labour practices in a factory staffed by female employees (Marcus, 2015). As Eagger herself noted, it was clear that, in the United States, *Miss Fisher* had become something of a 'little cult classic' (Eagger, 2016).

Critical Response

Reviewing the first series of *Miss Fisher* in *The Australian*, Graeme Blundell was extremely enthusiastic and particularly taken by Davis's performance, suggesting that rather than just playing Phryne Fisher, the actor seemed to 'collaborate with her' (Blundell, 2012). As a crime fiction reviewer as well as TV critic, Blundell was well aware of *Miss Fisher*'s origins, declaring himself to be a fan of the books and noting that 'the series is characterised by a charming facetiousness of style similar to that of Greenwood's writing' (Blundell, 2012). He also complimented the producers on their 'mastery of the crime thriller's tropes' and the director of photography, Roger Lanser, and production designer, Robert Perkins, for their elegant realisation of 'a decorous world' (Blundell, 2012).

Writing in *Metro* magazine, Carly Millar was less enthusiastic, suggesting that the series offered more style than substance (Millar, 2012). Despite the seriousness of the historical themes and issues, including 'cocaine smuggling, illegal abortionists, Melbourne's Chinese community, the anarchist and Zionist movements, union disputes and factory workers' conditions', Millar was of the opinion that without the show's 'brisk pace, playfulness and sense of whimsy' the plotlines would 'seem more than a little silly' (Millar, 2012, pp. 45–46). She also considered the scripts to be 'occasionally lacking', the murders 'outlandishly farfetched', the direction 'stagy', while conceding that 'the look of the show is its greatest strength' and drawing attention to the costume design of Marion Boyce and the 150 outfits she had created for Essie Davis (Millar, 2012, p. 47). In the end, Millar is willing to grant that *Miss Fisher* certainly achieved what it set out to do:

> *Miss Fisher* aims for light entertainment with a touch of whimsy, and succeeds admirably. As such, all of its flaws may be easily forgiven. It's precisely the kind of undemanding viewing that you can sit back and enjoy with a cup of tea (Millar, 2012, p. 47).

Meanwhile, the online feminist magazine *Jezebel* based in the US also reported on the first season of *Miss Fisher* on Netflix, with Rebecca Rose (2013) describing the title character as an 'independent, brash' woman of the 1920s who hops into bed with a relative stranger in the first episodes without apologies, regrets or thinking twice. This, Rose reported, appeared to have angered some Netflix viewers, whose comments were included:

> I love the look of the show. The costumes are amazing, the set is great, and the actors are quite good too. I just wish the lead charter wasn't such a (Netflix censored me here). If she wasn't giving it away to every other guy, the flirtations between her and Jack would be a lot more meaningful and much more entertaining to watch (Rose, 2013).

As well as:

> I just wish that Miss Fisher wasn't such a tramp. I mean she gives it away like Halloween candy. It is hard to respect some one with such little morality. It she had some romance with just ONE person, it would be a four or five star review (Rose, 2013).

Much was subsequently made of the apparent prurience of the American fans, with Davis herself invited to comment on the criticism that Phryne gave it away 'like Halloween candy', to which Davis responded 'She's just a woman who knows what she wants, and it's *not marriage*' (Meares, 2015). As Julie Ann Taddeo has noted, there were in fact only a 'handful of viewers' posting such negative comments (Taddeo, 2016, p. 57). Far more critical in the debate about Phryne's sexual politics was the initial response from the Australian screen industry. As Don Groves reported (2015), if the more conservative elements had had their way, *Miss Fisher's Murder Mysteries* might never have made it to the screen, or the protagonist could have been a very different character. Apparently, even after the show premiered, the battle to portray Phryne as a woman with a sexual appetite for exotic lovers was not over. As Deb Cox noted in an interview with *IF Magazine*:

> We relished the controversy but it was a reminder that, though the female protagonist has gained ground, that ground still needs defending (Groves, 2015).

As Cox told Sandra Sdraulig:

> We wanted to honour the character of the books, and we knew that she could not come across as a dilettante. I think we, and the network, were worried that if she was wealthy, drank too much champagne and bedded too many men, she might not be taken seriously. They were very serious about how many lovers she had in the first series (Sdraulig, 2014, p. 52).

Whether because of network concerns, or a recognition that fans were responding to the character of Detective Inspector John 'Jack' Robinson as played by Nathan Page, in seasons 2 and 3 the focus was not so much on Miss Fisher's lovers as on her flirtatious relationship with D.I. Robinson. A former competitive cyclist, the athletic Page as Jack Robinson was accorded a much stronger presence than in Greenwood's books, where the relationship with Phryne is one of mutual respect rather than romantic interest. As Julie Ann Taddeo noted, Jack Robinson was 'radically transformed' for television, possibly with good reason (Taddeo, 2016, p. 59). As the subsequent Phryne and Jack relationship evolved onscreen, it was clear that Page was himself a major drawcard for the fans. D.I. Robinson/Nathan Page began to dominate the YouTube fan tributes and fan fiction.[6] In Australia, The D.I. Jack Appreciation Society (DIJAS) Facebook Page began in July 2012, and was still operating in July 2023, providing a forum for debate on each episode and much more, while in the UK a Tumblr site was established for D.I. Jack Robinson and Nathan Page fans (McCorry, 2015).

The Fans

While the fan following for *Miss Fisher's Murder Mysteries* may have begun with the TV series, it was even more evident in the events surrounding the production of the spin-off film, *Miss Fisher and the Crypt of Tears*, before the film was made. In their efforts to raise the finance for the film, Eagger and Cox initiated a crowdfunding campaign 'to bring our fanbase along for the experience' (Every Cloud Productions, 2022). Initially established with a goal of $250,000 to be acquired in thirty days, that figure was reached within the first forty-eight hours, with the follow-up targets of $300,000 and $400,000 being reached in the next twenty-four hours, making it the most successful crowdfunding campaign for an Australian film ever (Moran, 2017). With half of the funders based overseas, $400,000 was leveraged from offshore sources while $500,000 was also secured from private investors (Every Cloud Productions, 2022). Speaking at the Sun Theatre in Yarraville, Melbourne before a screening of the film in February 2020, Eagger made it clear they knew from the start that *Miss Fisher and the Crypt of Tears* was going to be a film for the fans, although perhaps not the critics.

In the audience for that screening at the Sun Theatre, just ahead of what was to be the second wave of COVID-19 in Australia, were members of the Adventuresses' Club of the Americas dressed in their best 1920s ensembles as well as members of the Australian readers and writers network, Sisters in Crime. As it emerged, many of the assembled fans had also contributed to the crowdfund that had enabled the film to go into production, with many of the American fans having already travelled to Australia on several occasions to take part in *Miss Fisher*-related events. As reported by Every Cloud, more than 150 fans of *Miss Fisher* had travelled from the northern hemisphere to take part in the various *Miss Fisher* experiences on offer, including this event, with a calculated impact of over $6 million in terms of direct tourism (Every Cloud Productions, 2020c). On this occasion, the planned events included high tea at the Windsor Hotel (where Miss Fisher first stays when she arrives in Melbourne), punting in the Botanic Gardens and a champagne fuelled 'Fan Screening and Soiree' at the Classic Cinema in Elsternwick.

The second fan screening of the film at Yarraville's Sun Theatre was organised by Sisters in Crime Australia, with producer Fiona Cox and *Miss Fisher* creator, Kerry Greenwood, in attendance. Cox and Greenwood engaged with the audience in a Question and Answer session before the screening, chaired by Sue Turnbull, who can reliably report that watching *Miss Fisher and the Crypt of Tears* surrounded by American fans and members of Sisters in Crime Australia, many of them frocked up in vintage finery, was a memorable occasion, not least because it demonstrated the mutual affection between Miss Fisher's creator, her producer and her fans.

As the lights dimmed, the fans clapped and cheered as the film opened with a heavily-disguised Phryne in a voluminous black chador racing through the streets of Palestine to rescue a young woman who has been wrongfully detained. Foiling all attempts to capture her, at the end of the chase, Phryne sheds her robes to emerge in a sparkling gold dress framed against the skyline like the glamorous Bond-like hero she had indubitably become. As the audience cheered once again, it was clear that Miss Phryne Fisher was indeed an international fan phenomenon. It was, however, the ballroom scene that ultimately galvanised the attention of the audience at the Sun Theatre. As the camera panned across the guests, Kerry Greenwood and her partner, David Greagg, came into view seated at a table in the ballroom in their cameo appearance. At this point, there was a flurry of joyous recognition given that David and Kerry were also sitting in the front row. And as the camera continued to track around the ballroom, it became apparent that many of the onscreen guests were also sitting in the audience, including members of the Australian D.I. Jack Robinson Appreciation Society. These were the fans whose reward for their contribution to the successful crowdfund was to be cast as extras in the film.

Also evident as a result of the week's activities around the launch in Melbourne was the fact that the American fans of *Miss Fisher* were a highly organised group. *The Adventuresses' Club of the Americas*[7] has a website, a podcast, and regularly conducts simultaneous viewings in 'real time'. Its members have held annual fan conventions since 2014, although the 2020 convention had to be cancelled due to the COVID-19 pandemic. These conventions are where the fans share their scholarship and knowledge, not only of the show (and that's impressive in itself), but also of the fashion, poisons, the Hispano-Suiza automobile that features in the books and much, much more. In 2023, costume designer Marion Boyce was the VIP guest at the convention held in St Paul, Minnesota.[8]

As Paddy McCorry observed in 2015, fans of *Miss Fisher* were already using a variety of social media platforms including Facebook, Tumblr, Pinterest, Instagram, YouTube, fanfic sites and blogs to celebrate their love of the series and what they refer to as the Phryneverse, a term which lends *Miss Fisher's Murder Mysteries* a claim to be recognised as 'cult TV'. In his seminal essay addressing what defines a cult TV programme, Matt Hills (2004) outlines a number of key characteristics, with the first of these being 'a consistent narrative world'. As an example, Hills points to the 90s TV series *Buffy the Vampire Slayer* (1997–2003), which establishes a 'hyperdiegesis – or an extended, expansive narrative world'; a criterion that would also seem to be the case with *Miss Fisher's Murder Mysteries*. Eagger herself has described the fictional world of Miss Fisher as '... a fantasy world. It's a heightened world, and you're inviting the audience into that and you don't want them to trip up' (Neill, 2016, p. 49).

According to McCorry the lively, supportive and funny self-titled 'phandom' for *Miss Fisher* (a phryneolgism apparently being collected in a phractionary) functions as a system of networks where members share information and skills, comment, analyse, discuss and debate all things Phryne. Here fans engage in many forms of creative activity including posting photos, artwork, compilations and Photoshopped images, and as was observed at the Melbourne screenings for *Miss Fisher and the Crypt of Tears*, they make their own hats, jewellery and costumes to attend Phryne-related events. *Miss Fisher* fans have also organised 'ficathons' (a challenge in which each participant writes a fanfic based on another participant's request) and write 'drabbles' (a piece of fiction that is exactly 100 words long) while providing editing and review services to each other (McCorry, 2015).[9] In this way friendships between fans have been created 'across the globe' in both virtual and real locations.[10]

Flow-ons

As these fan engagements reveal, the value of *Miss Fisher* lies not only in the careers and opportunities in the screen industry that were generated locally and internationally, but also in terms of all the other activities the series and character have inspired. This inevitably includes the screen-induced tourism that has brought fans to Australia for the costume exhibitions, the afternoon teas, the visits to the stately homes, the streetscape walks, the trips to Queenscliff and the Great Ocean Road as well as the merchandise produced to coincide with the original show. As Eagger and Coz told Michael Bodey from *The Australian* newspaper, even before the second series was launched, the commercial arm of the ABC had already begun merchandising items for the second series, including a *Miss Fisher Cluedo* game. As Eagger observed, 'We realised we could extend the brand'. A limited edition of brooches, handbags and jewellery designed by Boyce also became part of this 'organic' expansion as Cox and Eagger looked for ways to keep the brand alive between series. As it happened, at least half the merchandising sales came from international markets, once again signalling the success of *Miss Fisher* overseas, where the fan base was apparently much younger than the 'predominantly older woman' watching the ABC. However, Eagger was also prepared to admit that in 2015, the merchandise had not really made any money for the production as yet, although it had served their purpose in supporting the show and extending *Miss Fisher*'s reach and fan base (Bodey 2015).

A Melbourne costume exhibition was also a quid pro quo with the National Trust in return for the access they had given the production to a number of its properties for filming as well as an opportunity to showcase the award-winning costume designs by Marion Boyce. The exhibition not only ensured that the production obtained cheaper rates for its location work, it also attracted 40,000 people to the National Trust buildings in its first iteration. On the strength of this outing, it was moved to another National Trust building, Sydney's Old Government House in Parramatta, in 2014. And in 2015, this extension of the Phryneverse included a Festival of Phryne, a series of events organised around the launch of season 3. This included a travelling exhibition of the costumes and fifty events from an afternoon tea and walking tour of Melbourne to a 1920s garden party with 400 fans and their guests attending a screening of the Series 3 Finale at The Australian Centre for the Moving Image. As Neill (2016, p. 49) reported in a *Metro* article discussing how *Miss Fisher's Murder Mysteries* had showcased the history of Melbourne to the world, the series had a significant impact on the 'real-world manifestations of the past it portrays', including helping to raise funds for the reconstruction of the roof at Rippon Lea.

In terms of value, there is clearly a feedback loop that proceeds from the fans' appreciation of the TV series, their pleasure and their creative engagement back to the economic and cultural benefits to be derived from the series and its spin-offs, generating more money for future projects. As reported by Every Cloud in August 2022, these included:

- A spin-off series (*Miss Fisher's Modern Mysteries*)
- A feature film (*Miss Fisher and the Crypt of Tears*)
- An overseas format (*Miss S*)
- Exhibitions and events
- 350,000 DVD and Blu-Ray units sold domestically
- Over fifty items of branded merchandise developed and sold both domestically and internationally (over 150,000 items sold)
- Games books
- Novelisations (*Miss Fisher's Modern Mysteries*)

In the planning stage at this time were a rest-of-world format sale, an original graphic novel prequel series in production with AMC, a stage play adaptation and an additional prequel TV series. *Miss Fisher*, it would appear, was the creative gift that kept on giving.

2015 FESTIVAL OF PHRYNE

As an extension of the Costume Exhibition for Series 3, Every Cloud Productions joined forces with the National Trust of Australia (Victoria) to put on the 'Festival of Phryne' – a series of glamorous events held throughout Melbourne from May to September 2015 to initially tie in with the transmission of Series 3 on ABC TV.

Every Cloud again partnered with the National Trust to produce a Travelling Series 3 Costume Exhibition that launched in Melbourne on 1 May until September 2015. It is touring nationally to:

- Victoria (Melbourne) @ Rippon Lea House, 1 May 2015 to 30 Sept 2015
- South Australia (Adelaide) @ Ayres House, 16 Nov 2015 to 14 Feb 2016
- New South Wales (Parramatta) @ Old Government House, Mar/Apr 2016 to Jun 2016
- Queensland (Brisbane) @ National Trust House, Aug 2016 to Oct 2016
- ACT (Canberra) @ National Film and Sound Archive Nov 2016

In partnership with the National Trust, the 'Festival of Phryne' produced fifty 'Miss Fisher' branded event sessions, including:

- 30× Afternoon Tea & Walking Tour of Melbourne sessions
- Pop Up Miss Fisher Speakeasy at the Melbourne Gaol
- 2× Miss Fisher Murder Mystery Dinners at Como House & Rippon Lea
- 6× Fashionable High Tea sessions at Labassa Mansion
- Meet the Makers of Miss Fisher & Afternoon Tea at the Rippon Lea Ballroom
- Miss Fisher Series 3 Finale Screening at ACMI
- Miss Fisher Merchandise Showcase & Inspiration talk
- 2× Friday Night After Dark – Jazz, Swing & Costumes

- 1920s Miss Fisher Garden Party
- Music & Miss Fisher Event – Live music from the series
- 1920s Beauty Salon & Swing Dance Workshop

In the first three months, from May to August 2015, the 'Festival of Phryne' has seen:

- 21,000 domestic and international visitors, to the Costume Exhibition – which is projected to overtake the previous exhibition's attendance record
- An additional 2,570 visitors attending public programs and events, which tie in with the exhibition and the Festival of Phryne
- Almost 400 fans and guests attending the Finale screening in Melbourne on 26 June 2015 at ACMI, sponsored by Film Victoria

Sources: Every Cloud Productions (2020c)

Cultural Impact

In identifying the cultural value and impact of *Miss Fisher*, it's clear that this would include many of the factors already raised above, including the initial move by Fiona Eagger and Deb Cox to embrace a complex female hero and to bring her to the screen in a production process that would involve as many women as possible. As Lisa French has noted, even by 2014, Screen Australia had no gender-based affirmative action programme to address a significant imbalance in the industry (French, 2014, p. 190). The fact that the original *Miss Fisher* series had two female producers was therefore culturally significant, because as director Sue Maslin has already noted, 'women producers not only give orders but are possibly more attuned to listening to their crew and observing outcomes' (Sue Maslin, cited in French, 2014, p. 190). This leads French to the conclusion that women may contribute to cultural change in workplace cultures because they are more encouraging, 'focused on relationships and effective communicators' (French, 2014, p. 190). Such a change, it was noted, would indeed mark a major cultural shift.

In terms of the representation of Miss Fisher herself, as Julie Ann Taddeo pointed out, both Greenwood's books and the original TV series explore the limits of women's liberation in the 1920s 'as well as the conflicted responses of viewers in a post-feminist media landscape to the sexualised "modern woman" of the past and present' (Taddeo, 2016, p. 49). Miss Fisher's sexual freedom and choice of lovers is a case in point here. While in the books, Miss Fisher continues her relationship with her wealthy Chinese lover, Lin Chung, after his marriage and with the agreement of his wife, with whom she becomes friends, this relationship ends in the TV series as the relationship between Phryne and D.I. Jack Robinson becomes the primary focus. As Taddeo observes, series 2 was much tamer in terms of sex, with a much greater focus on the Phryne/Jack story arc (Taddeo, 2016, p. 58). As noted earlier, the decision to constrain Phryne's sexual adventures may well have been an effect of network pressure, as well as a concern about how a sexually liberated woman might be perceived by more conservative members of the audience.

While the ABC (2011) teachers' study guide intended for senior secondary English students steers clear of specifically addressing Phryne's sexual appetites and the word feminism, in the section on representation it does invite students to reflect on Phryne's status as a woman and to compare this with the status of women in the present:

> In the first video, Kerry Greenwood, author of the Phryne Fisher books, talks about changing values and attitudes in the 1920s. Watch the video, and then answer the questions:
> - Identify three key differences for women in the 1920s and explain how these changes came about.
> - Write a paragraph to explain how men treated women in polite society, with a second paragraph to describe how and why this treatment has changed in contemporary times.
> - What imagery does the author use to illustrate the values and attitudes of the 1920s? (ABC, 2011)

In answering this question, the students would have much to draw on, even in the first episode. As Graham Blundell (2012) pointed out in his initial review of the series, when Phryne arrives in Melbourne and is ensconced in the fashionable Windsor Hotel, there is a scene in which she is 'swapping edgy jokes about the unnaturalness of celibacy and the medical problems of the 'wandering womb' with 'delightful Dr MacMillan', who is dressed in 'sexy men's clothes' and who has a completely 'no-nonsense approach to the rife male hypocrisy of the time'. Later in the episode Phryne has an affair with a Russian dancer while advertising the fact to her maidservant that she is using the latest birth-control device, as devised by the 'thoroughly modern' Miss Marie Stopes, who was a pioneer in female contraception (Blundell, 2012).

The study guide also quotes from the screenplay for episode 9, *Queen of the Flowers*, which directly references the predatory behaviour of a paedophile mayor, but steers clear of addressing this criminal behaviour in the questions. Instead students are invited to focus their attention on the effective use of language in the scene:

> Write a 200-word paragraph to explain how language is used to create tension in this scene, illustrating your answer with two examples (ABC, 2011).

Given that this study guide is intended for the study of English in a senior secondary school, one can appreciate the reasons for this choice. However, this directive to focus on language does tend to side-step some of the more pressing issues the series addresses, including drug-taking and abortion, as well as the disparity between rich and poor. Despite her inherited wealth, and possibly because of her disadvantaged childhood, Miss Fisher in the books and on the screen is decidedly left-leaning in terms of her politics, befriending two communist taxi drivers in the first episode (Taddeo, 2016, p. 52).

In her cogent analysis of the series, Julie Ann Taddeo concludes that the construction of *Miss Fisher's Murder Mysteries* is therefore 'multi-purpose'. While Phryne may provide 'evidence' for the ways in which the 'modern woman' was perceived in the 1920s, her investigations also appeal to our 'twenty-first century social sensibilities' in so far as she is frequently dealing with issues that would have been 'swept under the carpet' in the 1920s (Taddeo, 2016, p. 52). In this way, *Miss Fisher* appears to 'avoid the conservatively nostalgic impulse of the TV period drama' for which the creator of *Downton Abbey*, Julian Fellowes, has been criticised (Taddeo, 2016, p. 51). Inevitably this leads to the conclusion that what *Miss Fisher* offers is something of a revisionist take on history, as is confirmed in episode four of *The Adventuress Podcast* (Aldrich, 2019). Here British academic Jessica Meyer talks about her research into the experience of shell-shock in the First World War, and describes how she is fascinated by how the war is represented in the *Miss Fisher* world through the surviving male characters, while also being somewhat sceptical about the historical accuracy of Phryne's own career as an ambulance driver during the combat. As she confesses, despite these inaccuracies, Mayer herself is nonetheless a fan.

Over the course of a week in February 2021, a premiere in Sydney and two fan screenings, Sue Turnbull met with fans from America, Canada, the UK, Finland and Germany. This included two young women from Northern Europe, who had spent ten days travelling to every *Miss Fisher* location they could find, taking a steam train to Castlemaine and identifying an obscure alleyway in the Kensington wool sheds where they recreated significant moments from the series. These were highly intelligent young women, both medical students, who had bonded online over *Miss Fisher* and were enjoying the holiday of a lifetime, which had taken them off the usual tourist route and into the industrial corners of Melbourne.

All of the fans encountered during this month of Phryne-related events talked eloquently about the ways in which *Miss Fisher* had enabled them to make new friends across the world, to find like-minded others and to build communities of interest. At the same time, there was often a more intimate and confessional story of how they came to *Miss Fisher*, and how she and her world view were of personal value in difficult or trying times. These encounters were often framed in terms of how Miss Fisher inspired them to be a bit more powerful, more confident and a lot less scared of the world – 'like Phryne'. In their discussion of the show, and in their public pronouncements, the rhetoric was all about empowerment, but also the requirement to be unapologetically oneself. In this way they testified to the inestimable value of a fictional character who has found her way onto a global stage and into the hearts of her fans.

It has been suggested that one of the ways in which Phryne Fisher differs from the more conventional detectives of the Golden Age, such as Dorothy L. Sayers' Harriet Vane or Agatha Christie's Miss Marple, is 'her sense of adventure, her spiritedness and her active pursuit of criminals', which as Millar (2012) points out, often results in her placing herself and her nearest and dearest in danger. Although Greenwood herself may regard James Bond as the male counterpoint to Miss Fisher, in making her lady detective a 'modern woman' of the 1920s, she is in effect paying homage to (but also correcting the shortcomings of) the Golden Age detective novels, whose creators, and the times, still did not allow for a Miss Fisher. Authors like Sayers and Christie, though writing at the height of the first sexual revolution, simply did not put sexually modern women like Miss Fisher, with her 'taste for young and comely men' (Greenwood, 1989), in the lead role of crime solver. As Glenwood Irons notes, the woman detective featured in early twentieth-century fiction was 'seldom perceived as having an individuality equivalent to that of the male detective' (1995). On the other hand, Alison Light has argued that Golden Age detective fiction was in fact quite transgressive, feminising the genre with effete anti-heroes whose throw-away slang and penchant for cocktails was part of a larger reaction against the trauma of the First World War (1991: 66).

Perhaps the closest Golden Age comparison to Miss Fisher might be Christie's Prudence 'Tuppence' Cowley – former VAD nurse turned Bright Young Thing; with a black bob like Miss Fisher but without her deep pockets, Tuppence advertises her services as a 'Young Adventurer' for hire in post-war London and solves crimes with her fellow war veteran, Tommy Beresford, the kind of male/female pairing that has been a staple of the television crime drama series from *The Avengers* (ITV 1961–1969) to *The Bridge* (Turnbull, 2014, p. 168). In terms of genre, however, *Miss Fisher's Murder Mysteries* has more in common with the more arch tone of series such as the 'cosy' murder mystery *Midsomer Murders* (ITV 1997–), in that while serious social issues might be addressed, there is always a reassurance that the bad will get their comeuppance and justice will be done.

Another possible reassurance for those who need it is the fact that *Miss Fisher's Murder Mysteries* presents a version of Australia with strong ties to England, which while historically accurate, effectively conceals the Indigenous history of occupation and subsequent patterns of migration. While the Chinese character of Li Chun features prominently in the books, especially the most recent *Murder in Williamstown* (2022), his role is downplayed in the TV series. In fact, after the British, the Chinese are the oldest immigrant group to the continent, predating the infamous White Australia Policy introduced soon after Federation in 1901. *Miss Fisher*'s onscreen world is therefore predominantly monocultural which may also help to account for its international success, noting that the Chinese themselves decided to make Miss Fisher firmly their own by relocating her to Shanghai in the *Miss S* adaptation. In her favour, Miss Fisher herself, by virtue of her wealth and heritage, is very much an unconstrained cosmopolitan 'citizen of the world'. Although she was born into poverty, she has advanced into the British aristocracy, has lived in France, relocated to Australia, has a best friend who is gay, and acquires a range of lovers from a variety of different nationalities. Taken as a whole there are ways in which the series is both regressive and progressive.

While, as we have indicated, there are ways in which *Miss Fisher's Murder Mysteries* might be critiqued and found lacking, in terms of our study, what the series clearly represents is the ongoing viability of Australian content in a global marketplace now dominated by the streamers. The fact that Phryne is a modern, cosmopolitan woman whose life is largely unconstrained by border restrictions and anxieties about money, who lives life to the full in fabulous frocks while scaling tall buildings, is only a small part of the story when it comes to accounting for her success. Indeed, in terms of her total value to those involved in her creation and the global audience that has embraced her, as well as the multiple ripple effects the series has had in both local and national terms, this may well be inestimable.

Table 3.1 *Miss Fisher's Murder Mysteries* **(2012–2015)**

The makers

Commissioning broadcaster	Australian Broadcasting Corporation (ABC)
Production company	Every Cloud Productions
Distributor / international sales	All3Media International

The results

Sales	$20 million in sales (Aug 2022) reaching 179 countries and 247 territories (Feb 2020) (Every Cloud Productions, 2020b).
	In 2017, the first two series of *Miss Fisher* were respectively the second- and third-highest drama export supported by Screen Australia (George & Tansley, 2018; Groves, 2018a).
Awards	2 wins and 13 nominations
	Australian Academy of Cinema and Television Arts (AACTA) Awards
	• 2020 Nominee Audience Choice Award Favourite Australian TV Drama: Fiona Eagger
	• 2015 Nominee Best Television Drama Series: Fiona Eagger, Deb Cox (Series 3)
	• 2015 Nominee Best Costume Design in Television: Marion Boyce, Ep. 'Death Defying Feats (2015)'
	• 2014 **Winner** Best Costume Design in Television: Marion Boyce, Ep. 'Murder Most Scandalous (2013)'
	• 2013 Nominee Best Lead Actress in a Television Drama: Essie Davis
	Logie Awards
	• 2016 Nominee Best Actress: Essie Davis
	• 2016 Nominee Gold Logie: Essie Davis
	• 2016 Nominee Most Outstanding Actress: Essie Davis
	• 2014 Nominee Most Popular Actress: Essie Davis
	• 2014 Nominee Most Popular Drama Series
	• 2013 Nominee Most Popular Actress: Ashleigh Cummings
	The Equity Ensemble Awards
	• 2014 Nominee Outstanding Performance by an Ensemble Series in a Drama Series
	• 2013 Nominee Outstanding Performance by an Ensemble Series in a Drama Series
	Sichuan TV Festival
	• 2013 Nominee Gold Panda Best Writing for a Television Series: Deb Cox

Table 3.1 (*cont.*)

Awards (*cont.*)	NSW/ACT Awards for Cinematography • 2012 **Gold Award** for Telefeature, TV Drama and Mini Series: Roger Lanser, ACS
Audience demand	Episodes from the three seasons attracted audiences of more than one million in Australia. Its debut in France was seen by an audience of 3.28 million (Every Cloud Productions, 2020b). In 2015, *MFMM* was among the most popular programs on ABC iView, with a broadcast audience of 1.4 million and 600,000 iView plays (Inside Film, 2015). In June 2022, the movie *Miss Fisher and the Crypt of Tears'* free-to-air premiere on the ABC averaged a consolidated audience of 905,000, following a theatrical release earlier in the year (Every Cloud Productions, 2022). IMDb rating: 8.2/10 Rotten Tomatoes average audience score: 93%

Notes: AACTA: Australian Academy of Cinema and Television Arts; NSW: New South Wales; ACT: Australian Capital Territory; ACS: Australian Cinematographers Society.

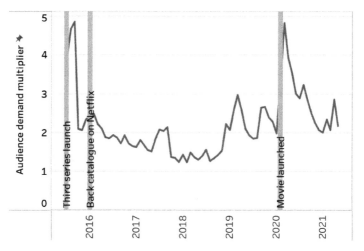

Figure 3.1 Audience demand multiplier for *Miss Fisher's Murder Mysteries*

Note: The audience demand multiplier benchmarks content relative to the market average of 1. If a show has 2× demand, it is two times more in-demand than the average TV show in the market.

Source: Parrot Analytics (2021).

Chapter 4

The Kettering Incident

In 2018 Screen Australia reported that in the previous year, the top-selling Australian TV drama internationally was *The Kettering Incident* (Showcase 2016), closely followed by the first two seasons of *Miss Fisher's Murder Mysteries* in second and third place (Groves, 2018a). While *Kettering* and *Miss Fisher* might have therefore been on a par in terms of their monetary returns and economic value to their producers and distributors, they may not have had quite the same kind of value for their Australian audiences, partly as a result of accessibility. Unlike *Miss Fisher's Murder Mysteries*, which initially found an enthusiastic audience on the ABC, a free-to-air public service broadcaster, *The Kettering Incident* was at first only available on the subscription television service Foxtel, which in 2016 had just 2.9 million subscribers in Australia and a penetration rate of 30 per cent.

Despite only being accessible to a small audience, the success of *The Kettering Incident* and the political thriller *Secret City*, another Foxtel commission, at the 2017 Logie Awards, was hailed as the culmination of what Foxtel's head of drama, Penny Win, described as a five-year plan. This entailed the creation of high-end quality drama that would help to drive subscriptions nationally while sitting comfortably alongside the HBO quality dramas on their Showcase platform. While Foxtel appeared to have achieved its goal in 2018 and there was a subsequent change of direction, it was interesting to note how few of the people we spoke to during the course of our study in Australia had seen either *The Kettering Incident* or *Secret City* when they first appeared on Foxtel. In fact both these series only became better known when they moved to international streaming platforms, thus proving, as Foxtel anticipated, that they would indeed have an extended shelf life. At the time of writing in July 2023, *The Kettering Incident* could be watched in Australia on Apple TV+ and Prime Video, while *Secret City* was available on Netflix, Apple TV+ and YouTube as well as Binge and Foxtel.

Of even more interest was the fact that both of these series reflected the influence of what was variously described in the press as 'Nordic Noir' or 'Scandi Noir' in terms of their look and their content, a fact that was not lost on reviewers. Clem Bastow, writing in *The Guardian* (2016), suggested that the pace of *The Kettering Incident* was 'languid' and that the show had more in common with 'Scandi-noir' than the HBO model of 'event television'. As it later emerged, *The Kettering Incident* had even more in common with the Swedish crime drama *Jordskott* (SVT & DR 2015–2017), including its narrative, supernatural elements, gothic overtones and ecological themes. But *Jordskott* was never mentioned in the press, possibly because the Swedish series did not appear in Australia until after *Kettering* in December 2017 when, promoting its launch on its VOD platform SBS OnDemand, public broadcaster SBS declared that '*Jordskott* goes beyond the usual Nordic Noir scenario with a very ... specific ... twist' (Cubis, 2017).

ABC Radio National identified *The Kettering Incident* as part of an emergent Aussie-noir trend, 'in particular Tasmanian Gothic, as the wild rugged landscape of Australia's most isolated state becomes its own malevolent character in the story' (Madden, 2016). The series was promoted as the brainchild of Tasmanian-based writer Vicki Madden, who was framed in the pre-publicity as the 'creative champion' of the series (Lotz, 2017), even though co-producer Vincent Sheehan was also credited as a co-creator. In her many interviews and appearances to publicise the show, Madden continued to reiterate how this was both a 'very personal story' and a 'very Tasmanian story' that enabled her to combine her 'life experiences' growing up in Tasmania with her extensive experience as a writer and producer for television both in Australia and in the UK (Bastow, 2016).

The Kettering Incident follows the trajectory of Dr Anna Macy (Elizabeth Dubecki), a Kettering native who left Tasmania at the age of fourteen following the mysterious disappearance of her best friend while on a cycling trip through the forest. Fifteen years later, Anna is working in London as a doctor when she is overtaken by blinding headaches, mysterious blackouts and nosebleeds. Returning to Kettering in search of answers (which frustratingly for many viewers never quite arrive), Anna finds the town in the midst of a dispute between environmentalists and local loggers. When the daughter of one of the latter, Chloe Holloway (Siano Smit-McPhee), also mysteriously disappears in the forest, Anna becomes engrossed in a quest to find out what has happened to both of the missing girls. Inevitably, this involves the local police, as represented by Officer Fergus McFadden (Henry Nixon) and Detective Brian Dutch (Matthew Le Nevez), who is investigating a potential drug ring. As the story proceeds, the supernatural elements begin to accumulate, with a surprise ending that renders *Kettering* a somewhat incomplete generic hybrid.

By way of comparison, and to demonstrate that this turn to the supernatural was already present in crime drama from Scandinavia, the plot of *Jordskott* series 1 unfolds as follows. Police Detective Eva Thörnblad (Moa Gammel) returns to her hometown of Silverhöjd, where her daughter Josefine is still missing after disappearing seven years ago beside a forest lake. Since Josefine's body was never found, the local police have determined that she has drowned. Upon Eva's return, another child disappears, this time a local boy who has been missing for a week, and Eva is certain that there is a connection between the two disappearances. At the same time, she is also dealing with the death and probate of her late father that involves his large timber felling, silver mining and processing business. Eva subsequently teams up with Göran Wass (Göran Ragnerstam), a Rikskriminalen detective (and member of a secret society), and Tom Aronsson (Richard Forsgren), a local detective. They discover that the children's disappearances are inextricably tangled with the conflict between locals who depend on the local industries and the mystical beings protecting the forest and surroundings.

Both series feature a blonde female central character whose whiteness is in stark contrast to the gloomy backgrounds of the forest and dingy interiors. Both feature a remote small town close to the forest that looms large as a presence and as a source of tension between those who wish to protect it and those who wish to exploit it. Both feature missing children and a puzzled but misdirected police presence. Both culminate in a revelation that there are supernatural forces at work. As a result, Coralie Sanderson's description of *Jordskott* as the quintessence of EcoNoir applies equally well to *Kettering*, since in both we have not only the troubled central female character familiar to the Nordic Noir trope but also:

> … the narrative presence of the police procedural… the missing child topos, the sublime landscaping gaze, the melancholic mood, the socio-political critique, and most importantly the presence of supernatural, mythological, folkloric and Gothic tropes (Sanderson, 2023, p. 88).

While this case study will explore the total value of *The Kettering Incident* to those who were involved in its creation, as well as to Tasmania and the screen industry both locally and nationally, it is interesting to note how there are three stories of origin here. While the first would encompass the global popularity of Nordic Noir, conceived as a brand with global currency (Hansen & Waade, 2017), the second would include Foxtel's stated desire to create high concept drama that would enhance their subscription base and find an international audience. The third, however, belongs to Vicki Madden as the 'auteur' and 'creative champion' of a series that was presented as a very personal undertaking. Ultimately, the 'success' of *The Kettering Incident* is probably more to do with the benefits it has generated for the Tasmanian film industry which, as Karl Quinn (2023c) has noted, has subsequently gone from strength to strength.

Making *The Kettering Incident*

Initial Development, Origins

> The Tasmania that I grew up with was a very gothic, isolating experience for me. My feelings here, my memories of childhood were always chaotic I suppose and frightening at times. Even coming back to Tasmania I wanted to reflect that. When I watch shows like *Twin Peaks*, or I watch shows like *The Killing* or *The Bridge*, I feel that very same connection with those shows because I think Tasmania is such a gothic noir-ish place and there are certain places around Tasmania that you can definitely feel the past, you can feel something eerie and malevolent in the ground. Maybe that's because I'm a writer…. (Madden, 2016).

Reflecting on her experience of growing up in Tasmania and on the cultural influences that had shaped her vision, it is interesting to note that not only does Madden mention two of the most significant and influential of the Nordic Noir crime dramas, *The Killing* (DR 2007–2012) and *The Bridge* (SVT & DR 2016–2019), but also David Lynch's cult TV series *Twin Peaks* (ABC 1990–1991). Indeed, reviewer Michael Idato in *The Sydney Morning Herald* was keen to point out that since both series feature sawmills, *Kettering* might well do for Tasmania what *Twin Peaks* did for Snoqualmie, Washington State by attracting tourists to a spectacular landscape (Idato, 2016). While *Twin Peaks* may have been one reference point, Idato went on to modify this connection by suggesting that in his opinion, *Kettering* was more reflective of Jane Campion's recent brooding crime drama set in New Zealand, *Top of the Lake* (Sundance TV 2013–2017), or another cult TV series of the 1990s, *The X-Files* (Fox 1993–2002), than David Lynch's brilliant, 'mad vision'. Idato's comments thus point to the rich legacy of television crime dramas that creators may inevitably draw on in the construction of their own, original drama.

For Madden herself, the 'biggest thematic baseline' in the show was that of 'people feeling isolated but trapped by their home town'. As Madden told an interviewer, when she returned to Tasmania after living in Ireland, she had a 'three-month meltdown' during which she felt disconnected from the people around her and her family, 'So being a writer, I started to capture that and put my finger on it. That was the formation of Anna Macy' (Martain, 2016). In this story of origin, the value of *Kettering* to Madden would appear to be a working through of her own trauma while also applying the skills she had acquired as a writer and producer for television in order to shape this into something that might have a different kind of value in a commercial context.

Having left Tasmania at the age of 18 to work in the television industry in the 1990s, Madden's apprenticeship as a screenwriter included work on a number of significant Australian TV crime dramas, including *Halifax fp* (Nine Network 1994–2002) and *Water Rats* (Nine Network 1997–1998), before moving to work in the UK. This included stints as a script producer with Lynda La Plante on her series *Trial and Retribution* (ITV 1997–2009) as well as two years on the long-running British police procedural, *The Bill* (ITV 1983–2010). Returning to Tasmania to care for her mother (Vinall, 2020), Madden pitched her original idea for *The Kettering Incident* to Screen Tasmania, who suggested that she team up with Tasmanian film producer, Victor Sheehan (Sangston & McPhail, 2017). Sheehan was the producer of the critically acclaimed Australian film, *Animal Kingdom* (2010), and had recently shot the film *The Hunter* (2011) in Tasmania despite being only able to employ eight Tasmanians out of a crew of fifty because of skilled labour shortages. Sheehan had, however, reportedly 'fallen madly in love' with Tasmania and was keen to work there again (Martain, 2016). In putting Madden and Sheehan in touch and providing seed funding, Screen Tasmania was clearly hoping that *The Kettering Incident* would attract further production to Tasmania and help build capacity in the state, as would indeed prove to be the case (Sangston & McPhail, 2017).

Sheehan approached Penny Win, then head of drama at Foxtel, with their pitch for the show, telling an interviewer that Win was the only person he thought would take on the project given that it was 'a genre no one had seen on Australian screens' (Mathieson, 2017). Win was apparently unfazed by the originality of the pitch, which was, as she observed later, very different from the *Kettering* that finally emerged (Crowley et al., 2017). According to Win, she really liked what she described as this noirish, Tasmanian, high concept genre with aliens, because it was 'brave' and would inevitably 'make a noise' (ibid). Win also hoped it would help reframe Foxtel's drama profile, telling Foxtel's director of content, Ross Crowley, 'We could get into that space and own it if we don't pussyfoot around the edges' (Crowley et al., 2017). The space in question was clearly Foxtel's aspiration to be Australia's version of HBO, with *Kettering* as the crime drama that would help them achieve this as part of the five-year plan that Win herself had drawn up for Foxtel drama (Crowley et al., 2017). As Win pointed out, she initially saw *Kettering* as a cross between *Broadchurch* (ITV 2013–2017) (the successful British crime drama set in a South-coast small town) and *The X-Files* with a little bit of *Twin Peaks* (Crowley et al., 2017).

When it came to the perceived Nordic Noir influence on *Kettering*, Win was adamant that in her opinion this had been thoroughly assimilated and transmuted in the process of the adaptation to a Tasmanian setting. As she told us, there was a time when everybody who came to Foxtel was pitching Scandi Noir: 'They were borrowing all the tropes and structure of *The Killing* and all those ones, but it didn't work' (Crowley et al., 2017). In Win's opinion, to make it work there had to be a distillation of these tropes into something like Australian noir, with the observation 'you've got to be yourself for it to be successful internationally' (Crowley et al., 2017). According to Win, Madden was able to deliver this because:

> She's totally influenced by the Scandis and she's been over there a number of times and met them all but she knew it had to be Tasmanian. And that's why it was successful, it didn't try to be Scandi, but it definitely was noir, making it true. It's being true to yourself and not trying to be anything else is what travels really well (Crowley et al., 2017).

As this comment reveals, Win is of the opinion that although Madden was 'totally influenced by the Scandis', she has managed to translate the Nordic Noir influence into something quintessentially Tasmanian.

Development and Production

After Channel 4 in the UK came on board, Foxtel was apparently involved in every part of the production, from the writer's room to the 'beat sheets' to the plotting. Most important of all, Win observed, was the acquisition of trust so that the creators would accept the feedback in what she described as a mapping process melded by both sides (Crowley et al., 2017). Madden herself reported that the experience of receiving feedback from Foxtel was 'difficult', telling an interviewer 'That's when you have to work very hard to keep the vision locked in. You've just got to "hold your nerve" and I think I had that written on my whiteboard for the first year' (Bizzaca, 2016a). As these contrasting perspectives reveal, there were clearly some creative differences to be negotiated, with Win determined to shape the show into one with global appeal and Madden determined to keep control of her story.

One of the ways in which Madden was able to maintain control was by assuming the role of 'showrunner', a designation already familiar in the US and the UK but not usually described as such in Australia. In explaining how she envisaged this role, Madden suggested that she had some experience of this when working on *The Bill* in the UK, and that she already knew she could 'put a show together' (Bizzaca, 2016a). According to Madden, being a showrunner involves the writer stepping into the role of the producer in order to 'steer the ship' while holding fast to the creative vision of the show (Bizzaca, 2016a). Writing in 2013, Don Groves suggested that while the emergence of the showrunner role was a relatively recent development in the production of Australian drama, it had clearly existed in the past with writer/producers in comedy who might well have been described as showrunner, such as Geoffrey Atherden on the sitcom *Mother and Son* (1984–1994). More recent Australian examples of people who might have qualified for the role included the involvement of writer/producer Tony Ayres in the adaptation of *The Slap* by Christos Tsiolkas, and Shelley Birse's role in the production of *The Code* (2014–2016).

If the role of the showrunner is to provide the 'single vision' that holds the production together, then this is clearly what Madden sought to provide, especially when overseeing what Clem Barstow in *The Guardian* described as 'a dream team of Australian film and TV talent'. This included writers Cate Shortland (who would go on to direct the Marvel film *Black Widow* [2021]); Louise Fox (who co-created the supernatural series *Glitch* [2015–2019] with Tony Ayres); and Andrew Knight, whose writing credits stretch from comedy (*The D Generation* [1986–1987]) to the *Jack Irish* series (2016–2021) based on the crime novels of Peter Temple, and who would go on to co-write the Tasmanian set comedy-thriller, *Bay of Fires*, in 2023 for the ABC.

In the exercise of her creative control over the show, Madden was also responsible for the choice of the cinematographer. After what Madden describes as a 'tonal meeting' in Sydney where she talked about the style she envisioned for the series (Bizzaca, 2016a), Ari Wegner secured the role by producing a 'mood board' for Madden, which effectively captured Madden's childhood memories of Tasmania:

> … right down to these dollops of light coming down through the trees to the forest floor and those puddles of reddish water. She [Wegner] called those puddles 'Kettering blood' and that was when I knew I'd fallen in love with her. It tied in perfectly with the song *Crimson and Clover*, which is used throughout the series. It's my mother's favourite song and it's also very haunting, nostalgic and melancholy, which is exactly the mood I wanted for the series (Madden cited in Martain, 2016).

For Wegner, who had shot two feature films, *Grey Matter* (2011) and *Ruin* (2013), but had not been involved in a TV series before, the eighteen-week shoot in Tasmania was the longest in which she had been involved. This meant that in order to maintain the 'winter feel' of the show, she needed to use digital effects, including precise measurements of the colour temperatures of each scene in order to match the look of the various locations (Pragier, 2016). According to Wegner, what they wanted to achieve was a sense of 'unease' reflecting Anna's vision so that the audience would feel as if they were experiencing the show from her point of view rather than simply 'watching' her from a distance (Pragier, 2016). The 'look' of *Kettering* is therefore tonally dark, as in the most iconic of the Nordic Noir series, with a predominant colour scheme of blue/grey with the occasional spark of red. For example, in the flashbacks depicting the disappearance of Anna's friend Gillian, she is wearing a red hooded coat as she disappears into the forest, in a visual echo of Little Red Riding Hood on her trip to Grandmother's house. Extensive use is also made of drone shots to capture the gloomy forest from above, while the opening night sequence with flashing torch beams recalls the opening of *The Killing* as a terrified Nanna Birk Larsen (Julie Ølgaard) runs through the woods pursued by her murderer.

While Wegner was from the mainland, *The Kettering Incident* employed 110 cast and crew members from Tasmania out of an approximate

200 people working on the show. This included thirteen attachments supported by Screen Australia, with three being allocated to the writing department. Madden herself was keen to point out her support for emerging creatives from Tasmania (Bizzaca, 2016a). One of those attachments was Shaun Wilson, the Tasmanian director of the successful web series, *Noirhouse* (ABC iView 2013–2014), who would move on from *Kettering* to another Tasmanian production, the comedy drama series *Rosehaven* (ABC 2016–2020), where he would direct a further thirteen episodes. As Madden observed, many of the crew who 'trained up' on *Kettering* would move on to *Rosehaven*, thus achieving what Screen Tasmania had initially hoped for – the skilling up of the local workforce and more jobs.

Even before the series began, the premier of Tasmania had been describing the projected $15 million production as a 'game changer' for the Tasmanian screen industry, with the promise of work for at least fifty cast and fifty crew members, a goal that appeared to have been met (Giddings, 2014). The Tasmanian Arts Minister, Vanessa Goodwin, also justified the Government's investment (through Screen Tasmania) of $1 million in the production on the grounds that it would help 'foster local talent' and build 'industry capability with trainees working across a range of departments, including the creative areas of scriptwriting and directing, as well as craft specialisations such as editing and art department' (ABC News, 2014a).

The Kettering Incident proved to be part of a flurry of production activity, including *Rosehaven* and the Oscar-nominated film *Lion* (2016), that influenced the development of Screen Tasmania's 2017–2021 Strategic Plan (Screen Tasmania, 2017). The Plan notes that while audiences for independent cinema are declining, 'high-end television' is increasingly the 'new cinema', with streamer revenues expected to increase markedly in the next five years (Screen Tasmania, 2017, p. 7). Screen Tasmania's outlook for the screen industry was hopeful, 'with Tasmania home to many young and eager people who are keen to be given opportunities in the screen industry'. To consolidate the jobs offered by *Kettering* and *Rosehaven*, Screen Tasmania presented a Workforce Development Plan that aimed to fulfil their mission 'To grow and develop a sustainable Tasmanian screen production industry to showcase Tasmanian talent, stories, creativity and our landscape' (Screen Tasmania, 2017, p. 10). It's an ambitious roadmap for the future which also aims to address gender, ethnic, geographic and Aboriginal imbalances in the screen production sector, delivering cultural impacts in addition to what are intended to be sustainable industry benefits. The final image in the brochure is of a cameraman on his knees filming a Tasmanian devil, one of Australia's many endangered species.

Financing, Distribution and Aggregation

Financing of *The Kettering Incident* came together in 2013, with Screen Tasmania investing $1 million in the series, Screen Australia committing $1.34 million and the BBC Worldwide contributing a distribution advance ('$15m television series to be filmed in Tasmania and broadcast around Australia', 2014; Screen Australia, 2015a; Whittock, 2013). At the April 2016 MIPTV conference in Cannes, BBC Worldwide announced that it had licenced *The Kettering Incident* amongst 2,000 hours of programming to clients across Europe and the Middle East (BBC Worldwide, 2016a). This included what was described as a 'mixed package agreement' for a suite of crime dramas including two British shows, series 4 of *Sherlock* (BBC & PBS 2010–2017), series 1 and 2 of *Happy Valley* (BBC One 2014–2023) and *The Kettering Incident*. Grant Welland, Executive Vice President of BBC Worldwide was reported as saying that these deals constituted a 'pipeline of quality content' that would ensure further growth for the company. As this press release reveals, Foxtel had achieved its goal of selling *Kettering* as a quality drama show that could sit alongside other quality TV shows in package deals that would ensure ongoing returns from an extended global market.

Four months later, BBC Worldwide North America announced via a press release that Amazon Prime Video would be the exclusive US Premium subscription home of the 'new Australian drama, *The Kettering Incident*' (BBC Worldwide, 2016b). Specifically mentioned in the first paragraph was the fact that the show had won the Special Jury Prize in the Series Mania Festival in Paris and that it starred 'Elizabeth Debicki (*The Night Manager*, BBC One & AMC 2016) and Matthew Le Nevez (*Offspring*, Network Ten 2010–2017)', comments suggesting that the show was being 'sold' to its audience on the strength of its international recognition and its stars, although the international currency of Le Nevez was clearly overshadowed by that of Debicki. Indeed, *Variety* magazine picked up on the Debicki connection in its coverage of the show, using an image of the star as Anna Macy from *Kettering* to illustrate its article (Barraclough, 2016), demonstrating that Debicki's rising star power was a significant factor in the promotion of the show internationally.

By 2017 *Kettering* had become Australia's best-selling drama overseas, with Don Groves reporting in *IF Magazine* that this included Sky Atlantic in the UK, Japan and Korea, while the BBC had also screened the eight-part drama on its channels or SVOD platforms. There were, however, some gaps, including Latin America, with Vincent Sheehan noting that he would have liked bigger numbers in some territories 'but producers always say that' (Groves, 2018a). Despite the territorial gaps, *Kettering* was reported to be the Australian show that was sold into the most territories during the relevant period, although Jane Campion's *Top of the Lake* (BBC UKTV & BBC Two) was claimed to be the show that had generated the most sales in its lifetime up to that point.

Non-Monetary Benefits to Creators

For Madden herself, there was not only the personal value of telling a story that reflected on her own experience, but also pride in the claim that she had helped bring a significant TV production to her home state:

> After working internationally and around Australia I'm excited about coming home and writing and co-producing a television series that will put Tasmania on the world stage ('$15m television series to be filmed in Tasmania and broadcast around Australia', 2014).

The fact that even before the series appeared on Foxtel it had won an international award was also a significant factor in the perceived success of the show. As David Knox reported in his *TV Tonight* blog, in April 2016 at the Series Mania festival in Paris, a jury headed by David Chase (who created the HBO drama *The Sopranos*) gave *Kettering* the Special Jury Prize with Vincent Sheehan being on hand to receive the award. Later that year at the Australian Academy of Cinema and Television Arts, *Kettering* would be nominated in eight categories, winning three (for Best Original Music Score, Best Telefeature or Miniseries and Best Lead Actress for Elizabeth Debicki). At the Logie Awards the following year, *Kettering* would win again for Best Miniseries or Telemovie, with Henry Nixon winning for Most Outstanding Actor (Table 4.1).

While such awards may be of value to the creative talent not only in validating their work, but also in raising their profile and helping to ensure their future employment in the industry, there is no doubt that these awards were of particular significance for Foxtel. As Craig Mathieson pointed out, at the 2017 Logies the industry-voted jury awards consistently went to shows made by Foxtel 'usurping the traditional free-to-air broadcasters' (Mathieson, 2017). In terms of Foxtel's five-year plan, *Kettering* therefore clearly achieved everything they wanted; it was a high-end drama that could hold its own alongside the quality HBO offerings on their Showcase platform; it was uniquely Australian but also had international currency; it was critically successful and it could be 'multi-played'. As Win explained, while overnight ratings might have some immediate significance, a show like *Kettering* which could be shown on many different platforms would have a long tail in economic terms, so that they were not worried about people missing it on first release (Crowley et al., 2017). As far as Foxtel was concerned, the series would inevitably find an intended audience that Win characterised as 'highly intelligent' on one platform or another (Mathieson, 2017), as has indeed been the case. Interestingly, Win explained that she herself followed audience reactions to the show on message boards and through the comments, and that they employed a social media team at Foxtel tracking reactions to shows online (Crowley et al., 2017).

Reception: Watching *The Kettering Incident*

Tasmanian audiences were given a sneak preview of the show at the Dark Mofo Festival in June 2015, when two episodes of the show were screened simultaneously at nine locations across Hobart (Goddard & Lehman, 2015). On its website, Dark Mofo is described as 'a midwinter festival in Hobart that celebrates the dark through large-scale public art, food, music, fire, light and noise, underpinned by the longest night of any Australian capital city'.[1] It might be noted that a similar event is beautifully parodied in the subsequent Nordic Noir spoof *Deadloch* (Amazon Prime Video 2023). Hobart in winter is the closest Australia comes to the sub-Arctic experience of Nordic Noir, but at the inverse time of the year. Asked about the feedback he had received from these screenings, Sheehan said it was gratifying that the audience was apparently just 'yearning for more' at the same time as it was perceived to have a 'very true Tasmanian voice' (Goddard & Lehman, 2015).

When the show screened on Foxtel in 2016, it was reported that the two-episode premiere drew 115,000 viewers to their screens (Knox, 2016d). While this might seem a relatively small figure, it nevertheless made *Kettering* the top non-sports programme on the Foxtel platform for that week. Accorded an audience score of 8/10, it was noted in the same review that not everyone had been taken by *Kettering*, with Debicki's performance garnering 'almost as much criticism as it did praise', as did the slow pacing of the show. However, the review went on, 'everyone agrees that the scenery is beautiful', while observing that this would hardly be enough 'to hold up the ratings for a whole series'. Nevertheless, Foxtel estimated that 532,000 people had watched the first episode of the series during encore presentations and recorded Foxtel iQ viewings, while the final episode attracted an audience of 151,000 viewers, the largest for any episode (Goodwin, 2016; Mediaweek, 2016). Capturing a wider range of activity than ratings alone, Parrot Analytics' audience demand shows that viewer interest in *Kettering* peaked not with its launch on Foxtel, but with the announcement that it had been acquired by Amazon Prime Video, when audience demand was fifteen times that for the average television show (Figure 4.1).

Critical Response and Online Reviews

Writing in *The Daily Review*, Raymond Gill rehearsed his objections to *The Kettering Incident* even before it appeared, suggesting that the show would merely confirm what everyone already believed to be true, that any story set in Tasmania tends to portray the state as gloomy, moody, creepy and gothic (Gill, 2014). Nor did he miss a reference to the prevailing fashion for Nordic Noir:

> Just as some people devour Scandinavian fiction for its tales of depressed, psycho killers skulking about on barren outcrops, rocky isthmuses, and spindly forests under leaden skies, we know that any story set in Tasmania will feature some hooded-eyed wacko channelling the inevitable ghosts of the past (Gill, 2014).

As Gill waspishly noted, while the prime minister might be welcoming the promise of jobs, a reinvigorated screen industry and tourist opportunities, he himself was profoundly sceptical.

When *Kettering* did appear, the press reviews were highly enthusiastic. Michael Idato in *The Sydney Morning Herald* praised the show's originality, describing it as unlike anything else on Australian television, while Graeme Blundell in *The Australian* proclaimed it 'as good as anything we've seen from overseas in recent years' (Blundell, 2016; Idato, 2016). On the Rotten Tomatoes website the show scored 67 per cent from all critics while the Top Critics (those working for established news outlets) scored it at 75 per cent, and on the IMDb website, 3,638 reviewers gave the show a weighted average vote of 6.7/10 (Table 4.1). Although critics from *The Guardian*, *The Sydney Morning Herald*, *News.com* and *The Sunday Times* shared their enthusiasm, Peter Crawley from the *Irish Times* wondered just 'how many genres a single show can keep in play before a globetrotting audience decides it would rather escape elsewhere' (Crawley, 2017). Steve Murray writing for ArtsATL[anta] described *Kettering* somewhat dismissively as a 'wannabe *Twin Peaks*'.[2] None of the major critics mentioned the Scandinavian series it resembled most closely, *Jordskott* (2015).

The Flow-ons

Even before production began, the Tasmanian Premier Lara Giddings was claiming that with its $15 million budget, and its fifty-strong cast and crew, *The Kettering Incident* would be a 'game-changer' for the Tasmanian screen industry (Giddings, 2014). As well as having long-term benefits in building the reputation of the local screen industry there would also be significant benefits for local businesses including equipment hire, caterers and accommodation providers (Giddings, 2014). This enthusiasm was echoed by the Tasmanian Arts Minister, Vanessa Goodwin, who considered the government's $1 million investment in the project to be money well spent (ABC News, 2014b). In a press release timed to coincide with the screening of the last episode, Goodwin claimed that the series had already generated a 'local spend' of $6 million and had provided 110 jobs for local cast and crew. She also suggested that the series would promote Tasmania to a worldwide audience (Goodwin, 2016).

Tourism

The possibility of increased tourism to Tasmania as a by-product of *The Kettering Incident* was mooted from the start, with Ben Neutze in the *Daily Review* suggesting that *Kettering* might do for Tasmania what the *Lord of the Rings* film trilogy had done for New Zealand. In an article that drew on his own experience of tracking down the apartment block in New York used in the long-running American sitcom *Friends* (1994–2004), Neutze (2014) noted that just as we fall in love with characters on film and TV, we fall in love with the places they inhabit. 'Get ready for the influx, Tassie', he concluded. In 2017, Screen Tasmania lauded the role *Kettering* played in showcasing Tasmania to the world and bringing 'Tasmania's talent, locations, stories and lifestyle to the nation' (Screen Tasmania, 2017). However, while an attachment to characters and place might certainly be a motivating factor for fans of Australia's other great TV export *Neighbours*, given that tours to Pin Oak Court and the Nunawading studios where the series was filmed in Melbourne began in the 1980s (Bowles, 1994), the question of whether or not Tasmania received a significant boost in tourist numbers following the worldwide circulation of *The Kettering Incident* is moot. Nor would *Kettering* seem to have been used in the state's promotional literature. Writing in 2022, we found no mention of *The Kettering Incident* on the Discovering Tasmania website[3] or on tasmania.com,[4] suggesting that tourism agencies have found little value in the show as a boost to tourism. Although it is possible that this could be because *Kettering* did not portray the region or its inhabitants in a particularly favourable light, the fact that other crime shows, such as the Nordic Noir dramas emanating from Denmark, have indeed boosted tourism (Waade, 2016) suggests that gloom and doom are not necessarily discouraging factors, although the border restrictions during the COVID-19 outbreaks in 2020 and 2021 may well have put a dampener on cultural tourism.

In an essay describing the tourism activities of British fans attending a Nordicana event celebrating Scandinavian crime drama in London 2014, Annette Hill and Koko Kondo (2022) explore the concept of 'entertainment mobilisation'. This concept, they argue, is useful in critically exploring how fans constitute themselves and manage their activities moving across the films, TV series, tourism and cuisine related to Nordic culture and the crime genre. At the height of the Nordic Noir wave in 2015 in the UK, British visitors to Copenhagen doubled, while visitors to Southern Sweden, the home of the TV series *Wallander* (TV4 2005–2013) and *The Bridge*, also increased by 29 per cent (Hill & Kondo, 2022). As one of their interviewees told them:

> When I watched the drama [*The Bridge*], I got an idea of taking a train all the way, I know you can go via Cologne and Copenhagen and Malmö then that will take me to the bridge. I am really thinking about it (Hill & Kondo, 2022, p. 181).

The bridge in question here is the Øresund Bridge connecting Sweden to Denmark, and the site of the discovery of the first body in the first season of the eponymous series. Thus, as Stijn Reijnders discovered in 2011, and Hansen and Wade reported in 2017, people are indeed motivated to investigate the scene of a fictional crime, whether this be in a book or TV series. Whether this mobilisation is motivated by an attachment to the character or the place or both is an issue that merits further exploration.

Cultural Impact

While *The Kettering Incident* gestured towards ecological themes, it was never as explicit in expressing what Coralie Sanderson (2023) describes as 'eco-anxiety' as the Swedish series *Jordskott*. While the loggers are certainly at war with the environmentalists who want to save the old growth forests in and around Kettering, this tension is not central to a plot which ultimately appears to be about a secret experiment in cloning, as evidenced by Anna's encounter with what appears to be a version of herself in the underground bunker at the end. In narrative terms, the series was ultimately frustrating, with a conclusion that hardly explained anything but with clear potential for a sequel. While this was envisaged at the time, and confirmed by none other than Foxtel executive director Brian Walsh ('Ratings resurgence at Foxtel', 2016), on 6 June 2018 Madden herself confirmed via Twitter that Foxtel had decided not to go ahead with season 2, by which time it would appear that she herself was already committed to a new series.[5]

Just one day before Madden's announcement, Patrick Frater, writing in the industry newsletter *Variety*, announced that the Australian-owned streaming service Stan had commissioned a new drama series by Victoria Madden to be distributed by Disney's ABC studios (Frater, 2018). Nick Forward, Stan's chief content officer, was reported as suggesting that the scale and scope of the production would be something that Australia had rarely seen before. Also noted in the article was the fact that at the time Stan was the only serious rival to Netflix in the Australian streaming sector (Frater, 2018). This new drama series was another Tasmanian production, *The Gloaming* (Stan, Starz & Disney+, 2020), for which Madden would again claim the role of showrunner. Shot mainly in and around Hobart, it made extensive use of the bridge over the Derwent River as a backdrop in ways that clearly echoed the use of the Oresund Bridge in the DR series *The Bridge*.

With its strong female heroine, Detective Mollie McGee (Emma Booth), who is paired with fellow detective Alex O'Connell (Ewan Leslie), the series echoed the set-up of both *The Killing* and *The Bridge*. Although she is a capable and good detective, Molly is portrayed as a less than attentive mother (shades of Sarah Lund in *The Killing*), while the brutal murder that they set out to investigate has connections to events in Alex's past (shades of Danish detective Martin Rhode's connection to the killer in *The Bridge* Season 1). The detectives also have a romantic backstory. Alex grew up in Hobart, was once a teenage boyfriend of Molly, but left for the mainland after a series of traumatic events which are relevant to the plot.

Once again, however, the most significant thematic parallels are with the Swedish series *Jordskott*, in that *The Gloaming* draws on both gothic and folklorish elements while also gesturing towards environmental concerns. Following the discovery of a woman who has been brutally murdered, wrapped in barbed wire and pushed down a spectacular waterfall, Molly and Alex are required to team up in an investigation that will lead to the discovery of a quasi-religious cult, The Crofters, who practice various forms of witchcraft and ritual. As a secret society with strong links to the business community, The Crofters are also caught up in plans to develop land hitherto deemed unsuitable for development. The final episode culminates in a mid-winter festival that in its use of fire and noise gestures towards Hobart's own Dark Mofo, but which ends in death and the revelation of the crimes against humanity of which the contemporary Crofters have been guilty in their lust for power and monetary gain. With another nod to *Jordskott* and the red earring belonging to her missing daughter that Eva wears on a chain round her neck, Alex also discovers a red earring belonging to a mysterious girl. In this case, the earring belonged to Jenny, the young woman he was with when she was shot many years ago in an encounter that he has suppressed and that is the source of his own trauma. Throughout the course of the investigation, like Eva, Alex ponders the earring at significant moments as they inexorably move towards the revelation of just what happened to Jenny and Alex, and why.

The Nordic Noir echoes did not pass unnoticed. While acknowledging *The Gloaming*'s nod to *Twin Peaks* (most specifically the body wrapped not in plastic but barbed wire) *Guardian* reviewer Luke Buckmaster usefully compared the series to Madden's previous Tasmanian production:

> Like *Kettering*, *The Gloaming* is bathed in frosty moonlight and ensconced in fog and haze. It has a Scandi-noirish atmosphere and a plotline drawn from a more defined genre playbook: the police procedural thriller (Buckmaster, 2019).

As Buckmaster observes, following Jennifer Kent's period film *The Nightingale* (2018) and Foxtel's gothic drama *Lambs of God* (2019), *The Gloaming* is but the latest in an 'emerging trend of Tasmanian-based productions that view the island state as a place of terrible beauty, located somewhere south of the mainland and west of hell'.

While *The Gloaming* demonstrates once again Madden's appropriation of Nordic Noir tropes in a setting that is determinedly Tasmanian, and while the inhabitants of Tasmania might object to their island being represented as a place of 'terrible beauty', there is no doubt that *The Kettering Incident* and *The Gloaming* have contributed to a renaissance in the Tasmanian screen industry. This was not, however, the first time that a homecoming Tasmanian screen creative had attempted to stimulate the screen industry in Tasmania. On ABC Radio Hobart in 2017, Paul McIntyre described how, long before *Kettering* and *Rosehaven*, Tasmanian-born Hollywood star Louise Lovely returned home in the mid-1920s determined to get a local film industry started – in contrast to Tasmania's other more notorious film star export, Errol Flynn, who never returned to the island although the house in which he once lived still stands (Bevan, 2016). While ten films were subsequently made, only one was set in Tasmania, the celebrated *Jewelled Nights* (1925) based on a book by Tasmanian novelist, Marie Bjelke Petersen and filmed at Savage River on Tasmania's west coast. Lovely herself wrote the screenplay, directed, produced and starred in the film, while Petersen's account of the filming is in the Tasmanian Archives and Heritage Office (Claydon, 2018). Sadly, only two minutes of this film, described as a lost classic, remain. Furthermore, while *Jewelled Nights* was hugely popular in Australia, there were no international sales and the film made a loss, signalling that even 100 years ago, the Tasmanian screen industry was inevitably dependent on success in the global marketplace.

The Value of *The Kettering Incident*

When compared with *Miss Fisher's Murder Mysteries*, the value of *The Kettering Incident* would appear to be primarily to its producers, Foxtel; its creators including Vicki Madden, but more specifically to the Tasmanian screen industry. Writing in the *Sun Herald* in July 2023, Karl Quinn pointed to the current ubiquity of crime shows from Tasmania, including the Nordic Noir spoof *Deadloch* on Amazon Prime and *Bay of Fires* on the

ABC. Revisiting the history of recent international film productions set in Tasmania, including *The Hunter* (2011) starring Willem Dafoe, *Lion* (2016) with scenes shot in Hobart, and *The Light Between The Oceans* (2016), not forgetting Jennifer Kent's challenging portrayal of Tasmania's colonial past in *The Nightingale* (2018), Quinn suggests that such big film productions tend to be infrequent and short-term, with little opportunity to develop local talent. What really made a difference to the local industry, it is suggested, were the recent television productions led by *The Kettering Incident*. Following the *Kettering* shoot, many of the cast and crew moved on to the comedy drama *Rosehaven* (ABC 2016–2021), which ran for five seasons and forty episodes. According to Alex Sangston, executive manager of Screen Tasmania, the longevity of *Rosehaven* changed everything: 'It was a complete gift for us, because it gave our crews better and better experience over five years' (Quinn, 2023c). Despite the fact that this meant productions could now be crewed largely by experienced Tasmanians, the industry was still facing a number of challenges. As Quinn points out, there is no film studio in Tasmania and most of the specialist gear has to be imported from the mainland (Quinn, 2023c). Sangston's final point is even more revealing given that with a population of just over 500,000, the local production teams were over-stretched. After the more recent productions of *Deadloch* and *Bay of Fires*, 'they were all just cooked' (Sangston, quoted in Quinn, 2023).

It's an interesting problem, and one that is rarely rehearsed, but too much work would appear to be just as difficult to manage as no work at all. Tired people, however, will recover and will need to work again if the Tasmanian arm of the Australian screen industry is to carry on. While there is unlikely to be a sequel to either *The Kettering Incident* or *The Gloaming*, it remains to be seen if either *Deadloch* or *Bay of Fires* might lead to a second season. Inevitably this will depend as much on international interest and rapidly-evolving streamer economics as it does local ratings success. Whatever the outcome, it is clear that both *The Kettering Incident* and *The Gloaming* were part of a renaissance of the Tasmanian screen industry of significant value for the island, and for the Australian screen industry more generally in terms of attracting international attention and sales. The fact that these series did so by harnessing the legacy of Nordic Noir clearly demonstrates their inherent international ambition as well as their determination to showcase Australian stories in an Australian setting to the world. The brilliance of *Deadloch*, however, is that it effectively flips the Nordic Noir genre on its head in a delightful spoof that sends up the narrative, aesthetics and familiar tropes of the genre in ways which are also profoundly Australian. How well such a send-up will travel, and how it will be received given the amount of profanity and argot it contains, remains to be seen.

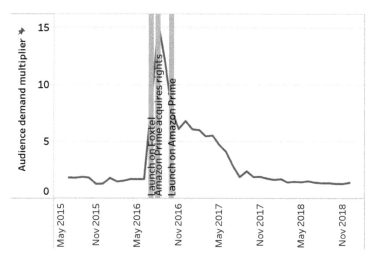

Figure 4.1 Audience demand multiplier for *The Kettering Incident*

Note: The audience demand multiplier benchmarks content relative to the market average of 1. If a show has 2× demand, it is two times more in-demand than the average TV show in the market.

Source: Parrot Analytics (2021).

Table 4.1 *The Kettering Incident* (2016)
The makers

Commissioning broadcaster	Foxtel
Production company	Porchlight Films and Sweet Potato Films
Distributor / international sales	BBC Worldwide

The results

International sales	2017: Top-selling adult TV drama supported by Screen Australia (Groves, 2018a).
Awards	5 wins and 9 nominations Logie Awards • 2017 **Winner** Most Outstanding Actor: Henry Nixon 2017 Nominee Most Outstanding Actress: Elizabeth Debicki Casting Guild of Australia Awards • 2016 Nominee Best Casting in a TV Miniseries or Telemovie: Kirsty McGregor Camerimage • 2016 Nominee Jury Award Best Pilot: Ari Wegner, 'The Kettering Incident: Anna (#1.1)' Australian Academy of Cinema and Television Arts (AACTA) Awards • 2016 Nominee Best Guest or Supporting Actress in a Television Drama: Sacha Horler, Ep. 'The Search (2016)' • 2016 Nominee Best Guest or Supporting Actress in a Television Drama: Sianoa Smit-McPhee, Ep. 'Anna (2016)' • 2016 Nominee Best Direction in a Television Drama or Comedy: Rowan Woods, Ep. 'Anna (2016)' • 2016 Nominee Best Screenplay in Television: Vicki Madden, Ep. 'Anna (2016)' • 2016 Nominee Best Cinematography in Television: Ari Wegner, Ep. 'The Search (2016)' • 2016 **Winner** Best Original Music Score in Television: Matteo Zingales, Max Lyandvert, Ep. 1 • 2016 **Winner** Best Telefeature or Miniseries: Vincent Sheehan, Vicki Madden, Andrew Walker • 2016 **Winner** Best Lead Actress in a Television Drama: Elizabeth Debicki Australian Writers' Guild • 2015 Nominee Awgie Award Television Miniseries Original: Vicki Madden, Andrew Knight, Cate Shortland, Louise Fox Series Mania Festival • 2016 Winner Special Jury Prize
Audience demand	The top non-sport program on Foxtel in July–August 2016, with a cumulative audience of 532,000 people watching the first episode by the end of the series (Goodwin, 2016). IMDb rating: 6.7/10 Rotten Tomatoes average audience score: 67%

Chapter 5

Secret City

Like *The Kettering Incident* (Showcase 2016), *Secret City* (Showcase & Netflix 2016–2019) is an Australian crime drama that first appeared on the subscription platform Foxtel in fulfilment of its obligation as a subscription broadcaster to spend 10 per cent of its drama expenditure on the creation of new Australian drama. As outlined earlier, head of drama at Foxtel, Penny Win, had been working since 2012 towards creating a production slate of high-end drama that included not only *The Kettering Incident*, but also *Wentworth* (SoHo & Showcase 2013–2021) – a prison drama that 'reimagined' Australia's highly successful cult soap opera series *Prisoner/Prisoner: Cell Block H* (Network Ten 1979–1986) for a contemporary audience (Batty et al., 2021). In an interview with the authors that included Foxtel's director of content, Ross Crowley and Tony Pollitt, Win told us that Foxtel wanted 'aspirationally to be HBO'. As Win explained, 'We want to be critically successful. The production values have to be incredibly high. Everything we commission sits on the Showcase Channel where we have the-best-of-the-best HBO' (Crowley et al., 2017). Crowley elaborated on this ambition suggesting that because Australia absorbs both British and American dramas, there is an opportunity to produce what he described a 'hybrid' drama that might work in both spaces and that would appeal to what he identified as a global niche audience for genre television, a comment that echoes Tom O'Regan's (1993) observation that Australian television has always 'looked both ways'.

In terms of inspiration, while Win was keen to dismiss any suggestion that Foxtel might be tempted to make anything that looked like 'Scandi Noir', *Secret City* announces a stylistic debt to Nordic Noir right from the start, although it is avowedly Australian in its geo-political concerns and Canberra location. While the first pre-title sequence is that of a young woman setting fire to herself in a protest on behalf of Tibet outside a pagoda in a city which the caption tells us is Beijing, the second features a young man running across a bridge at night, illuminated only by the streetlights and the headlamps of the cars that are pursuing him. Although the caption tells us this is Canberra, which Australians might have guessed from the distinctive flagpole of Parliament House in the background, the setting immediately recalls the opening of *The Bridge* (SVT & DR 2011–2018) in season 1, when the night traffic driving over the now unmistakeable Øresund Bridge separating Sweden from Denmark is halted by the discovery of a body. After the running man pauses to swallow a SIM card from his phone, he jumps into the water to escape his pursuers and the title sequence begins. The ominous orchestral music in a minor key is reminiscent of another series that has been often included in the Nordic Noir canon, the Danish political drama *Borgen* (DR1 2010–2022), set in the Danish capital of Copenhagen. Featuring helicopter and drone shots, the *Secret City* title sequence then presents a collage of Canberra locations and buildings, as well as Lake Burley Griffin and a pine forest, all colour-coded in the noirish moody blues that echo the Nordic Noir aesthetic.

In the drama that subsequently unfolds, *Daily Nation* journalist Harriet Dunkley (Anna Torv), who works in the Federal Parliamentary Press Gallery in Parliament House, discovers a conspiracy revolving around the scheming Attorney General, Catriona Bailey (Jacqui Weaver), who is manipulating both American and Chinese interests in her ambitions to become the head of a police state through the passing of a Safe Australia Bill. While the first death to occur is that of a young CIA agent, the second is that of Harriet's former husband Kim Gordon (Damon Herriman), who has transitioned as a woman and is working for the Australian Signals Directorate, the statuary agency that provides foreign signals intelligence and cyber security services to the Australian government. The scenes shot in this building with low lighting and dark workspaces are reminiscent of a much earlier American crime drama series set in a counter-intelligence agency, *24* (Fox 2001–2010), once again pointing to the ways in which the Australian crime drama has continued to borrow stylistic elements from a range of different sources.

What further distinguishes *Secret City* from *The Kettering Incident* is that it is a political thriller. The plot hinges on what actor Dan Wylie, who plays Defence Minister Mal Paxton, has described as Australia's ongoing predicament 'sandwiched between two heavily armed super-powers'. On the one hand, Australia is a close ally of the United States as a source of military protection and support; on the other, China is Australia's most significant trading partner and the health of the economy depends on this alliance. Upsetting the balance is the fact that China has continued to build military bases in the South China Sea and has stated an ambition to annexe the independent country of Taiwan. As a political drama, *Secret City* was therefore well ahead of the game in pointing to the tensions with China that have resulted as a consequence of Australia's ongoing alliance with the US.

Secret City thus belongs to a cycle of quality television drama from the Nordic region, including *Borgen*, the Norwegian speculative thriller *Occupied* (TV2 2015–2020), and the Danish series *Thin Ice* (TV4 2020) set in Greenland, that have been identified by American scholar Robert (Saunders, 2021, p. 1) as signalling television's geo-political turn in the new millennium. However, while the shows that emanate from Northern Europe may be concerned with 'the post-Cold war challenges of globalisation, neoliberalism, and right-wing nationalism' as they unfold in Europe (Saunders, 2021, p. 2), *Secret City* has its gaze firmly on Asia and Oceania and the political tensions that are operational in this region in terms of how they resonate in Australia. *Secret City* therefore represents both an appropriation and a relocation of the political, aesthetic and stylistic tendencies of Nordic Noir in a drama that rehearses the particular geo-political tensions of Australia as a nation.

The Making of *Secret City*

Origins

Like *Miss Fisher's Murder Mysteries* (ABC 2012–2015), *Secret City* also began as a series of crime novels, albeit one that was itself inspired by television. As journalist Steve Lewis told Caris Bizzaca (2016b), he was frustrated by the lack of Australian political drama on television during an era when American series such *The West Wing* (NBC 1999–2006) and the Danish series *Borgen* were enjoying significant popularity. Lewis shared his thoughts with fellow political journalist Chris Uhlmann, who had already been toying with a television script while longing to write a political thriller. The two journalists joined forces, and published *The Marmalade Files* in 2012. As Lewis explained:

> We did really want to deal with the big things facing our nation – such as the decline of mainstream journalism, the loss of faith in our political

institutions, and the big dance between nations where Australia finds itself caught between China and the US – but in an entertaining romp that people wanted to read (Burke, 2019).

The pair were already embarked on a sequel, *The Mandarin Code*, when they approached the ABC about turning their books into a television series.

Development and Production

While the ABC did not take the bait, Uhlmann and Spicer were advised to contact producer Penny Chapman at Matchbox Pictures (Bizzaca, 2016b). In an extended interview with the authors, Chapman explained how she and Tony Ayres, co-founder of the independent production company Matchbox Pictures, shared a pre-existing interest in Canberra as a setting and were very receptive to Uhlmann and Lewis's initiative (Chapman, 2019). As Chapman admitted, she had always wanted to do a political drama in Canberra, where she had studied at the Australian National University, thus revealing the specific personal value that this project had for her as a producer. In adapting the novels for the screen, Chapman was of the opinion that *The Marmalade Files* was more of a satirical comedy than a political thriller and needed additional narrative complexity to sustain a six-hour series. Another key change was that of the gender of the central character: Harry Dunkley thus became journalist Harriet Dunkley, as played by Australian actor Anna Torv. A team of experienced writers including Greg Waters, Belinda Chayko and Matt Cameron were hired to work on the adaptation. As Chapman explained, once they had their three writers in a room, and after deciding on the two opening scenes, they knew they were dealing with 'something quite rich' (Chapman, 2019). As she explained, when it comes to television 'it's about the writers, it's not about the directors… if you go in with a writer who's got a track record for being a great script showrunner, then you'll get heard, you'll get listened to, you will absolutely get attention' (Chapman, 2019).

Despite an insistence on the significance of the writers, getting the 'palette' right for the series was also important since the style template they were aiming for was indeed 'Scandi-noir' as in *The Killing* (DR1 2007–2012) and *Borgen*. According to Chapman (2019), there are three people in the production design who need to be 'joined at the hip' in determining the 'visual nuances' and the style of a TV show. In this instance this included the director (Emma Freeman), the production designer (Felicity Abbott) and the cinematographer (Mark Wareham and subsequently Garry Phillips). Chapman revealed the significance of Nordic Noir drama in their thinking 'because Canberra is such a Scandinavian looking city' while admitting that *The Bridge* was indeed one of their key visual references. Chapman also suggested that they were influenced by other American series, without being specific, although echoes of the espionage thriller *24* are indeed evident. For director Emma Freeman, one of the most exciting aspects of the shoot was the opportunity to use film locations that had never been used before, including the Prime Minister's courtyard and the offices of then Prime Minister Tony Abbott's Chief of Staff, Peta Credlin (McCredie-Dando & Karlovsky, 2016). As producer Joanna Werner explained, such unprecedented access was a direct result of Chris Uhlmann and Steve Spicer's connections with the Press Gallery and Parliament House. Werner was also keen to point out that the cultural specificity of shows like *The Bridge* and *The Killing* were clearly part of their appeal to an international audience and she fervently hoped that the uniquely Australian setting of Canberra would be of interest internationally (McCredie-Dando & Karlovsky, 2016).

As it happened, the uniquely Australian setting and geo-political specificity did indeed impress Matchbox Pictures' parent company NBCUniversal (NBCU) in Los Angeles and the production team was told to 'double down' on the Canberra locations (Barrett, 2016). As Chapman told us:

> I got from the Vice President of Scripted in LA an email saying, 'Holy fuck, right. This is fucking amazing. This is so stylish. And oh my god, you have turned around what we thought was a domestic drama into something interesting, into something really, really sellable and really smart'. ... I mean, the head of the head of NBCUniversal looked at all six episodes on an international flight and said 'this is the best looking drama to come out of Australia, in my view'. Not that he's seen every drama that's come out of Australia, but... but it felt sophisticated. To them, it felt really stylish. It felt American, I think, or, or European. It felt international. ... And so they were beyond excited, about a project that they thought would at best do alright in the domestic market and not be able to be sold internationally because it was it was so domestic (Chapman 2019).

NBCU subsequently sent the production team 'notes' and emails revealing that the American executives were largely unaware of China's activities in the South China Sea, an observation that suggests the value of a crime drama in educating people around the world about the geo-political issues that affect people and nations beyond their own immediate horizons. Note also the words used by Chapman to characterise how the series was perceived; 'sellable', 'sophisticated', 'stylish', 'American', 'European' and 'international', but not Australian. And this despite the fact that that the series was unequivocally Australian in terms of both its Canberra location and its political concerns.

As Chapman herself admitted (Barrett, 2016), the use of Canberra proved to be a considerable boon when it came to selling the series internationally. In her opinion, this was because people are interested in dramas set in an unfamiliar location that serves the plot in convincing ways. As a result, unlike the experience of producers in Canada in the late 1990s as described by Serra Tinic (2005, p. 13), who were told that they should avoid cultural specificity and aim for the 'homogenous or universal' if they wanted to find a global audience, by 2016 a significant shift seems to have occurred in the perception of the producers, the buyers and the distributors of television for an international market: a shift suggesting that cultural specificity was now an advantage rather than a disadvantage in terms of the sellability of a product. As we argue here, the transnational success of Nordic series such as *The Killing*, *The Bridge* and *Borgen* that had resonated with audiences worldwide had a major part to play in demonstrating that dramas set in nations hitherto perceived to be on periphery might be of value in the international market for televisual content.

Finance and Industry

Because the initial expectations for the series were apparently low (given the parent company NBCU considered it to be 'just' a domestic drama), Matchbox Pictures was only able to leverage what Chapman described as 'a very mean budget' for the series, with Screen Australia investing $999,000 and commissioning broadcaster Foxtel providing some 'development money'. This resulted in a number of tussles with the head of production at Matchbox, who suggested they might need to cut back on their budget for the aerial shots (Chapman, 2019). Chapman, however, apparently stood firm given that in her opinion these sweeping aerial shots were essential to the whole tone and look of the show, as indeed they were. According to Chapman, calls for cutbacks always happen in

Australia, where the money for ambitious domestic productions is limited. However, one effect of the tight budgets is that fact that 'We make these shows on the smell of an oil rag', demonstrating in the process that 'We're the little engine that could' (Chapman, 2019). And the results, she added, were often surprising, with *Secret City* being one of those surprise successes, although not in immediate rating terms. Clearly one of the key values of the series for Chapman was the fact that it demonstrated the resourcefulness of her company to deliver a high-quality production that demonstrated the skill of its creatives and production team on a tight budget, a triumph of frugality.

Setting the series in Canberra also enabled a collaboration with Screen Canberra (then ScreenACT), a not-for-profit industry group funded by the federal and territory governments with a clear mandate to bring productions and jobs to the region. As Chapman told us, Matchbox was keen to employ as many people as possible from the Australian Capital Territory (ACT) either as actors, crew or attachments, given that one of the company's mantras is the need to ensure ongoing development of new talent, including producers and writers (Chapman, 2019). The benefits for the then ScreenACT were immediately apparent, with the ACT Government once again awarding the small agency $250,000 in 2016 to continue their work attracting high-end productions to the ACT. As the Chief Minister noted, 'ScreenACT has been hard at work in recent years attracting film and television productions to the capital', with the result that apparently 'production companies were now flocking to the capital' (Raggatt, 2016). Monica Penders, Director of ScreenACT, was keen to follow up on this assertion in a press release, pointing out that '*Secret City* has demonstrated that Canberra is an amazing backdrop for good quality story-telling, with ease of access, world-class recognisable locations and clear unpolluted high-altitude light' (Raggatt, 2016).

Three years later, the ACT Government (2019) published an article on their website in which Penders reiterated her commitment to supporting and growing the ACT screen industry. Referring to *Secret City* in particular, Penders noted that there had been paid attachments on the shoot that had enabled local industry professionals to 'grow and develop' their expertise. 'Large film (sic) projects' like *Secret City*, Penders concluded, have a significant impact on the local economy, not least in terms of tourism given the series' international career. While film tourism is a well-known phenomenon, the popularity of Nordic Noir has also had a significant impact on tourism to the Nordic, as many scholars have noted (Hansen & Waade, 2017; Reijnders, 2011). Whether *Secret City* did indeed attract any subsequent tourism to the ACT is, however, hard to trace. A tour of the Visit Canberra website makes no mention of any film or TV series shot in the region.

This is despite the fact that, as the recently renamed Screen Canberra website reveals, since the appearance of *Secret City* in 2016 the ACT Government has supported a number of other drama series set in the capital. These include a second season of *Secret City*, subtitled *Under the Eagle*, in 2019 and another political drama set in the halls of the Parliament House, *Total Control* (ABC 2019–2024). Produced by Blackfella Films, founded in 1992 by Indigenous filmmaker Rachel Perkins, *Total Control* set a new direction for the Australian political thriller by placing at its centre the portrayal of an Indigenous politician, Alexandra 'Alex' Fielding (Deborah Mailman), who is persuaded to enter politics by serving prime minister Rachel Anderson (Rachel Griffiths) in a somewhat cynical effort to shore up her own majority in the House of Representatives. While the geo-politics of this series encompass American interests in Australia in terms of the establishment of a new military base on Indigenous land, the series is primarily concerned with issues of Indigenous dispossession and the incarceration of black youth. In a move that was somewhat ahead of Australia's unsuccessful referendum on an Indigenous Voice to Parliament which unfolded in 2023, in seasons 2 and 3, *Total Control* went on to address the issues of Indigenous representation in Parliament, once again signalling the ways in which an Australian drama destined for global distribution might rehearse for the world issues of national concern that have international resonance when it comes to the treatment of Indigenous people more generally.

Reception

When asked whether Matchbox Pictures had conducted any audience research to gauge what audiences might be looking for in a crime drama, Chapman told us that that although the company does not conduct formal research, they do attempt to stay abreast of what programmes appear to be working. She reported that their Managing Director had just returned from a trip to London and LA to explore whether there might be some interest in the raft of shows that they already have in development (Chapman, 2019). This suggests that knowing what audiences want is still a guessing game, built partly on past successes but also on hopeful predictions about what people will watch, and that it is still largely controlled by the international gatekeepers and distributors of content identified by Cunningham and Jacka (1996) as playing a decisive role in the transnational trade in television content. As the case of *Secret City* would seem to suggest, while the success of a television series might depend on the right idea at the right time, good writing, clear production values and style, as well as excellent performances and a memorable location, whether a project is greenlit depends on the knowledge and assumptions of decision-makers well up the line, and factors such as distribution deals and strategic marketing.

Although the first season of *Secret City* attracted an audience of only 80,000 on the Foxtel Showcase platform, it was the top-rated non-sports show on subscription television for the week in which it was released (Knox, 2016c), with Parrot Analytics' demand multiplier showing it was attracting audience interest of more than ten times that of the average title at the time of its launch (Figure 5.1). In hindsight, Chapman was of the opinion that *Secret City* would probably have attracted a lot more attention if it had appeared on the ABC rather than on Foxtel given that the ABC has a much bigger reach. As she noted somewhat ruefully, it was only after the show was picked up by Netflix that 'many, many people said to me, "my god, I've just seen *Secret City*, it's really good"' (Chapman, 2019). As we noted at the time, there appeared to be some unease in our discussions with Chapman and with Foxtel about the reasons why *Secret City* was not promoted as avidly as it might have been when compared with the much bigger noise around *The Kettering Incident*. This inevitably led to speculation that there may have been some political interference/sensitivity about *Secret City* in terms of then current China/US relations that may have led to the launch being somewhat muffled.

Despite the fact that *Secret City* failed to make a big splash on first release, Chapman was keen to express her pride in the series and what they had managed to achieve at Matchbox Pictures (Chapman, 2019). This pride seemed to be well-placed given that *Secret City* won a number of significant awards (more than *Kettering*, in fact) and excellent reviews. These included a *New York Times* article alerting American viewers to *Secret City*'s arrival on Netflix, describing it as one of the three shows to watch 'this week' (Lyons, 2018):

> If you like foreign political thrillers with main characters so icey they'll freeze to your tongue, try this Australian import ... *Secret City* is an easy binge, though it's violent and often quite down on the human condition. It's not as fun and sudsy as *Scandal*, but it has some of that show's 'everybody knows everybody – and everybody's a liar' attitude, with some of the aesthetics and frigidness of *House of Cards* and some of the panic and sorrow of *London Spy*. A second season is in the works (Lyons, 2018).

Although Chapman may have regretted the subdued attention to *Secret City* at the time of its release, this was not a problem for Foxtel. As Penny Winn explained, as in the case of *The Kettering Incident*, they were not worried that people may have missed the show on its first appearance because it could be subsequently multi-played and shown on different platforms (Crowley et al., 2017). According to Ross Crowley, in the new global landscape for television, shows like *Secret City* eventually find their 'specific homes' in English-speaking territories such as America and Britain and beyond. In Crowley's opinion, drama series have gone from being 'vertical national drama' to 'global drama' in that a show's potential popularity and reach has been enabled by the emergence of global niche audiences for specific types of television on subscription platforms:

> If you are making gothic, you are making it for a global gothic audience. If you make noir, you're making it for the global noir audience, regardless of where you are born (Ross Crowley in Crowley et al., 2017).

For Win and the rest of the Foxtel team, the immediate ratings were therefore of secondary importance. What they hoped for instead was that their new dramas would become 'subscriber drivers', attracting media attention through critical reviews and social media while driving a long revenue tail through the many different distribution deals. Online demand metrics certainly indicate ongoing demand: the Parrot Analytics' demand multiplier peaked to 6x with the release of the second series on Foxtel and Netflix in 2019 (Figure 5.1), and in April 2023, the show was still finding an audience on Netflix of around 6000 views per week (IMDbPro, 2023).

Awards

Despite its initially limited reach, the first season of *Secret City* was recognised for its quality by the screen industry in Australia. At the 2017

Logie Awards Anna Torv and Damon Herriman won Logies for Most Outstanding Actress and Most Outstanding Supporting Actor for their roles as Harriet Dunkley and Kim Gordon, with Herriman also winning Best Guest or Supporting Actor at the Australian Academy of Cinema and Television Arts Awards (AACTA). At the Australian Director's Guild Awards, Emma Freeman won for Best Direction in a Television Drama Series, and composer David Bridie won a Screen Music Award for Best Music for a Mini-series or Telemovie (Davidson, 2016; Knox, 2017). While these awards clearly pleased Chapman, they also delighted Foxtel, who took home seven Logie Awards for their drama productions on the one night (including two for *The Kettering Incident*) with Foxtel CEO Peter Tonagh describing this recognition as 'an amazing milestone for our company' (Knox, 2017). Foxtel's (and Penny Win's) ambition to produce world-class drama that would get the network noticed would therefore appear to have been achieved by 2017, although by 2019 Win had left the company and drama production appeared to have stalled, even though Foxtel insisted that they were committed to producing four new drama series a year (Groves, 2019). One of those new programmes included the second season of *Secret City* in what was announced to be a new co-production partnership between Foxtel and Netflix after the latter picked up the distribution of season 1 (Morphet, 2019).

Secret City: Under The Eagle subsequently premiered on March 4, 2019 on Foxtel's FOX Showcase platform, with considerably more media attention, especially to the political landscape in which it appeared. As Penny Chapman told the Canberra *Courier Mail* (Kristy Symonds et al., 2019), with a federal election looming, the timing could not be better for a second season of a political thriller intended to shed light on the machinations taking place in the Canberra corridors of power. *Secret City: Under the Eagle* picked up the story in season 2, with Harriet Dunkley on parole after serving a sentence for treason resulting from illegal activities in the first season. Once again, the narrative concerned itself with secret dealings behind the closed doors in Canberra, this time with a focus on the kinds of clandestine military operations conducted on Australian soil that have long been a feature of Australia's relationship with its American ally. Regarding Australia's geo-political ties with Asia, the focus shifted to Pakistan and the illegal arms trade. However, while a strong cast of female characters, including Harriet once again, took centre stage, the series received very few reviews or accolades in comparison with the first season. While there are a number of possible reasons for this, in our opinion, the fact that season 2 largely eschewed the Nordic Noir aesthetic may have been at least one factor.

Social and Cultural Value

When it comes to assessing the social and cultural value of a series like *Secret City*, it's hard to assess the impact it may have had more broadly. As the comment from the NBCU executive cited by Penny Chapman above reveals, it certainly drew attention to a political issue of which many people had little current knowledge: the build-up of China's military operations in the South China Sea. As it happens, these issues became even more pertinent in 2021, when Australia entered into a trilateral security pact with the UK and the US (AUKUS) that would enable Australia to acquire nuclear-powered submarines. American Ambassador to Australia, Caroline Kennedy, suggested that this deal would provide a 'lot of deterrence' in the Indo-Pacific region as China continued its 'economic coercion' (Hurst, 2022). Meanwhile, former Labor Prime Minister Paul Keating described Australia's commitment to AUKUS and the purchase of the American submarines as the 'worst international decision' by a Labor government since 1916 (Karp, 2023). *Secret City* season 1 was therefore prescient in signalling the potential problems for Australia as an ally of two major international powers engaged in a power struggle in the South China Sea. For actor Dan Wyllie (who plays the Minister of Defence Mal Paxton), the memorable experience of filming in Parliament House and witnessing the political environment was one he was keen to share:

> It's very complex, very meaty... It's about the Australian-American alliance and the Chinese intrusion into the South China Sea. Labor versus Liberal. It's incredibly current and we were shooting it thinking 'I hope these events don't overtake the show before it gets on'. So we're really riding the wave of currency. It's incredible how pertinent the show is (Dan Wylie in Knox, 2016b).

For Wyllie, the memorable experience of filming in Parliament House and witnessing the political environment was one he was keen to share:

> At the tail end of the shoot when we only had a couple of days to go, the Turnbull spill happened. [Malcolm Turnbull replaced Tony Abbott as

> Liberal Prime Minister.] So it was absolutely electric. We had incredible unfettered access to the place. You go through the bowels of the place and it's like airport security to get in. The carpet is six inches thick and you feel like you're drowning in it. You can really feel white man's power in the place. It's incredibly dense and claustrophobic (Dan Wylie in Knox, 2016b).

Wylie did not need to worry about the series' currency; political intrigue is universal, even while events and even countries might change. In the US, commentators immediately found parallels with the machinations of the Trump presidency. Writing for online review site *Decider* in 2018, Sean T. Collins described the series as 'more relevant than ever… The point is that unencumbered nationalism, unchecked intelligence and surveillance agencies, and unscrupulous politicians are a toxic mix no matter when or where they come together, fictionally or not' (Collins, 2018).

And while Wyllie may have been aware of 'the white man's power' in an institution that is indeed still male-dominated, what's interesting about *Secret City* is that the focus in both season 1 and 2 is firmly on the female characters, who are the prime movers of the drama. As one reviewer observed, 'there's something of a feminist edge to the second series. Women seem to shine in every scene' (Hardy, 2019). In terms of the gender politics, *Secret City* therefore once again demonstrates its alignment with the Scandinavian dramas such as *Borgen* and *Thin Ice* that foreground the female protagonists in ways that might well be calculated to appeal to a female viewing audience.

As Harriet Dunkley, Anna Torv has a commanding onscreen presence. An Australian-born actress, like Elizabeth Debicki in *The Kettering Incident*, Torv had also enjoyed success internationally in the Fox science fiction thriller *Fringe* (2008–2013): success that would no doubt have appealed to NBCU, and later Netflix, in backing the series. Incidentally, Torv is also related to the owners of Fox, since her aunt Anna was married to Rupert Murdoch for thirty years ('Torv is her own mistress', 2008). As the tall, blonde, athletic Harriet, dressed primarily in shades of grey and blue, Torv exudes a cool calm in season 1 that might well be described as 'Nordic'. Her performance is also carefully calibrated and pared back. As an investigative journalist it is Harriet's compulsion to find out what happened to the gutted body discovered by the lake that ultimately leads to the death of her former partner Kim, who had tried to help her. This is a death for which Harriet feels responsible, and which drives her to relentlessly pursue the truth even when faced with the charge of treason.

While the first victim is male, and the second a transgender woman, neither of the victims fit comfortably into the trope of the young white female victim identified by Barbara Klinger in her analysis of the transnational serial crime drama (Klinger, 2018). Examples of such white female victims begin with *Twin Peaks* as the 'primal show', which Klinger suggests may have in turn influenced *The Killing*, as well as *Top of the Lake*, *Jordskott* and *The Kettering Incident*. As Klinger argues, in many of these series it is the body of the white female victim, which she describes as the 'gateway body', that is the 'hook' or the 'apparatus of capture' that draws us into the narrative (Klinger, 2018, pp. 521–523). Klinger's primary focus, however, is on *The Killing* and the 'feminist paradox' that emerges when programmes with female leads are investigating crime committed against female victims. As Klinger argues, the 'gateway figure' of the 'white female victim' now functions as a 'workhorse for crime TV in transnational distribution', while the lead female investigator, who is often up against it in terms of her own position within a male-dominated workforce, continues to face the problem of male violence that they cannot solve (Klinger, 2018, p. 531). In other words, while the gender of the investigator may have changed, nothing else has.

Although Klinger is certainly correct in pointing to the failure of these dramas to solve the problems of male violence that they address, it might be pointed out that this is indeed the grim reality of noir crime fiction and drama more generally. While the crime itself might be solved, the social problem of which it is a symptom may be insoluble. And while the female investigator may indeed be up against the patriarchy, the very fact that the narrative draws attention to this should also be applauded in terms of the ways in which such series invite the audience to think critically about gender politics. As has been argued, therein lies the value of the crime drama, which highlights the fault lines in the society it represents (Saunders, 2021; Turnbull, 2014).

In terms of the gender politics of *Secret City* in season 1, Harriet is a journalist, and a good one at that, who is by no means disadvantaged as a woman in the press room. She gives as good as she gets from her sniping male colleague, Griff (Marcus Graham), and has a close relationship with her male boss that is both friendly and caring. Adding to the feminist edge is the fact that the origins of the crime she is investigating appear to be located in the machinations of two powerful women – the Attorney General, Catriona Bailey, and the wife of the Chinese Ambassador. While Bailey power lunches with the (male) American Ambassador and (male) head of the Military, the Chinese Ambassador's wife is conducting an affair with the Minister of Defence Mal Paxton and spying on him at the same time. Women, in other words, are at the heart of this narrative, both in terms of the clandestine crimes that are committed and the investigation that will lead to their revelation.

When it comes to the victims, while the first body is that of a young male CIA agent and thus defies the 'white female victim' trope, the second is that of a transgender woman, which brings with it another set of cultural complications. The fact that Kim is murdered could be said to buy into what has been identified as the 'bury your gays' trope. As Haley Hulan (2017) effectively argues, whenever a LGBTQI+ character is depicted on screen, they will inevitably die. In her history of the trope, Hulan describes how the trope emerged in literature at the end of the nineteenth century in novels featuring a same-gender romantic couple, one of whom had to die by the end of the book in order to avoid the social backlash that might ensue for the author, who could be perceived to be promoting homosexuality (Hulan, 2017, p. 17). Hulan traces the evolution of the trope through literature, film and television to arrive at the influx of gay characters dying on television in the 2016 season, even though there are no longer the same societal and cultural prohibitions in place. Hulan's conclusion is that creators need to be aware of these patterns in order to avoid the potential stereotypical narratives that kill off queer characters. With Kim, she is killed by her lover, an ASIO agent who is seeking information (given to Kim by Harriet) about his agency's involvement in a deal to exchange the female Tibetan protestor for Chinese dissident students operating in Canberra. Whether this motive is ultimately as compelling as it might be, it certainly echoes the trope of 'bury your gays', even as the murder of Kim is a key plot move giving Harriet, who still loved her, a convincing motive for pursuing the truth about her death.

Within the genre of television crime, as in crime fiction, it is generally accepted that someone has to die in order for an investigation to proceed since murder is regarded as the most serious of crimes. However, when it comes to the choice of victim, there may well be a difference between what is portrayed in the fictional world as opposed to what is happening in the real world. For example, the Australian Bureau of Statistics suggests that in 2021, there were 370 victims of homicide in Australia and that the majority (70 per cent) were male (ABS, 2023b). However, when it comes to physical assault (affecting 1.9% of the population), it was reported that in 2021 women were more likely than men to experience assault by a family member or intimate partner, although less likely to experience physical assault by a stranger (ABS, 2023a). As a transgender woman, Kim is assaulted by an intimate partner and dies as a result. This is a likely although unfortunate scenario. Nevertheless, a question then arises about the value of crime as entertainment, as it manages a number of competing agendas that might include an obligation to reflect what is actually happening in the world or an obligation to tell stories that imagine an alternative (and better) reality, not forgetting the obligation to hold and entertain an audience through compelling storytelling and performances that ring true.

There is, however, another problem in the representation of Kim, since while it is possible to argue that having a transgender character with a successful career and people who love her portrayed onscreen is of value in itself, we also run into the problem that actor Damon Herriman is not himself transgender. This was an accusation launched at Australian actor Hugh Sheridan when he was cast in the role of Jonathan Larson in Larson's autobiographical musical, *Hedwig and the Angry Inch*, in 2020 (Byrne, 2023). Although Sheridan was in the process of coming out as both bisexual and non-binary at the time, he was 'dumped' from the production at the request of 'activists'. Despite the producers subsequently inviting Sheridan back, the production was cancelled and 'We all lost our jobs' (Byrne, 2023). The politics of representation, and whether actors or indeed writers can inhabit and create characters who are not like them, is fraught. As it is, *Secret City* largely avoided a critical outcry at the time of its first season, largely because, it might be argued, the audience was so small and public commentary on the show largely absent.

As Penny Chapman told Dan Barrett, they were well aware of the issues involved in portraying a transgender character on screen:

> We had some interesting conversations with NBCU when the scripts were being written and one of the things that became obvious was that the issues with her story were not about her being transgender. They were about her pursuing secrets that she shouldn't have pursued. She happens to be transgender. We were absolutely concerned that we must not make her a stunt (Penny Chapman in Barrett, 2016).

Within the same article, Damon Herriman described his approach to the character:

> I wanted to be respectful and as truthful as possible. I did as much research as I could. There's no question that every scene there would be something that I would be thinking, 'Is this the way I would be behaving if I was transitioning myself?. I hope the transgender community is accepting of it and okay with a non-transgender actor playing the role and that they feel like I portrayed the character in a realistic and respectful way (Damon Herriman in Barrett, 2016).

Whatever the transgender community may have thought of Herriman's performance, it was clearly applauded by the industry, attracting a number of the awards that inevitably contribute both personal and economic value to an actor's career. For Herriman, his short period of time on screen in two episodes was clearly worth the risk.

There was, however, another character on the show whose role was both remarkable but unremarked: that of Indigenous actor Miranda Tapsell as Harriet's extremely smart, gay, newsroom associate Sasha Rose. Arguably, this was an example of 'colour-blind' casting, as Sasha's Indigeneity was never mentioned and neither was her efficiency, although both were convincingly demonstrated onscreen as she supplied Harriet with background information, covered for her, and generally backed the senior journalist up. One of the stars of the successful Australian film *The Sapphires* (2012), loosely based on the true story of a 1960s female singing group who travelled to Vietnam to entertain the troops, Tapsell also starred in the television drama series *Redfern Now* (ABC 2012–2015), produced by Blackfella Films that, as we shall argue later, was part of a wave of television series produced by Indigenous creative talent and featuring Indigenous actors that contributed to the increasing visibility of Indigenous stories on screen.

Political Drama: The Value of Nordic Noir

Secret City was not the first Australian drama to deal with politics and crime, but as we have argued here, it was the first to employ what we have described as the Nordic Noir aesthetic to tell the story in order to appeal to the global niche audience for Nordic Noir. If this were in any doubt, a comparison with an earlier Australian political thriller, *The Code* (ABC 2014–2016), supports this claim. Created, written and produced by Shelley Birse for Playmaker Media and the ABC, the first season of *The Code*, set in Canberra and outback Australia, focussed on journalist Ned Banks (Dan Speilman) and his brother Jesse (Ashley Zukerman).

When Ned is sent a thumb drive containing footage of a car accident, Jesse, who is a brilliant computer hacker on the autism spectrum, helps him to recover the missing images. As a result of Ned's enquiries, the brothers become involved in the disclosure of a government cover-up involving the leaking of partially enriched uranium intended for sale to Pakistan. The first victim here is a young aboriginal girl who dies as a result of a collision with a truck carrying the uranium out of the fictional town of Lindara.

With a cast including internationally successful Australian star David Wenham as the duplicitous Deputy Prime Minister and Minister for Foreign Affairs and Trade, and Lucy Lawless, the star of *Xena: Warrior Princess* (1995–2001), as a local Lindara schoolteacher, it is clear that like *Secret City*, *The Code* had its sights set on international distribution deals and a transnational career. In terms of style, however, *The Code* hearkens back to American productions like *The Wire* (HBO 2002–2008) and *NYPD Blue* (ABC 1993–2005) in the deployment of hand-held camera work, fast editing and the use of blurring. While the contrast between the red dirt of outback Australia and the cooler tones of the architecturally splendid Canberra anticipates the visual contrast of another political drama, *Total Control*, the gender politics are very different from that of *Secret City*. From the two brothers driving the action, to the politicians running the show, the men are centre stage. This is not the case in either *Secret City* or *Total Control*, which more closely resemble the gender shift of the Nordic Noir dramas.

Co-created for the ABC by internationally recognised actor Rachel Griffiths, who stars as the embattled female premier Rachel Anderson, and Darren Dale from Blackfella Films, *Total Control* also revisits the dramatic terrain explored by *Borgen* in a number of interesting ways. Over three seasons, like the central character Birgitte Nyborg in *Borgen*, newly elected Indigenous Senator Alex Irving (Deborah Mailman) has to fight for her political ideals and her commitment to the community she represents while also navigating the challenges of being a (single) mother. The action therefore oscillates between the dusty outback town of Winton in Queensland and the halls of the Parliament House in Canberra. Like Birgitte, Alex emerges as a consummate media performer and expert tactician, achieving in the end what still seems like an impossible dream, the election of an Indigenous Prime Minister. Striding through the halls of Parliament House in her dark suit and heels, there is a moment in season 2 when the camera captures Alex from above, immediately recalling the title sequence of *Borgen* in which Brigitte, also seen from above, strides purposefully into and out of view.

Like *Borgen*, *Total Control* also anticipates the Australian swing away from the major parties, with the balance of power being held by (predominantly female) independent candidates. As Rachel Griffiths noted in an interview, 'We could never have imagined, really, the sea change of the last few years, so I don't really think we predicted. It was the trend that was there' (Quinn, 2022). Even more significant and on trend is the focus on Indigenous issues, with *Total Control* echoing the attention in the last season of *Borgen* given to the plight of the Greenlander people, also a politically marginalised nation under the control of a government that barely recognises them. The key difference, however, is that in *Total Control*, as in the crime drama *Mystery Road*, which we will discuss next, attention to Indigenous issues is front and centre all of the time.

In Sum

In thinking about the total value of *Secret City*, it's therefore easy to point to the value that the show had for Foxtel in terms of their international ambitions to produce television that could sit alongside the HBO series on their Showcase platform with a subsequent financially rewarding long tail. It's also evident that the series was of value to the creatives involved, including Uhlmann, Spicer and Chapman, who were so determined to get Canberra onscreen in an Australian political drama intended to emulate *The West Wing*, *House of Cards* or *Borgen*. For Canberra, the series represented a coup in terms of attracting another screen project to the ACT that would create more jobs at the same time as it showcased the modern architecture of the capital city. But perhaps most of all, the series was of value in terms of the geo-political issues it rehearsed. While it was argued by Morley and Robbins in 1995 (p. 1) that with the new transnational trade in television, audio-visual geographies were 'becoming detached from the symbolic spaces of national culture and realigned on the basis of more "universal" principles of international consumer cultures', *Secret City* demonstrates that twenty years on, the opposite was also true. A television drama series concerned with geo-political issues of national significance could indeed find an international viewership as a result of the emergence of a global niche audience for Nordic Noir able to appreciate the familiar aesthetic and the attention to ethical, social and cultural themes, but also the originality of its Australian location and concerns.

Table 5.1 *Secret City* (2016–2019)

The makers

Commissioning broadcaster	Foxtel
Production company	Matchbox Pictures
Distributor / international sales	Universal Media Studios International

The results

International sales	The first series was acquired by Netflix, with the second series co-commissioned by Foxtel and Netflix. Both series are available on Netflix in 48 countries, including Australia.
Awards	4 wins and 13 nominations Australian Directors Guild Awards • 2020 Nominee Best Direction in a TV or SVOD Drama Series: Tony Krawitz • 2017 **Winner** Best Direction in a Television Series: Emma Freeman Logie Awards • 2019 Nominee Most Outstanding Actress: Danielle Cormack • 2019 Nominee Most Outstanding Drama Series • 2017 Winner Most Outstanding Supporting Actor: Damon Herriman • 2017 **Winner** Most Outstanding Actress: Anna Torv Australian Writers' Guild Awgie Awards • 2019 Nominee Television Series or Miniseries of more than 4 hours duration: Matt Cameron Australian Academy of Cinema and Television Arts (AACTA) Awards • 2019 Nominee Best Drama Series: Stephen Corvini, Penny Chapman, Matt Cameron, Penny Win, Carly Heaton • 2019 Nominee Best Lead Actress in a Television Drama: Anna Torv • 2019 Nominee Best Cinematography in Television: Mark Wareham, Ep. 1 'Run Little Rabbit (2019)' • 2019 Nominee Best Production Design in Television: Elizabeth Mary Moore, Ep. 1 'Run Little Rabbit (2019)' • 2019 Nominee Best Male New Talent: Frederick Du Rietz Screen Music Awards, Australia • 2016 Nominee Best Music for a Miniseries or Telemovie: David Bridie Australian Production Design Guild Awards • 2016 Nominee Design on a Television Drama: Felicity Abbott Casting Guild of Australia Awards • 2016 Nominee Best Casting in a TV Miniseries or Telemovie: Kirsty McGregor
Audience demand	The first season attracted nightly audiences of 70,000 to 80,000 (Tonight, 2016). IMDb rating: 7.4/10 Rotten Tomatoes average audience score: 70%

116 Transnational TV Crime

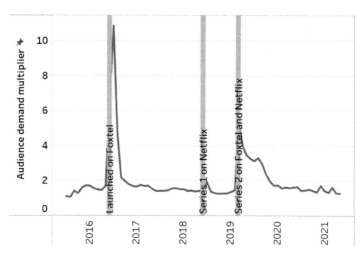

Figure 5.1 Audience demand multiplier for *Secret City*

Note: The audience demand multiplier benchmarks content relative to the market average of 1. If a show has 2× demand, it is two times more in-demand that the average TV show in the market.

Source: Parrot Analytics (2021).

Chapter 6

Mystery Road

Mystery Road (ABC 2018–) marks a significant moment in the history of the TV crime drama in Australia in both its attention to Indigenous storytelling and its depiction of the Australian landscape. With its origins in two earlier films, *Mystery Road* (2013) and *Goldstone* (2016), both written and directed by Indigenous filmmaker Ivan Sen, the TV series built on the tropes of the western thriller genre that characterised the original films to create a series that was branded 'outback noir' in the press (Buckmaster, 2018), although producer David Jowsey described the series as 'tropical outback gothic noir' (Dubecki, 2020). Rachel Perkins, the Indigenous Australian director of the first season and founder of the Indigenous production house, Blackfella Films, expanded on the concept of 'outback noir' and the intention of the show as follows:

> The 'outback' is not only a description of a place beyond the city, but it is also a way of life. It is where rules are broken, where people go to hide. There is a wildness to the outback that we embraced in the making of *Mystery Road*, but we also embrace the tropes of the genre; the male cop, the loner. There is no femme fatale that he falls for, but an older woman, his equal, who challenges him in a battle of wills that is the dynamic centre of our story. We hope that fans of the noir genre will find appeal in our show as it draws on well-established traditions, but we also hope they enjoy the journey as we dig deeper to bring layers of history, race and feminism to the fore (Hopewell, 2018).

These comments signal both Perkins' knowledge of the tropes of film noir, as well as the intention to update these in a geo-political setting very far from the urban locations of more traditional noir films and fiction. As Hansen and Re (2021) suggest, crime dramas inspired by the success of Nordic Noir series such as *The Bridge* (DR & SVT 2011–2018) were increasingly being set in peripheral locations in Europe during the same period.

Much has been written about the use of landscape and location in Australian art and literature (Stadler, 2016), commentary that may include references to the traditions of the oldest living civilisation on earth, the history of white settlement, indigenous dispossession, the romanticisation of 'the bush' in literature and film, and the identification of the 'outback' as a location that is at once both dangerous and beautiful. Of relevance also are the ways in which Australian crime fiction has reworked the noir traditions of American crime fiction in the portrayal of urban locations such as Sydney and Melbourne, before a more recent turn to what crime writer Garry Disher has identified as 'rural noir' in regional settings (Disher, 2021). When it comes to Australian television crime drama, a similar pattern can be identified in the shift from the urban locations of Australia's first television crime drama *Homicide* (Seven Network 1964–1977) set in and around Melbourne, or *Water Rats* (Nine Network 1996–2001), with its tourist gaze on Sydney Harbour, to more recent crime dramas set in remote outback locations, including all three series of *Mystery Road* and *True Colours* (SBS & NITV 2022), both of which feature Indigenous police officers.

While *The Kettering Incident* was frequently described as Tassie Noir, and *Secret City* with its focus on Canberra was labelled Aussie Noir, the first season of *Mystery Road* immediately stood apart in its use of the spectacular landscapes of the Kimberley in Western Australia. The first episode opened with the image of an abandoned utility vehicle (generally referred to as a 'ute') in an expanse of cracked brown earth. Using time lapse photography, the camera circled the ute as a spectacular sunset unfolded, the prelude to an equally spectacular starry night, followed by another blisteringly hot day in which the ute is surrounded by dusty Brahman cattle before being discovered by two backpackers on a quad bike from the local cattle station. As television critic Debi Enker noted:

> The first striking thing about Mystery Road is the landscape: a vast night sky sparkling with stars, expanses of baked earth, bulbous boab trees, imposing mountain ranges and outcrops of red rock (Enker, 2018).

Although *Mystery Road*, the film, was described by Jane Goodall (2018) as a 'Western with a crime story at its heart', *Mystery Road* the TV series is a crime drama that echoes the western in terms of its iconography and setting but also has a keen eye on recent developments in the TV crime drama. Like a cowboy, Indigenous Detective Jay Swan dresses in boots and jeans with a white hat to shield his eyes from the sun while the imposing landscape recalls John Ford's framing of Monument Valley in his iconic Westerns. However, the series also embraces the aesthetics of Nordic Noir in its use of a double narrative, strong female central characters, slow pacing and the frequent deployment of drone shots to establish a sense of geo-physical location. There are also a number of scenes shot at night in which headlights and torches punctuate the dark, transforming the sumptuous red landscape into thick blackness. With its initially antagonistic relationship between a strong female character, Senior Sergeant Emma James (Judy Davis), and Detective Jay Swan (Aaron Pedersen), the series also echoed the gender dynamics of Nordic Noir series such as *The Killing* (DR1 2007–2012) and *The Bridge*, in which two investigators of the opposite sex are forced to work together in a testy relationship to investigate a crime of violence.

Produced by David Jowsey (who co-founded Bunya Productions with Ivan Sen) and Greer Simpkin, *Mystery Road* was one of a series of television dramas first shown on Australia's first public service network, the ABC, that sought to address Indigenous issues in the new millennium. With the ABC's public charter obligations to broadcast programs 'that contribute to a sense of national identity and inform and entertain and reflect the cultural diversity of the Australian community' ('The ABC Act', 1983), it could be argued that this attention was overdue but timely. Central to this move was the appointment in 2009 of Indigenous filmmaker Sally Riley, as the inaugural Head of the Indigenous Department at the ABC before becoming Head of Scripted Production in 2016. This position was created by the ABC's then Director of Television, Kim Dalton, with the explicit instruction to 'get Indigenous material out of the ghetto', and Riley was given an unprecedented A$5 million a year to achieve this (Davis, 2017). This entailed commissioning a number of significant drama series, including the award-winning social drama set in Sydney, *Redfern Now* (ABC 2012–2015), and the docudrama telemovie *Mabo* (ABC 2012), both involving director Rachel Perkins and her company Blackfella Films. Another urban drama, *The Gods of Wheat Street* (ABC 2014), produced by Every Cloud Productions of *Miss Fisher* fame, was followed by a dystopian speculative drama, *Cleverman* (ABC 2016–2017), produced by Goalpost Pictures, drawing on Indigenous Dreamtime stories, but also reflecting contemporary issues such as border protection, asylum seekers and refugees.

Although attention has been paid to the portrayal of Indigenous characters and stories on film in Australia in the past, relatively little attention has been paid to the representation of Indigenous people on television, with some notable exceptions, including the work of John Hartley and Alan McKee (2001), Chris Healy (2008) and Graeme Turner (2020). While this lacuna may well have to do with the fact that Aboriginal and Torres Strait Islander people have been largely absent from mainstream television and film production, this began to change in the 1990s. As Therese Davis has argued (2017), the development of a vigorous Indigenous screen production sector over the next thirty years was largely the result of targeted screen policies and industry support that coincided with significant national debates about Indigenous governance at that time. These debates were inspired by a series of important political initiatives during the 90s, including the establishment of the Aboriginal and Torres Strait Islander Commission in 1990; the Council for Aboriginal Reconciliation in 1991; the High Court's Mabo judgment in 1992; the Royal Commission into Aboriginal Deaths in Custody in 1991; and the 'Bringing Them Home' report emerging from the National Inquiry into the Separation of Aboriginal and Torres Strait Islander Children from their Families in 1997. All of these initiatives point to the serious social issues that would find their way into the story lines of subsequent film and television productions telling Indigenous stories, including *Mystery Road*.

In their landmark book, *Australian Cinema after Mabo*, Felicity Collins and Therese Davis (2004) provide a comprehensive overview of Australian cinema from 1993 to 2003, discussing a number of films that review the colonial past, including *Yolngu Boy* (2001) and *The Tracker* (2002). Returning to this topic in 2016, Collins describes the critical mass of Indigenous film and television production that emerged post-Mabo as the Blak Wave, noting in particular the affective response to specific films, such as Indigenous director Warwick Thornton's film *Samson and Delilah* (2009), which achieved international recognition when it was awarded the Camera d'Or at the Cannes Film Festival in 2009. Thornton would go on to further international success with his historical film *Sweet Country* (2017), also produced by Bunya, which won the Special Jury Prize at the 74th Venice International Film festival in September 2017. As casting director Anousha Zarkesh (2022) explained, such awards not only signal international recognition of the quality of the production, but also attract the interest of international buyers and distributors, who are then more likely to invest in future ventures.

It might be noted that following the lead of Indigenous Director Rachel Perkins in season 1 of *Mystery Road*, with fellow Indigenous

Director Wayne Blair, Thornton would go on to direct episodes in season 2 of *Mystery Road* (2020). Thornton's son, Dylan River, was the award-winning director of season 3, *Mystery Road: Origin* (2022), while Rachel Perkins' son, Tyson, also won an AACTA Award for cinematography (see Table 6.1).

Development, Production and Post-Production

Originally established by Ivan Sen and David Jowsey, the name of the Bunya Productions derives from the Bunya Mountains, to which both Jowsey and Sen had a cultural connection through their families. According to Jowsey, 'we're an Indigenous company in effect…. Ivan owns half the company and he's an Aboriginal filmmaker so it's having that Indigenous influence over the company that is probably the main feature' (Bizzaca, 2018). In Jowsey's opinion, the collaboration with Sen has influenced the ways in which they work with other Indigenous creatives, in that their policy is to share their intellectual property; 'That way everyone's got a seat at the table, everyone's a partner, everyone's got an equal stake in the project and the commitment is clear' (Bizzaca, 2018). In 2015, Sen and Jowsey were joined by Greer Simpkin, whose prior role was as Deputy Head of Fiction at the ABC. According to Bunya's website, one of the key reasons Greer was brought into the company was her experience in producing and financing large television projects.

As outlined on their website, Bunya's key operating principles include hiring Indigenous crews where available and employing locals as interns on all their productions, especially since these are often set in remote locations where the conditions are tough and hot, as they were on the first series of *Mystery Road*. Jowsey has described the process of negotiating access to these locations and acquiring the permission of local communities to go on country as a privilege rather than an obligation, suggesting, 'It's relatively easy if you are actually interested and are open. It really is something that opens you up to this incredible experience and generosity of Aboriginal communities' (Bizzaca, 2018). As Greer Simpkin observed, while *Mystery Road* may have been designed as a crime show, it was also intended to showcase Australia's Indigenous cultural heritage (Fry, 2018).

Inverting the familiar gateway trope of the missing/dead white girl (Klinger, 2018), the initial crime represented in season 1 of *Mystery Road* is the disappearance of two young male station hands, one of whom is a local Indigenous football star, Marley Thompson (Aaron McGrath), and the other a young white man, while out checking water pumps on the vast Ballantyne cattle property. The current white owner, Tony Ballantyne (Colin Friels), is planning to sell the farm to a mining company that is interested in the underground aquafers, which the Indigenous people know are vital to the health of the land. Underpinning the original crime of dispossession and stolen property are the more immediate crimes, involving the sale of illegal drugs in remote communities and the false imprisonment of Marley's uncle, Larry Dime (Wayne Blair), for the rape of a minor. As it emerges, this assault was conducted by the local head of the Aboriginal Council, Keith Groves (Ernie Dingo), a crime that unwaveringly points to current issues in remote Indigenous communities where sexual violence and abuse is a serious problem. As has long been acknowledged, such crimes can be ascribed not only to gendered violence, but also the social disadvantage experienced by Aboriginal and Torres Strait Islander communities which has ensued as a result of successive government policies since Australia was first invaded and the Indigenous population dispossessed. Indeed, it was not until a referendum in 1967 that the Australian Constitution was amended to include Aboriginal people in the national Census, effectively recognising them as humans rather than as 'fauna'. In November 2023 another referendum was held, which sought to alter the Constitution in order to give Indigenous people a 'Voice' to the Australian Parliament and to make representations directly to Executive Government on matters relating to Aboriginal and Torres Strait Islander people. The primary goal of the Voice initiative was to enable self-determination in the task of addressing the severe inequality that still faces Indigenous communities. However, only the Australian Capital Territory voted in its favour, and the Voice campaign was regrettably unsuccessful (Australian Government, 2023).

Although the crimes represented in *Mystery Road* may therefore be specific to the Australian context, the themes explored connect to similar trends in recent transnational television crime dramas from Northern Europe. For example, the dispossession of Indigenous Australians and their social disadvantage recalls the experience of the Sami people, as represented in the Nordic Noir crime drama *Midnight Sun* (SVT 2016), while the portrayal of an extreme and spectacular landscape under threat from industrial exploitation and the associated climate change invites a comparison with the arctic locations of multiple transnationally successful Nordic crime dramas over the last decade. These include the British series *Fortitude* (Sky Atlantic 2015–2018), set in a fictional arctic town, the Icelandic series *Ófærð/Trapped* (RÚV 2015–), and the Danish series *Thin Ice* (TV4 2020), set in Greenland. These issues are also raised in the fourth season of the Danish political drama *Borgen* (DR1 2022), which addresses the geo-political tensions that ensue after the discovery of a large oil field in Greenland, an island nation that is effectively still under the control of the Danish state. Like *The Kettering Incident* (Showcase 2016) and *Secret City* (Showcase & Netflix 2016–2019), *Mystery Road* is an Australian series that seeks to embrace global trends in the crime drama genre by addressing political and social issues of immediate concern to Australia, but with international relevance, in a visually distinctive location.

As season 1 director Rachel Perkins explained:

> We went to great lengths to shoot our series in some of the remotest and most spectacular landscapes in Australia. This landscape also has a deep history, of black and white conflict which we mine to give greater layers. It is a universal story of colonization, which is the undercurrent of what on its surface seems to be a cop show, but also has something to say about our country, our history and a future where two cultures must exist together and reconcile their past (Hopewell, 2018).

The potential for *Mystery Road* to find an international audience in terms of its 'universal story' and its spectacular locations was clearly part of its attraction as a project. As Penny Smallacombe, then head of Screen Australia's Indigenous department, suggested:

> Television audiences around the world are embracing Indigenous stories and with Rachel Perkins at the helm, a stellar cast on board and stunning locations, the series is set to be a success both in Australia and internationally (Frater, 2017).

This ambition was underlined by David Swetman, Vice President of Acquisitions for the distribution company All3Media, who extolled the series for its 'sumptuous, cinematic outback noir character' while proposing that it was a 'ground-breaking, genre-defining drama' (Fry, 2018). *Mystery Road*'s ambition to find an international audience therefore depended on a number of factors, not least the hope that the audiences might 'embrace Indigenous stories' and find some cultural and social value in them. There were, however, many other kinds of value to be derived from this show, not least in the process of the production itself.

Casting *Mystery Road*

In 2017, an ABC news release described the experience of a South Australian horse trainer, Jim Willoughby, who was involved in the making of the first season of *Mystery Road* (Fowler, 2017). Having worked on an earlier Bunya production, the period film *Sweet Country* in Alice Springs, Willoughby was invited to Western Australia to source and train local horses and riders for *Mystery Road* season 1 and to assist in the mustering of the cattle for several scenes in the film. A former station hand himself, Willoughby described how he was able to talk both the language of filmmaking and the language of the station to achieve the look that the director wanted. Three boys enrolled in an agricultural course at the local Kununurra District High School were employed as extras, one of them riding as a stunt double for a lead actor. As Greer Simpkin reported, the production also involved 100 extras from Wyndham and another 100 in Kununurra, noting that the crew were embraced by the local community during the ten weeks of the shoot (Fowler, 2017).

Casting Director Anousha Zarkesh confirmed Simpkin's observations in her account of the process involved in recruiting local acting talent for all three of the *Mystery Road* series (Zarkesh, 2022). With her experience working on previous television and film productions telling Indigenous stories, including *The Gods of Wheat Street*, *Redfern Now*, *Cleverman* and *Sweet Country* (2017), Zarkesh had already established herself as an award-winning casting director with a particular expertise in locating Indigenous talent. As Zarkesh (2022) explained, 'it's the hardest, and it's hard work. So no one could do what I do' since this involves direct engagement with local communities to source as much new talent as possible. While there are sound economic reasons for this localism, Zarkesh observed that there is also a payoff in terms of how the communities have responded to the series as a result of their involvement:

> When I'm embedded with the community, I literally arrive and I'll go out to the community, it's like, I'll drive out and I'll knock on doors if I'm looking for kids. I'll talk to all the schools and there's a lot of closed doors, a lot of people go 'Forget it not interested' …. But as *Mystery Road* and *Redfern Now* [were seen] it has become more of a vocation and people stepped up a bit. And they were kind of proud. They saw themselves on screen and said 'I could do that, too'. So it just got easier and easier that people would come forward (Zarkesh, 2022).

Characterising the process as 'pretty organic' and 'loose' and 'never what you think it's going to be', Zarkesh recounted how she would travel with her camera, 'shooting on the run' and invite people to play out scenes with her, possibly at the local pub, with often surprising results in terms of the improvised screen tests. Given that the storyline might involve talking about the Stolen Generation (a shameful period in Australian history when Aboriginal children were forcibly taken from their parents), or about the police treating Indigenous people with disrespect, or a racist scene, apparently these improvisations would often reduce everyone to tears and a lot of hugging would ensue: 'it's raw and authentic and truthful', Zarkesh explained (Zarkesh, 2022).

While this might seem a confronting experience, Zarkesh firmly believed the value of these encounters lay both in the process of people feeling confident enough to come forward in the first place and the outcomes. For the women in these communities, this was often a learning experience and one in which they took pride in the fact that they had 'pushed themselves' to participate, especially when they were employed on the production. As Zarkesh told Jane Goodall (2018), the process of blending local extras with professionally trained actors and established stars is a challenge that any casting director might face, but in *Mystery Road* it is central to what appears onscreen. While Zarkesh's task involves first finding the individuals with the distinctive physical and personal qualities who are willing to participate, there comes the challenge of shaping them into an ensemble capable of portraying 'the surface tensions and underlying bonds of an enduring community' (Goodall, 2018).

As a result of her engagement with the local communities, Zarkesh was of the opinion that the cultural impact of the production had been 'enormous' both for the Indigenous cast and the audience. When asked to explain how, Zarkesh suggested that a show such as *Mystery Road*, like the earlier *Redfern Now*, can 'change the psyche of the country' since many people who would not as a rule engage in Indigenous storytelling have now watched the show, and as a result have learned about cultural practices that they would not otherwise have encountered (Zarkesh, 2022). In making this point about the cultural value of the series, Zarkesh pointed to the storyline in season 2 in which a Swedish archaeologist is digging up Indigenous artefacts while a group of women protest the appropriation of their cultural heritage, an issue that is extremely pertinent to Indigenous peoples.

According to Greer Simpkin, the casting of Sofia Helin, who played Saga Noren in *The Bridge*, as the Swedish archaeologist Professor Sandra

Elmquist was a 'wish-list sprung to life', since Simpkin herself was a firm fan of Nordic Noir drama. This casting decision suggests Bunya Productions did indeed have their eye on the international career of *Mystery Road* in terms of the global niche audience for Nordic Noir, who would be attracted to the series by Helin's presence (Dubecki, 2020). As Zarkesh told us, the attachment of a 'name' can make all the difference in terms of raising revenue for a project based on its likely distribution – and Helin was clearly a 'name' for those familiar with Nordic Noir. There was, however, another motive for casting Helin. Season 1, which also featured a strong female central character, played by acclaimed Australian actor Judy Davis as Senior Sergeant Emma James, had sold very well into Europe. Given that feedback to the producers suggested that there was a very positive reaction to a mature female lead 'who has her own power and strength', there were then very good business reasons for the inclusion of Helin's character in season 2 (Dubecki, 2020).

Helin herself was apparently attracted to the role for a number of reasons, not least that the script called for a 'Woman, aged 30–60 years'. As she explained in an interview, 'Normally it says "Woman, 30 years old, beautiful". It makes me want to puke' (Dubecki, 2020). Characterised as 'Saga Noren gone Indiana Jones' and dressed in an Akubra hat, work boots and cargo pants, Helin is mired in sweat and red earth from the start to finish of her scenes, an experience she clearly embraced: 'Yesterday I had to film a fight scene where I roll around in the dust…. It was such fun' (Dubecki, 2020). Having been welcomed to country through an Indigenous smoking ceremony, Helin described how during the course of the shoot she not only came to learn about the repatriation of stolen Indigenous artefacts, but also about land rights, the dire incarceration rates for Aboriginal people, and the need for a constitutional voice to Parliament (Dubecki, 2020). As Helin's comments reveal, there were cultural and social values to be derived from this series that involved educating both the non-Indigenous cast and the audience about issues affecting First Peoples that simply cannot be measured in any quantitative way.

For actor Aaron Pedersen, who was cast by Ivan Sen and David Jowsey to star in the original *Mystery Road* film (2013) and its sequel *Goldstone* (2016), the value of his participation in the television series has been considerable in terms of the ongoing recognition he has received both nationally and internationally for his work. Having been nominated for eighteen awards over the course of his career, Pedersen has to date won eight, seven of them for his performance as Detective Jay Swan in both films, and more recently an AACTA International Best Actor Award for season 2 of the television series. As noted on the AACTA website, the International Awards honour screen excellence 'regardless of geography' and are intended to add a 'uniquely Australian voice to the international awards season alongside the Oscars, BAFTAs, Emmys and Golden Globes' (AACTA, 2023).

Interviewing Pedersen for *The Guardian*, Luke Buckmaster (2018) asked, 'Is the *Mystery Road* star one of the greatest actors of his generation?' before going on to discuss the 'strength and vulnerability' Pedersen brings to every role. According to Buckmaster, if there is one thing that defines Pedersen's work, it is 'gravitas' and his ability 'to project both great strength and great sorrow'. In this article, Pedersen describes how Ivan Sen directed him to play Jay Swan in *Mystery Road* the film, characterising Sen's approach as 'old school', in that he expects actors 'to have conversations not just with dialogue but with silences' (Buckmaster, 2018). Apparently Sen's primary instruction to Pedersen was 'Don't rush it, Aaron. Take your time. Breathe'. As TV critic Jane Goodall (2018) noted, Pedersen clearly adhered to this advice, given her observation that 'Pedersen has superb timing, often stretching out a response till you are unsure he has one, but he can also startle with a lightening comeback'.

In Goodall's opinion, while a cast featuring esteemed Indigenous actors such as Pedersen and Deborah Mailman as well as Anglo-Australian actors such as Judy Davis and Colin Friels might seem like an invitation to nominate 'outstanding performances', the ensemble approach ensured that every performance was both disciplined and nuanced. According to Goodall, *Mystery Road* was the first Australian drama series in a long time that truly deserved an international audience (Goodall, 2018). Producer Greer Simpkin also commented on the depth of the ensemble acting by the predominantly Aboriginal cast, crediting Anousha Zarkesh with her work in achieving this (Goodall, 2022).

Financing, Distribution and Aggregation

With the imprimatur of the ABC, the first series of Mystery Road received $700,000 in funding support from Screen Australia, and support from Screenwest and Create NSW. All3Media was on board from the outset, handling international sales (Frater, 2017; Screen Australia, 2017). The second and third seasons of *Mystery Road* also attracted $700,000 and

$921,000 respectively from Screen Australia's Indigenous TV Drama Production Fund, Screenwest and Screen NSW, and international distribution deals with all3media (ABC, 2020; Screen Australia, 2019, 2022a; Screenwest, 2021). Screenwest support for the second season of $2.8 million in production funding and $20,000 in internships and regional development planning through the WA Regional Film Fund highlights the expectation that the series would deliver on multiple fronts for the remote filming locations, Wyndham and Kununurra for season 1, the Dampier Peninsular for season 2 and Kalgoorlie-Boulder and Coolgardie for season 3. These included the economic benefits from expenditure on goods and services in regional and remote areas of the state, facilitating tourism and building capability and building capacity in the state's production and post-production sectors, and the requirement that any Indigenous content or participation complies with Indigenous Cultural and Intellectual Property Rights protocols (Arts Law Centre of Australia, 2023; Screenwest, 2022). With *Mystery Road: Origin* shot during the COVID-19 Delta variant outbreak of July 2021, while strict border closures were in place, 80 per cent of the crew were from within the state. The border closure meant that moving cast and department heads from the eastern states to Western Australia and then subsequently keeping them in Western Australia added to the production costs, which were covered by the ABC (ABC, 2022b).

In the weeks following *Mystery Road*'s ABC premiere in June 2018, All3Media proceeded to confirm international distribution deals. Later in the same month, it was announced that the North American streaming service Acorn TV had acquired the series, which would be available to US audiences from August, and had also bought the secondary rights for the UK, Ireland, Australia and New Zealand. In September, the BBC announced it had acquired the first season, which it would air as a weekly double bill (Whittingham, 2018a, 2018b).

With *Mystery Road* the film having screened in the Special Presentation section at the Toronto International Film Festival in 2013 – and having been a rare foreign screening at the 2014 Pyongyang International Film Festival in North Korea – international festivals were an important means of exposure for the television franchise. In 2018, before being acquired by Acorn TV, *Mystery Road* screened at Series Mania Festival in France – where *Kettering* had such success in 2016 winning the Special Jury Prize (Knox, 2016a) – and at the Banff World Media Festival. At the time the acquisition was announced it had screenings scheduled at the SeriesFest in Denver, the Munich Film Festival and the Saint-Tropez Film Festival. The second series premiered at the Berlin International Film Festival, alongside another ABC drama, *Stateless* (2020), the only Australian series selected (ABC, 2021; Dams, 2020). *Mystery Road: Origin* also made its international premiere at a festival, selected for the 2022 Toronto International Film Festival Primetime program, alongside the fifth season of *The Handmaid's Tale* (Lattanzio, 2022).

Professional Recognition – Awards

As Bunya reports on its website, by July 2023 the *Mystery Road* franchise held the highest number of AACTA nominations for a TV series in the history of the awards. While seasons 1 and 2 were nominated for twenty-one awards, winning eight including the AACTA Award for Best Television Drama, season 3 featuring Mark Coles Smith as the young Jay Swann also swept the board at the 2022 AACTAs. With Warwick Thornton's son Dylan River winning for best direction and Rachel Perkins' nephew Tyson Perkins winning for best cinematography, it is probably fair to conclude that the ensemble nature of this production extended from the cast to all the Indigenous creatives involved.

The first season also did remarkably well at the 2019 Logies, Australia's popular audience awards, nominated in eight categories and winning two, for Most Popular Drama Program and Most Popular Actress for Deborah Mailman (Table 6.1). Usually dominated by the commercial free-to-air broadcasters, in 2019 a concerted effort by ABC personality Tom Gleeson saw ABC viewers flocking to vote for their favourite programs the first time: neither the second nor third seasons of *Mystery Road* have won a Logie.

Reception

The first series of Mystery Road was an immediate success when it first appeared on the ABC. As Mathieson (2018) reported, it didn't just 'get off to a good start, it had a victory', the first double episode drawing a healthy audience of 786,000 in the five state capitals. This was particularly impressive since the series was up against a sensational interview with a current senior politician (Barnaby Joyce) regarding his sex life on a rival free-to-air commercial network. Only weeks into its run, *Mystery*

Road was reported to be the most watched non-children's series on the ABC catch-up service iView (Groves, 2018b), even though audiences appeared to be watching it in the traditional weekly, delayed gratification style, rather than bingeing in one hit (Quinn, 2018). The audience for the second season was similarly impressive, with the highest ratings for any Australian adult television drama series on free-to-air television in 2020 (Bunya Productions, 2023), and a Parrot Analytics demand multiple showing audience interest as being eight times above the average (Figure 6.1). The third season premiered in the Top 10 rated programs and as the most popular drama in its launch week, attracting 635,000 viewers in its free-to-air time slot (Crikey, 2022).

The critical reception for the first season was also very positive. Writing in the Australian newspaper, Graeme Blundell acknowledged cinematographer Mark Wareham's intention to honour the original western aesthetic of the original two movies:

> The characters are reduced to their most elemental emotions, terse and strangely indifferent, as are the red hills that hem in the township, and the austere and silent country beyond (Blundell, 2018).

While for Blundell the critical reference points were the Coen brothers' dystopian film *No Country for Old Men* (2007) and the TV series *Fargo* (FX 2014–), for TV blogger David Knox it was all about an Australian interpretation of Nordic Noir:

> Rachel Perkins brings a slow-burn Scandinavian style to the piece, but it is punctuated by a rock & roll and bluegrass soundtrack, and the outback light helps to avoid it becoming too brooding (Knox, 2018).

Indigenous academic and journalist Larissa Behrendt was also enthusiastic in her *Guardian* review, suggesting that Mark Wareham's cinematography not only gave the series a cinematic feel, but also gave the land 'such a strong presence that it feels like an antagonist in the story' (Behrendt, 2018). Her conclusion being that:

> Between the landscape as a protagonist and the explorations of community relations in small towns, *Mystery Road* reminds us of the distinct voice Indigenous creatives can bring to visual storytelling. The result is a deftly made drama that will satisfy the contract with the audience regarding its genre, but also leaves open broader questions about how history haunts all Australians, whatever their colour (Behrendt, 2018).

Over in the UK, television blogger Andy D noted the TV series' origins in the largely ignored (but highly recommended) 2013 film *Mystery Road* and its sequel *Goldstone*, suggesting that while the films had suffered from the problem that the women were presented as largely helpless victims or a 'voiceless motive' for male vengeance, the TV series had corrected this through the character of police officer Emma James, played by the 'incomparable Judy Davis' (Andy D, 2018). Writing in the *New York Post*, Mike Hale commented that while the mystery story itself ('with its topics of drug-trafficking, child sexual abuse and shady land deals') was 'fairly pedestrian', the show is a 'visual knockout, an evocative succession of desert, ranch and starscapes' (Hale, 2018). Acknowledging the work of director Rachel Perkins and cinematographer Mark Wareham, Hale went on to make some important points about the portrayal of the Indigenous characters, suggesting:

> It's also bracing to see the way in which the lives and concerns of the Indigenous characters are given precedence without the self-consciousness, or self-congratulation, that sometimes marks American productions' treatment of African-American or Native American characters in similar stories. That tends to be true of Australian TV and film in general… (Hale, 2018).

Writing in the *Houston Chronicle*, Arts and Entertainment writer Cary Darling (2018) also commented on the portrayal of the Indigenous characters, quoting Aaron Pederson himself on the issue:

> I think it's getting better… We are still romanticizing the indigenous image of the native but for me it's more of the sense of the inner being. We're getting a chance to dig deep into the emotional soul of people and understanding them as the framework of who they are, which is no different from anybody else. It's giving credibility to us as being quality contributors to society (Pedersen in Darling, 2018).

Flow-ons

Following the success of series 1 of *Mystery Road* both at home and internationally, a further two seasons of the show were subsequently produced, with the third, *Mystery Road: Origin*, constituting a 'prequel' exploring Jay Swan's backstory in 1999 after returning to his hometown of Jardine to join the local police force. Shot in the Goldfields area around Kalgoorlie,

Boulder and Coolgardie in Western Australia, the third series was again very well received after what some identified as the somewhat disappointing second series. As Graeme Blundell in *The Australian* observed, series 2 'got lost in too many misplaced plot diversions' while Sofia Helin's role was undeveloped and something of a diversion resulting in a 'narrative mess' (Blundell, 2022). Peter Craven (2022), also in *The Australian*, was somewhat kinder, describing season 2 as 'just as grandly filmed, just as unremitting' as season 1, before going on to rave, somewhat incoherently, about season 3 and the achievement of the series as a whole:

> ... the 18 episodes of *Mystery Road* inevitably punch at us as well as captivate us. They bring us closer than we might readily imagine to what Germaine Greer argued long ago in her Quarterly Essay, *Whitefella Jump Up*. When Australians look in the mirror they see an Aboriginal face. It hits like an epiphany as we watch these dynamic Indigenous actors that this captivating bit of outback crime diversion actualises the kind of conviction that could shape the Statement from the Heart, however it is finally parsed (Craven, 2022).

The Statement from the Heart referred to here is the petition produced by Aboriginal and Torres Strait Islander leaders in 2017, recommending a change to the Constitution of Australia to provide Indigenous people with a Voice to Parliament, a proposal defeated in the 2023 referendum (Uluru Dialogue, 2023). Nevertheless, Craven's comments signal the important political role that *Mystery Road* could play in helping White Australia understand and respond to the Indigenous call for constitutional recognition. What is also interesting about Craven's comments is the suggestion that as a television series, *Mystery Road* reflects a new Indigenous identity for all Australians. As Craven goes on:

> Yes, it's just television but it's television of such vibrancy and such power that it collapses the them/us distinction that structures so many of the stumbles we have made with our own Aboriginal inheritance in the past. This is epoch-making television (Craven, 2022).

Cultural Impact

While *Mystery Road* clearly had an epiphanic impact on reviewer Peter Craven, it is important to acknowledge that the series sits within an ongoing history of Indigenous representation in film and television that arguably reached something of a high-water mark in 2022, when the ABC announced their National Aboriginal and Islanders Day Observance Committee (NAIDOC) Week celebrations, with *Mystery Road: Origin* heading the bill (ABC, 2022a). In a press release celebrating 'the culture and achievements of the world's oldest continuous storytellers', Sally Riley, from her position as Head of Drama, Entertainment and Indigenous at the ABC, informed viewers that the ABC had come a long way:

> The ABC's history of Indigenous programming is explored in our TV special *Looking Black*, revisiting key moments from our 90-year history. It demonstrates how far the ABC has come in representing Aboriginal and Torres Strait Island voices and the issues important to their communities (ABC, 2022a).

The documentary *Looking Black* (ABC 2022) did not return to the beginning of Indigenous representation onscreen, but focussed on a period from the 1980s to the present, with Indigenous presenter and writer Dan Bourchier suggesting that this was a period in which, far from being 'cut out of the narrative', Indigenous creatives had become 'the main storytellers' (*Looking Black* 2022). The documentary began with an account of how the ABC pro-actively recruited Indigenous journalism cadets in the 1980s in order to ensure an Indigenous perspective in their newsrooms. However, as Senator Malarndirri McCarthy pointed out, this was not always ensured, since as a young journalist she herself had been effectively cut out of an important story she had been working on at the last minute. Of particular relevance to this account of the impact of *Mystery Road* was the appearance of a very young Aaron Pederson as one of those first news recruits, going on to be a co-host of the Indigenous current affairs series *Blackout* (ABC 1989–1995). Commenting on the success of *Blackout*, Indigenous writer, actor and director Leah Purcell described how the series was in effect 'teaching Australians another way to see our people through our eyes' (*Looking Black* 2022).

Blackout was followed by another Indigenous current affairs programme on the ABC, *Message Stick*, eventually axed after thirteen years by Sally Riley when she became Head of the Indigenous Department at the ABC. Riley suggested that this was largely because the series had failed to find an audience and because she was determined that the ABC should go on to 'bigger things': one of those 'bigger things' being the drama series *Redfern Now* (ABC 2013). According to Riley, the critical and ratings success of this series was a game changer in that 'the whole of the ABC felt they owned that show' (*Looking Black* 2022).

Empowered by the success of *Redfern Now*, as well as the sketch comedy series, *Black Comedy* (ABC 2014–2020), and the science fiction drama *Cleverman* (ABC 2016–2017), Riley reported that the question they were asking of themselves in the Indigenous department at that time was 'What other genre can we colonise?': to which the answer appeared to be, the crime drama. In developing *Mystery Road*, Riley therefore suggested that one of the perceived drawcards of the series was that the central character as portrayed in the two earlier films was a 'noir, Indigenous, sexy cowboy' (*Looking Black* 2022).

While the character of Jay Swan as embodied by Pedersen might have been critical to the pitch, what *Mystery Road* the series achieved was clearly much more than a new take on a familiar genre. Weaving together the Western iconography of the original with the noir melancholy of Nordic Noir, in a format that privileged strong female characters alongside a sensitive male figure, in a double narrative that unfolded at a gentle pace with languorous shots of a spectacular landscape under threat that carried with it the symbolic weight of a colonial past, *Mystery Road* not only presented Indigenous Australia from an Indigenous point of view, but it also made some telling political points. Reviewer Craig Mathieson (2022) was alert to these, noting:

> …. whenever you think [*Mystery Road*] *Origin* has settled for comfortable homage, you're swiftly reminded that in telling the story from an Aboriginal viewpoint, with a great slew of Indigenous characters who cover a complete spectrum, there's a harsh intimacy at work. At one point Jay regards the renovated interior of the Jardine pub, ripping away the pricey wallpaper to reveal the racist colonial-era mural that was covered up but never refuted.

Mathieson goes on:

> The handful of cases that are intertwined through *Mystery Road: Origin* are divided between the past's errors and the future's opportunities. Sometimes the push and pull they embody is breath taking, as when Jay stands in the Southwell house, a family friend, and looks upon a display stand of neck collars that were once used to imprison his forebears and are somehow now historic art. The hypocrisy is brutal, the impact immense (Mathieson, 2022).

As Therese Davis has argued, there's a clear difference between didactic documentaries that endeavour to teach non-Indigenous Australians about their history and the 'sharing of knowledge' through dramatic storytelling (2017). While the former assumes an 'us and them' approach, the latter involves a different kind of reciprocal relationship between the Indigenous screen creatives and onscreen characters with their mainstream audience, thereby 'opening out possibilities for greater respect and understanding of Indigenous knowledge of this country' (Davis, 2017, p. 248). Much earlier in 1993, Indigenous scholar Marcia Langton had pointed out that films and television are 'powerful media', since it is from these that most Australians 'know' about Aboriginal people (Langton, 1993, p. 33). If this is indeed the case, then the national and international success of a humanising and powerful crime drama such as *Mystery Road* is therefore of immeasurable cultural value in educating non-Indigenous audiences in Australia and across the world about the history and politics of Indigenous experience.

A further two drama series telling Indigenous stories are of interest here. The first is the four-part crime drama series *True Colours* (SBS & NITV 2022), produced by Australia's second public service broadcaster, SBS, in conjunction with the National Indigenous Television Service (NITV), which also featured in the seven-day slate of new fiction and documentary works for NAIDOC Week. In a familiar crime drama series trope mirroring the storyline of *Mystery Road: Origin*, Indigenous detective Toni Alma (Rarriwuy Hick) is sent back to her (fictional) hometown of Perda Theendar from her posting in Mparntwe (Alice Springs) to investigate a crime. In this instance, it's the mysterious death of the independent 18-year-old Mariah Cawood (Janaya Kopp) in a fiery car accident which occurred on land sacred to secret men's business outside town. According to reviewer Luke Buckmaster (2022), one of the most interesting aspects of this series is the way in which it demonstrates how Indigenous customs and laws 'rub up against white-oriented policing'. For example, in some situations Toni discovers that her official badge carries no weight at all. While *True Colours* is a competent television drama making important points about Indigenous culture, it nevertheless lacks both the cinematic ambition and Nordic Noir flair of *Mystery Road* as well as the commanding onscreen presence of Aaron Pedersen, Judy Davis or Mark Coles Smith as lead characters. That the series is aware of the cultural impact of Nordic Noir crime dramas is evident in episode 2 when, asked to provide an alibi for the night in question, one of the characters replies he was at home watching season 2 of *The Bridge*.

In April 2023, Screen Australia released *Seeing Ourselves* 2, the second of its reports on 'Diversity, Equity and Inclusion in Australian TV Drama', in which CEO Graeme Mason suggested that 'screen stories that authentically reflect us and our place in the world are important for helping to grow our cultural identity' (Screen Australia, 2023b, p. 3). While the report noted that there had been increases in the levels of diversity in terms of cultural background, disability, gender, sexual orientation and occupational status among main characters in TV dramas generally, of particular note was the 'strong and growing level of Indigenous representation on screen' (Screen Australia, 2023b, p. 7). Although Anglo-Celtic characters might still dominate Australian drama at 71 per cent of main characters, even though those who identify as Anglo-Celtic constitute only 53 per cent of the total population of Australia, for the first time ever, the proportion of Indigenous main characters was almost double (7.2 per cent) the proportion of Indigenous people in Australia (3.8 per cent). This achievement, the report noted, represents the culmination of over thirty years of work in the industry to support Indigenous practitioners and stories (Screen Australia, 2023b, pp. 27, 33). As a result, the report concluded, Australia was doing by far the best in terms of the representation of Indigenous people when compared with similar studies in the US, Canada and New Zealand. On the downside, the report noted that Indigenous characters were less likely to have high occupational status and were more likely to appear as sketch comedy characters, supernatural characters, children, students or criminals (Screen Australia, 2023b, p. 30). What was also notable is that with the exception of the TV series *Wentworth* (commissioned by subscription broadcaster Foxtel), the majority of the television dramas mentioned were made in conjunction with a public service broadcaster.

There are a number of points to be teased out of these findings, not least the significance of the ABC, SBS and NITV in the commissioning of Indigenous drama, although in relation to the latter, as Graeme Turner (2020) has pointed out, NITV has only a very limited budget to produce content to fill a twenty-four-hour schedule. Faced with competition from those with 'deeper pockets' – even with the support of Screen Australia's Indigenous Unit – this inevitably has an effect on what appears onscreen. Another key point relates to who is actually watching these Indigenous dramas. As has long been acknowledged, the viewership for the ABC in Australia continues to skew older, and as Dibley and Turner (2018) reported in 2018, 65 per cent of 18–24 year olds surveyed for a project on changing Australian tastes reported that they watched no free-to-air television at all, begging a question about what other platforms they might be using. For example, it is quite possible that a series like *Mystery Road* might be watched on iView, Stan, Acorn TV, Apple TV or Google Play some time after its initial appearance on the ABC, reinforcing over time the cultural and economic value of its 'long tail' in showcasing Indigenous storytelling.

Although unsuccessful, the fact that in 2023 Australia was poised on the brink of a decision that would give Indigenous people constitutional recognition and a Voice to parliament suggests that a shift has occurred over the last ten years. Indeed, the daily Acknowledgements of the traditional owners of the land that are spoken at every meeting and event when people gather together on a formal occasion are evidence that Indigenous identity and experience of country are now central to the ways in which life in Australia is now understood for everyone. If, as Benedict Anderson (2006) suggested, underpinning the concept of a nation is the idea of an imagined community, then that community is in the process of being re-imagined to incorporate an Indigenous perspective, a perspective that has been communicated by and large through media representations such as *Mystery Road*.

Table 6.1 Overview of *Mystery Road* series

Series	Date	Director	Cinematographer
Series 1 6 episodes	2018	Rachel Perkins	Mark Wareham
Series 2 6 episodes	2020	Warwick Thornton (3 episodes) Wayne Bair (3 episodes)	Warwick Thornton
Series 3 6 episodes	2022	Dylan River	Tyson Perkins

Table 6.2 *Mystery Road* (2018–)
The makers

Commissioning broadcaster	Australian Broadcasting Corporation (ABC)
Production company	Bunya Productions
Distributor / international sales	All 3 Media International

Table 6.2 (*cont.*)
The results

International sales	Acquired by Acorn TV in the US, BBC4 in the UK, CMore in Denmark, Finland, Norway and Sweden, Ivi in Russa. Acorn also acquired secondary rights for the UK, Ireland, Australia and New Zealand. In Australia it is available on Stan and Acorn TV as well as the ABC ('BBC Four acquires Australian drama Mystery Road', 2018; Clarke, 2018; Hazelton, 2018).
Awards	16 wins and 38 nominations AACTA International Awards • 2021 Nominee Best Drama Series • 2021 **Winner** Best Actor in a Series: Aaron Pedersen The Equity Ensemble Awards • 2021 **Winner** Outstanding Performance by an Ensemble in a Drama Series • 2019 **Winner** Outstanding Performance by an Ensemble Series in a Drama Series Australian Directors Guild Awards • 2021 Nominee Best Direction in a TV or SVOD Drama Series Episode: Wayne Blair • 2019 **Winner** Best Direction in a TV or SVOD Drama Series: Rachel Perkins, s. 1 Asian Academy Creative Awards • 2020 Nominee Best Drama Series • 2019 Nominee Best Actor in a Supporting Role: Wayne Blair • 2019 Nominee Best Actress in a Supporting Role: Deborah Mailman • 2019 **Winner** Best Cinematography: Mark Wareham Australian Academy of Cinema and Television Arts (AACTA) Awards • 2020 Nominee Best Lead Actor in a Television Drama: Aaron Pedersen • 2020 Nominee Best Guest or Supporting Actor in a Television Drama: Rob Collins • 2020 Nominee Best Guest or Supporting Actor in a Television Drama: Callan Mulvey • 2020 Nominee Best Guest or Supporting Actress in a Television Drama: Ngaire Pigram • 2020 Nominee Best Guest or Supporting Actress in a Television Drama: Tasma Walton • 2020 **Winner** Best Drama Series: David Jowsey, Greer Simpkin • 2020 Nominee Best Lead Actress in a Television Drama: Jada Alberts • 2020 Nominee Best Direction in a Television Drama or Comedy: Wayne Blair, Ep. 4 'Broken (2020)' • 2020 Nominee Best Direction in a Television Drama or Comedy: Warwick Thornton, Ep. 6: 'What You Do Now (2020)' • 2020 Nominee Best Screenplay in Television: Kodie Bedford, Ep. 4 'Broken (2020)' • 2020 Nominee Best Cinematography in Television: Warwick Thornton, Ep. 4: 'Broken (2020)' • 2020 Nominee Best Editing in Television: Nicholas Holmes, Ep. 6 'What You Do Now (2020)' • 2020 Nominee Best Sound in Television: Wes Chew, Luke Mynott, Michael Newton, Trevor Hope, Ep. 4 'Broken (2020)' • 2020 Nominee Best Production Design in Television: Herbert Pinter, Ep. 6 'What You Do Now (2020)'

Awards (*cont.*)	- 2020 Nominee Byron Kennedy Award: Aaron Pedersen in Mystery Road (2013) - 2018 Nominee Best Lead Actor in a Television Drama: Aaron Pedersen - 2018 **Winner** Best Television Drama Series: David Jowsey, Greer Simpkin - 2018 Nominee Best Lead Actress in a Television Drama: Judy Davis - 2018 **Winner** Best Guest or Supporting Actor in a Television Drama: Wayne Blair - 2018 **Winner** Best Guest or Supporting Actress in a Television Drama: Deborah Mailman - 2018 Nominee Best Guest or Supporting Actress in a Television Drama: Tasma Walton - 2018 Nominee Best Direction in a Television Drama or Comedy: Rachel Perkins, Ep. 'Silence (2018)' - 2018 Nominee Best Screenplay in Television: Timothy Lee, Kodie Bedford, Steven McGregor, Michaeley O'Brien, Ep. The Waterhole (2018) - 2018 Nominee Best Cinematography in Television: Mark Wareham, Ep. 'Silence (2018)' - 2018 **Winner** Best Editing in Television: Deborah Peart, Ep. The Waterhole (2018) - 2018 **Winner** Best Original Music Score in Television: Antony Partos, Matteo Zingales, Ep. 'Silence (2018)' Casting Guild of Australia Awards - 2020 Nominee Best Casting in a TV Drama: Anousha Zarkesh - 2018 Nominee Best Casting in a TV Drama: Anousha Zarkesh ARIA Music Awards - 2020 Nominee Best Original Soundtrack, Cast or Show Album: Matteo Zingales, Antony Partos Edgar Allan Poe Awards - 2019 Nominee TV Episode Teleplay: Michaeley O'Brien, Episode 1 Logie Awards - 2019 Nominee Most Outstanding Actress: Judy Davis - 2019 Nominee Most Outstanding Drama Series - 2019 Nominee Most Outstanding Actor: Aaron Pedersen - 2019 **Winner** Most Popular Actress: Deborah Mailman - 2019 Nominee Most Outstanding Supporting Actor: Wayne Blair Location Managers Guild International Awards (LMGI) - 2019 Nominee Outstanding Locations in a Contemporary Television Series: Brett Dowson, Hugo Cran Australian Writers' Guild Awgie Awards - 2018 **Winner** Television Series or Miniseries of more than 4 hours duration: Michaeley O'Brien, For episode 'Gone' - 2018 Nominee Television Series or Miniseries of more than 4 hours duration: Timothy Lee, For episode 'The Waterhole' Australian Guild of Screen Composers Australian Screen Music Awards - 2018 **Winner** Best Music for a Mini-Series or Telemovie: Antony Partos, Matteo Zingales Australian Screen Editors Awards - 2018 Nominee Best Editing in a Television Drama: Deborah Peart Screen Producers Australia (SPA) Awards - 2018 **Winner** Telemovie or Miniseries Production of the Year

Table 6.2 (*cont.*)

Audience demand	Season 1 ranked as the most-watched non-children's series on the ABC's iView platform. iView attracted an average of 246,000 viewers per episode and broadcast episodes 846,000 in mainland capitals. 800,000 viewers watched the premiere on the ABC in June 2018 (Crikey, 2022; Groves, 2018b).
	Season 2 attracted the highest ratings for any Australian adult television drama series on free to air television in 2020 (Bunya Productions, 2023).
	Season 3 premiered in the top 10 rated programs and as the most popular drama in its launch week, attracting 635,000 viewers in its free-to-air time slot (Crikey, 2022).
	IMDb rating: 7.5/10
	Rotten Tomatoes average audience score: 75%

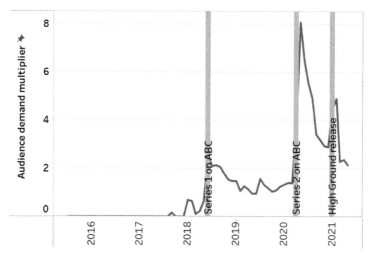

Figure 6.1 Audience demand multiplier for *Mystery Road*

Note: The audience demand multiplier benchmarks content relative to the market average of 1. If a show has 2× demand, it is two times more in-demand than the average TV show in the market.

Source: Parrot Analytics (2021).

Chapter 7

Valuing the TV Crime Drama

While in the final stages of writing up our case studies in July 2023, two Australian crime dramas set in Tasmania appeared on our screens. While one of these, the Nordic Noir spoof *Deadloch*, launched on Amazon Prime Video, the other, *Bay of Fires*, was broadcast on the ABC and available on their catch-up service iView. During the same time frame, Australia was preparing to vote in a referendum that sought to grant Indigenous Australians recognition through a Voice to Parliament that would be enshrined in the Constitution, and the establishment of a Makarrata Commission for agreement-making and truth-telling. This was intended to help ameliorate the systemic disadvantage suffered by Indigenous people since colonisation, the impact of which has been so effectively reflected in the television drama series *Mystery Road* (ABC 2018–), *True Colours* (SBS & NITV 2022) and *Total Control* (ABC 2019–). What struck us about the coincidence of these events was the way in which they chimed with the ongoing and inevitable debates about the value of the Australian screen industry as well as the geo-political implications of their production. While these two Tasmanian crime drama series might appear to represent the economic and industrial value to be derived from investment in regional screen production in Australia, as was envisaged during the making of *The Kettering Incident* (Showcase 2016), the Indigenous drama series set in outback Australia demonstrate the cultural and social value of the television crime drama in bringing the experience of Indigenous people to both national and international attention at a definitive moment in the nation's history.

In relation to the latter, a powerful two-minute advertisement supporting a 'yes' vote in the forthcoming referendum also appeared on free-to-air television and was shared online. Produced by the Sydney-based advertising agency, The Monkeys, this was part of a campaign funded by the Uluru Dialogue, a group of Indigenous people from across Australia hosted by the Indigenous Law Centre at the University of New South Wales. Directed by acclaimed Indigenous director Warwick Thornton and cast by Anousha Zarkesh, both of whom have played significant roles in the recent history of Australian screen production and crime drama series as detailed in Chapter 6, the advertisement featured a family watching transformative moments in the history of Australia as they unfolded on television screens, beginning with the 1967 referendum, which gave Indigenous people the right to vote. To the accompaniment of John Farnham's powerful anthem 'You're the Voice', these moments included the ruling on Eddie Mabo's campaign for Indigenous land rights in 1992, Indigenous athlete Kathy Freeman's Gold Medal win at the Sydney Olympics in 2000, Prime Minister Kevin Rudd's apology to Indigenous people in 2008, as well as the Uluru Statement from the Heart in 2017. The advertisement culminated with the now older and extended family setting off to vote 'Yes'. Clearly designed to have an emotional impact, the ad also dramatised the somewhat idealised role of broadcast television in the formation of ideas about nationhood and national identity.

This nostalgic construction of television as a witness to history is of particular relevance in an era when the ways in which television is watched in the home is changing, not only in relation to the multiplicity of screens now available, but also because of the access to different sources of content from international distributors on the range of streaming platforms now available. As reported by the *Australian Financial Review* in May 2023, while 61.5 per cent of households in Australia subscribe to at least one streaming service, the average number of subscriptions per home was 3.4 (Buckingham-Jones, 2023). Although this might suggest that television audiences are fragmenting, there is striking evidence that there are still occasions when households will gather round a screen for a shared experience. For example, during the FIFA Women's World Cup in August 2023, the Seven Network's streaming service, 7plus, recorded an average audience of 7.2 million for seven games, with an audience of 11.15 million for the semi-final match featuring Australia versus England, almost half the Australian population. This remarkable statistic was subsequently described by a Seven West executive as 'the biggest broadcast and digital viewing event in Australian history (Perry, 2023). While the fact that this was a sporting event rather than a television drama underlined the centrality of sport in Australian life (Cunningham and Jacka 1996, p. 55), what it also revealed was that people do still come together to watch a televised event when it is perceived to be of significance.

There was even a suggestion at the time that it might have been un-Australian not to watch the Australian team, the Matildas, in action. Given that broadcast television was introduced to Australia in order to coincide with the 1956 Melbourne Olympics, it has long been the case that sport brings Australians together more than any other television experience, including the coronations and royal weddings that are part of Australia's colonial heritage. For example, in comparison to the 11.15 million for the Matildas, the coronation of King Charles in May 2023 attracted an audience of just over 1 million each on the ABC and the Seven Network and just over 700,000 on the Nine Network (Meade, 2023).

Our study, however, is primarily concerned with the value of television drama about which there has been so much concern and debate over the years, particularly in relation to the need for government policy and intervention to support its production with ongoing evidence of market failure. Ever since television was introduced, there have been calls for more Australian content, particularly when it comes to drama. In 1963, a Senate Select Committee argued, in what came to be known as *The Vincent Report*, that there was so little Australian content on Australian screens 'as to be almost non-existent', especially when it came to drama (Australian Senate, 1963). The report found that 83 per cent of the drama programs shown on Australian television were of American origin and 13 per cent were from the UK, with only 4 per cent being of Australian origin. The report's seventy-nine recommendations included both tax incentives and a quota system to ensure the production of Australian drama and its availability to Australian audiences, recommendations that have been implemented in various ways over the intervening years.

As Cunningham and Jacka have noted, the underlying thrust of *The Vincent Report* was that over-exposure to American programs was essentially harmful in that the 'rising generation' were receiving only 'the most inadequate picture of Australia, her national traditions, culture and way of life' (Vincent Report as cited by Cunningham & Jacka, 1996). While expecting drama programs to generate cultural and social value by promoting a unified national imaginary is problematic, according to Cunningham and Jacka the Vincent Report was ahead of its time in arguing that Australia should be producing content for the international market in order to support the industry. This latter suggestion, however, was largely ignored until the late 1980s and 1990s, when international co-production became essential in funding expensive high-end drama (Hoskins et al., 1998).

Writing at the time of the 1988 Bicentennial marking 200 years since the invasion of Australia, Susan Dermody and Liz Jacka noted that Australian screen production had long been suspended between arguments about cultural value versus an economic discourse that encompassed the employment possibilities, profitability and 'the language that money speaks' (Dermody & Jacka, 1988, p. 11). In terms of the options for a film industry seeking to compete on the international stage, Dermody and Jacka argued that this had resulted in two strategic responses. While the first might involve embracing an exportable 'national type', as in the film *Crocodile Dundee* (1986), the second might necessitate effacing any hint of an Australian origin, as in the film *Mad Max: Beyond Thunderdome* (1985) (Dermody & Jacka, 1988, p. 14). In either case, the intended audience for these films was international rather than national. When it came to the fate of Australian television content in the international market place, while the middle-brow Australian soap operas *Neighbours* (Seven Network & Network Ten 1985–) and *Home and Away* (Seven Network 1988–) had enjoyed considerable success in the UK (but not in the US), the high-end miniseries dramas reflecting Australian history and experience that rated so well with domestic audiences during the 1980s were apparently deemed 'too parochial' by international buyers (Cunningham & Jacka, 1996, p. 54).

What was subsequently described as the 'golden age' of the Australian miniseries during the 1980s was a direct result of government policy initiatives intended to support the film industry, including the 10BA Producer offset tax incentive. During this period over eighty drama productions were broadcast on both public service and commercial television screens, showcasing key moments in Australia's history from the days of the penal colony (*For the Term of His Natural Life*, Nine Network 1983) to the Australian experience of the Vietnam War (*Vietnam*, Network Ten 1987), as well as the politically sensitive and controversial dismissal of an elected government by the Crown in 1974 (*The Dismissal*, Network Ten 1983). As Ina Bertrand (1990) pointed out, twenty-six miniseries were shown in the Bicentennial year alone, varying in length from three to thirteen hours each. While the commercial networks dominated these listings, the recently appointed head of drama at the ABC, Sandra Levy, had as her goal in 1986 the production of 100 hours of drama a year that would, according to the ABC charter, 'contribute to a sense of national identity, and reflect the cultural diversity of the Australian community': a goal she subsequently achieved (Jacka, 1991, p. 28). This was an era during which the television industry could be seen to be heavily invested in providing Australian drama content for Australian audiences, content that inevitably reflected Australian history and social concerns. As such, it could be argued that Australian television in the 1980s was engaged in a form of identity politics dramatising just what it might mean to be a citizen of Australia.

The production of these series also underpinned the concept of the 'Australian look' first introduced in a report from the newly established Australian Broadcasting Tribunal (ABT) in 1977, which called for the establishment of an Australian television service that 'looks unmistakeably Australian' (quoted in Cunningham & Jacka, 1996, p. 64). As Cunningham and Jacka suggest, the concept of the 'Australian look' came to be a source of subsequent conflict during the 1987–1991 Inquiry into Australian Content on Commercial Television, eventually resulting in a new standard for commercial television licensees that reverted to 'off-screen indicators' to measure the Australianness of a production. In other words, cultural value as represented by what was appearing onscreen was deemed more difficult to identify than the benefits to the Australian screen industry from ensuring that a minimum number of Australians were involved in key creative roles on the production.

As Terry Flew observed, by the mid-1990s, the concept of Australianness as reflected onscreen was being further undermined by a number of national and international factors (Flew, 1995, p. 76). Taking into account the increasingly multicultural nature of Australian society, the historic devaluation of the role and concerns of women and the dynamism and distinctiveness of Aboriginal Australian culture, Flew suggests that the unifying discourse of an 'imagined community' that had hitherto underpinned the concept of the nation state in contemporary world capitalism could no longer hold sway in Australia as elsewhere (Flew 1995, p. 76). As Flew suggests, the unsettling of television's role in producing such a unifying national discourse was the outcome of a number of cultural and technological factors, including the development of cable and satellite delivery systems in the 1990s and later the digitisation of free-to-air broadcasting and the arrival of the streaming services that have fragmented audiences for drama. Another factor was the globalisation of the screen industry as increasing production costs had resulted in screen production companies having to 'go global' in order to find new markets and audiences. Meanwhile, the concept of the largely passive watcher as a 'cultural dope' had been replaced by the image of the viewer as a 'sovereign consumer' exercising 'popular discrimination' in the choice of their viewing pleasure (Flew, 1995, p. 82). As Flew concludes,

> All these tendencies point to an increasing asymmetry between the economic and industrial imperatives in an era of globalisation, and the cultural objectives of representing Australia to Australian audiences through television product (Flew, 1995, pp. 84–85).

This is the asymmetry that has continued to haunt the Australian screen production industry over the last seventy years, articulated most recently by Sandy George (2022b) in her platform paper 'Nobody Talks About Australianness on our Screens', in which she nostalgically laments the absence of what she perceives as onscreen Australianness. It's an argument that would suggest a television crime drama series like *The Tourist* (BBC One, Stan, HBO Max & ZDF 2022–) – a British television production shot in Australia with an Australian crew and Australian actors, but one in which any direct reference to Australia, even the ubiquitous blow flies, appears to have been erased – is the direction in which the Australian screen industry is inevitably headed in its quest for survival in the global screen industry: a direction that was prefigured in Dermody and Jacka's discussion of *Mad Max Beyond Thunderdome* (Dermody & Jacka, 1988).

However, as our case studies have demonstrated, the erasure of Australianness in the quest for an international audience is not the only possible response to the economic, industrial, social and cultural upheavals that have impacted the production of Australian crime dramas over the last fifteen years. As our analysis has demonstrated, it is entirely possible to create an Australian television crime drama series set in an identifiable part of Australia and which reflects Australian issues and concerns, that will also be of interest to a global audience. Not only that, but it is precisely the Australianness of the content which lends currency to these crime drama series in the international marketplace given the ways in which the genre has developed and travelled over the last twenty years.

Genre as a Form of Global Currency

One of the reasons why television crime dramas are able to travel is no doubt because of the familiarity of the audience with the crime drama as a genre. While from the 1950s onwards, Australian audiences were acquainted with both imported American and British crime dramas, the game changer in the new millennium has been transnational success of the Nordic Noir TV dramas. The success of series like *The Killing* (DR1 2007–2012) and *The Bridge* (SVT & DR 2011–2018) in the UK and the US as well as Australia demonstrated that there was a niche audience for quality TV crime dramas produced by countries perceived to be on the 'periphery' of the screen production industry, even when these were subtitled. The fact that Nordic Noir dramas then inspired a wave of television productions that drew on their aesthetics, narrative structures, themes and social concerns, while overlaying these with their own cultural concerns, effectively demonstrated how the television production industry is now a truly global industry, looking outwards at the same time as it looks inwards.

As Graeme Turner has observed, what is striking about television in the post-broadcast era is the emergence of television drama series, and here he cites Nordic Noir dramas such as *The Bridge*, that are 'more narratively and morally complex' and 'more socially and politically nuanced' than might be possibly expected for series targeted solely at a 'single national mass market' (Turner, 2020, p. 292). According to Turner, the most productive location for new forms of inquiry into ideas about television citizenry in the post-broadcast era is therefore to be found in new forms of entertainment, including quality niche drama (Turner, 2020, p. 293). This then raises the question of how a television crime drama series, intended for a transnational TV audience rather than just a local, regional or national audience, might play a role in the formation of a type of 'global citizenship' rehearsing matters that are of not just national but of global concern.

For example, with regards to the case studies presented here, while *Miss Fisher* joins in a global conversation about feminism and women's role in society, *The Kettering Incident* engages in environmental concerns while *Secret City* explores political corruption and global politics. *Mystery Road*, on the other hand, draws attention to the ways in which Indigenous people have been marginalised and disinherited, thereby joining a sub-genre of crime drama that includes the Swedish–French co-production set in Finland, *Midnight Sun* (SVT 2016), which considers the plight of the Sami people of Sapne, or *Thin Ice* (TV4 2020–), which addresses the situation of the Greenlandic people who are still under the rule of Denmark (2020). More recently the American series *Dark Wind* (AMC 2022–), set in the 1960s, follows the career of Navajo Nation police officer Joe Leaphorn and his wife, who is a nurse concerned about the enforced sterilisation of the First Nations women in her care; in effect a form of genocide. It might be noted *Dark Wind* is based on the crime novels of the late Tony Hillerman, who was in turn inspired to write about Leaphorn after reading the Australian crime novels of Arthur Upfield featuring the Indigenous policeman Napoleon 'Bony' Bonaparte, on which two Australian television series were produced (Stead, 1988). The point of this detail being that the transnational circulation of crime fiction as a genre both precedes and underpins the transnational circulation of the TV crime drama, from early televisual representations of Sherlock Holmes to the many screen iterations of Swedish writer Henning Mankell's Wallander series and Steig Larsson's Millenium series, both of which were televised during the 1990s and early 2000s and which preceded the breakthrough transnational circulation of *The Killing* in 2007.

When it comes to how these series might contribute to a notion of 'global citizenship', as James Curran wrote in 2011, entertainment is connected to the democratic life of a society in four key ways. It provides a space for exploring and debating social values; it offers a means of defining and refashioning social identity; it affords alternative frameworks of understanding, and it provides a way of assessing, weakening and revising the public norms that are an integral part of the way we govern ourselves (Curran, 2011, p. 75). In order to achieve this, however, a television crime drama must first engage the viewer. As Annette Hill has demonstrated in her research into the reception of *The Bridge*, this engagement is dependent not only on a multi-layered narrative, but also on the 'strong characterisation' that effectively 'pulls' the audience into the 'here and now of storytelling' (Hill, 2018, p. 76). According to Hill, while television dramas can be theorised as public narratives, 'constructing, mediating and framing our social and individual identities', their impact inevitably depends on the ways in which they engage the emotions of the viewer through their affective structures (Hill, 2018, p. 78). This Hill illustrates through an account of how the character of Saga Noren is constructed and performed in ways calculated to maximise viewer engagement and affect.

When it comes to identifying just how a television crime drama might contribute to the ways in which people imagine the world and perform their citizenry there is clearly a need for more qualitative audience research on a global scale. While this is beyond the immediate scope of this study, what the transnational success of the Australian television crime dramas that we have been discussing here suggests is that they may indeed be contributing to a re-imaging of what it means to be a citizen, not just of one's country of origin, but of a world that has never been more inter-connected in terms of screen entertainment. And this is so even as political divisions both between and within nation states continue to unfold, given that as a viewing experience, the transnational television crime drama has the potential to engage the audience in a series of affective moments that enable people to recognise the shared plight and problems that are faced by the characters onscreen that may well override the self-interested imperatives of nationhood that still prevail in a globalised world. This brings us back to the concept of total value stated earlier, evidenced through 'phronesis' and the pursuit of the common good.

Total Value

As we have demonstrated, each of the Australian crime drama series we have discussed can be shown to generate value across all four dimensions of the concept of total value outlined in Chapter 2. This encompasses the industrial, creative, cultural and social value to be derived from each series, although different kinds of value may be clearer in each case. For example, in the case of *Miss Fisher's Murder Mysteries* (ABC 2012–2015), we have a period crime drama produced by the independent production house Every Cloud Productions for an Australian public service broadcaster, the ABC, that was both a success with older viewers in terms of ratings, but also attracted a younger viewership as the series went on. Following a distribution deal with All3Media, *Miss Fisher* proved extremely popular overseas, including in America, where it gained a loyal fan base after it appeared on the streaming platforms Netflix and Acorn TV. Even more surprisingly, *Miss Fisher* was the first ever Australian production to inspire a Chinese remake (*Miss S*, Tencent 2020–). In creative and economic terms, *Miss Fisher* was indeed of considerable value to the Australian screen industry, but there were also significant social and cultural benefits to be derived from this success as well.

For example, the series was also of significant personal value to the creators, including Kerry Greenwood, who wrote the original crime novels, as well as Every Cloud producers Fiona Eagger and Deb Cox, who shared a vision in terms of wanting to say something important about women's lives. This feminist intention was carried over into the production itself in terms of the number of women who were employed on set. The series also generated significant cultural benefits from the large number of spin-off activities it inspired, including the various costume exhibitions and events around Australia that generated funds for the National Trust in its preservation of the Heritage buildings in which these events took place.

Even more significant was the social value to be derived from *Miss Fisher* in terms of the audience experience. Whether this involved simply joining an online group or engaging in fan activities, such as attending *Miss Fisher*-themed events, *Miss Fisher* appeared to draw people together in communities of interest that were of significant personal value to those involved. In terms of viewers, it is clear that the character of Miss Fisher, as embodied and performed by Essie Davis, carried an affective charge that inspired women around the world to be less scared and more confident in their dealings with the world, 'like Phryne'.

When it comes to *The Kettering Incident* (Showcase 2016), there is as yet little evidence of audience engagement as a significant social value, although this may have transpired. While the enigmatic and troubled character of Dr Anna Macey, as portrayed by Elizabeth Debecki, did not appear to affectively engage viewers in the same way as Saga Noren in *The Bridge* or Miss Fisher, commentators appeared to be much more impressed in cultural terms by the portrayal of the Tasmanian landscape and the achievement of a Nordic Noir aesthetic. However, unlike the Swedish series *Jordskott* (SVT & DR 2015–2017) to which *Kettering* bore a striking resemblance, the environmental themes were largely tangential to the main plot.

The value of *Kettering* would therefore appear to lie primarily in the contribution that the series made to the development of the Australian screen industry in general and Tasmania in particular, given that in 2018 *Kettering* was Australia's top selling drama internationally. Tucked behind the Foxtel paywall, the viewing numbers for *Kettering* in Australia were in fact very small, although this didn't appear to be an issue for the Foxtel executives to whom we spoke given that Foxtel's central ambition at this time was the production of a 'high-end' quality drama series that could sit on their Showcase platform alongside the HBO dramas perceived as benchmarks in the field. The fact that even before *Kettering* screened in Australia, it won the Special Jury Prize at Series Mania Festival in Paris, appeared to suggest that this ambition had been achieved. The critical reception of the series was also strong in Australia, with *Kettering* winning a number of industry awards at the 2016 AACTA awards and 2017 Logies.

Kettering was also something of a personal career milestone for Victoria Madden, who was the creative champion of a show that encapsulated her experience of returning to Tasmania. While the promised sequel never eventuated, Madden would go on to create the crime drama *The Gloaming*, which would once again employ the aesthetics and tropes of Nordic Noir to tell a story about Tasmania as a place of exile and dark deeds. For Madden, there was clearly a personal value in telling these stories, even as they generated work and benefits for the Tasmanian communities in which they were filmed. The *Kettering* production, supported by investment from Screen Tasmania and Screen Australia, who also funded a number of attachments, involved a large cast and crew. The ongoing strength of the Tasmanian screen sector, as envisaged in Screen Tasmania's workforce plan, would see a number of subsequent television crime drama productions filmed on location across the state, including *Bay of Fires* (ABC 2023) and *Deadloch* (Amazon Prime Video 2023).

Location was also a significant value in the case of the political crime drama, *Secret City* (Showcase & Netflix 2016–2019), set in Canberra. Produced by Matchbox Pictures for Foxtel with investment support from ScreenACT, another state-based government agency keen to bring skills and jobs to its region, *Secret City* was another of Foxtel's series intended for a global niche audience for high-end quality drama. For producer Penny Chapman, setting the drama in Canberra provided an opportunity to showcase the architecture and modernist aesthetic that she loved about the national capital. The series also fulfilled Chapman's dream of producing an Australian political thriller in the style of the Nordic Noir drama *Borgen* (DR1 2010–2022), with a similar focus on the female characters at the centre of a political intrigue. Stylistically the first season of *Secret City* successfully evoked the Nordic Noir aesthetic of *The Bridge* in terms of its colour palette and pacing, although this was largely abandoned in the second season.

Like *Kettering*, *Secret City* did not rate particularly well when first shown on Foxtel, but proved to have a long tail when shown on Netflix. Like *Kettering*, *Secret City* also attracted a number of industry accolades, including two Logies and an Australian Directors Guild Award in 2017. In terms of cultural and social value, however, *Secret City* is probably most important for demonstrating that Australia could produce a political drama about the nation's geo-political predicament 'sandwiched between two heavily armed super powers' that had international relevance in terms of the political tensions between the US and China. In an era characterised by unencumbered nationalism and unscrupulous politicians, *Secret City* drew attention to the ways in which political power, rather than supporting the public good, can be used to undermine this.

Political awareness is also central to the TV crime drama *Mystery Road* (ABC 2018–), which represents a high watermark in the history of Indigenous screen production. In this case, however, the politics involved relate to the ways in which Aboriginal and Torres Strait Islander people have been disinherited and abused since colonisation, with the inevitable social effects that are visible in contemporary communities as portrayed onscreen. Combining an Australian appropriation of the Western with a Nordic Noir reframing of the television crime drama, *Mystery Road* was immediately hailed as a type of 'outback noir', going on to win the highest number of AACTA Awards ever in the history of the Awards themselves.

Made for the ABC with its ongoing commitment to Indigenous storytelling under the leadership of Indigenous film maker Sally Riley as Head of Scripted Production, *Mystery Road* was clearly intended for an international market from the start, with screenings at international festivals, a distribution deal with All3Media and subsequent sales to BBC4 in the UK and the Acorn TV platform in North America. With the casting of Swedish actor Sofia Helin in season 2, the series once again overtly signalled its international intentions, although for many critics this season was something of a disappointment in narrative terms. As Swedish archaeologist, Sandra Elmquist, Helin's character failed to evoke the kind of affect that her portrayal of Saga Noren generated in *The Bridge*, pointing more to a failure in the scriptwriting than a failure in Helin's performance. When it came to generating the type of affect that would engage the viewer, this was primarily achieved through the character of Jay Swan as performed by Aaron Pedersen in seasons 1 and 2, and by Mark Coles Smith in the prequel *Mystery Road: Origin*. Both actors were lauded for their work by critics and the industry alike.

In terms of the concept of total value encompassing the industrial, economic, cultural and social benefits, what *Mystery Road* emphatically demonstrated was the strength of the Indigenous screen sector, from the production team at Bunya to the long list of creative talent who worked on the show. This included Indigenous directors Wayne Blair, Warwick Thornton, Rachel Perkins in seasons 1 and 2, and the sons of Thornton and Perkins, Dylan River and Tyson Perkins in the *Mystery Road* prequel. However, as casting director Anousha Zarkesh (2022) revealed, the pride that was instilled in remote communities through the recruitment of local talent was immense. Although it might be argued that such engagement would only be fleeting and temporary, there are other kinds of social and cultural benefit that are immeasurable. For the Indigenous communities involved, there was clearly a benefit to be derived in knowing that attention is being paid to the issues that concern them and that Indigenous storytellers are sharing stories that reflect on their experience of dispossession and the social impact this has had. Although Zarkesh was firmly of the opinion that Indigenous storytelling has the capacity to 'change the psyche of the country', this remains to be seen given that when it comes to how effective a television crime drama series can be in changing the ways in which people think, it all depends who is watching and what they bring to that experience.

Total Value Revisited

In terms of our original question – How does value accumulate through the production, distribution and reception of a television crime drama? – it is clear from the account we have given here that this is complicated. As we have demonstrated, it is rarely a case of weighing up the economic versus the cultural value of a series, since every series we have discussed can be shown to create value, from the generation of the original story idea through to the reception and potential flow-ons that the series generates. Nor are these benefits easily quantifiable, with the potential exception of the financial values that are routinely reported as evidence of the health or otherwise of the Australian screen industry. Too significant to ignore is how a television crime drama may contribute to the common good, recalling the concept of phronesis, revealing the ways in which they can address social and political issues that are not just of local and national interest, but also of global concern.

Notes

Chapter 3 Valuing Miss Fisher

1. These include Netflix, Acorn, Channel 5 UK, UKTV's Alibi Channel, France 3, Rai (Italy).
2. There have been other successful TV exports, including the prison drama *Prisoner* (1979–1986), also known as *Prisoner: Cell Block H*, and its more recent spin-off *Wentworth* (2013–2021), and the long-running soap opera *Neighbours* (1985–2022). However, when it comes to the genre of the television crime drama series, the success of *MFMM* would appear to be unparalleled.
3. The line is 'Ciel, mes bijoux!' as confided to Sue Turnbull by Kerry Greenwood in 1990.
4. Every Cloud Productions (2022) reports gross receipts of $20 million dollars for international sales of *Miss Fisher* seasons 1, 2 and 3.
5. The Parrot Analytics demand multiplier benchmarks TV content against the market average by quantifying demand from household use of search engines, wikis and information sites, fan and critic rating sites, social video and social media platforms, peer-to-peer apps and open streaming platforms. A demand multiplier of ×1 represents the market average. If a TV show has 10× demand, it is 10× more in-demand than the average TV show in that market. https://helpcenter.parrotanalytics.com/en/articles/7219894-what-is-the-demand-multiplier
6. See *Miss Fisher's Murder Mysteries* Fan Fiction Archive on FanFiction.net (Taddeo, 2016, p. 59).
7. https://www.missfishercon.com/
8. https://www.missfishercon.com/vip-2023
9. These definitions are available on the Fanlore wiki site. https://fanlore.org/wiki/
10. Examples of fan sites include www.nathanpagetheactor.wordpress.com, and Essie Davis/Phryne Fisher www.theadventuressesclub.com/miss-fisher-fans. Both sites link to an MFMM discussion forum.

Chapter 4 *The Kettering Incident*

1. https://darkmofo.net.au/about
2. https://www.rottentomatoes.com/tv/the_kettering_incident/s01
3. https://www.discovertasmania.com.au/places/hobart-and-south/kettering/
4. https://tasmania.com/points-of-interest/kettering/
5. https://twitter.com/sweetpotato12/status/1004287861711966213

Bibliography

$15m television series to be filmed in Tasmania and broadcast around Australia. (2014, 10 February). *Australian Government News*.

AACTA, A. (2023). *ACCTA International Awards Overview*. Retrieved 12 September 2023 from https://www.aacta.org/aacta-awards/aacta-international-awards/12th-aacta-international-awards/overview/

ABC. (2011). Miss Fisher's Murder Mysteries: *Student Activities English Senior Secondary*, Miss Fisher's Murder Mysteries Classroom, Issue. http://abc.net.au/phrynefisher

ABC. (2020, 9 March). *Australia's favourite drama* Mystery Road *returns for season two*. Retrieved 8 February 2024 from https://about.abc.net.au/media-room/australias-favourite-drama-mystery-road-returns-for-season-two/

ABC. (2021, 15 January). *World premiers for* Stateless *and* Mystery Road *at Berlin International Film Festival*. Retrieved 8 February 2024 from https://about.abc.net.au/press-releases/world-premieres-for-stateless-and-mystery-road-at-berlin-international-film-festival/

ABC. (2022a, 1 July). *ABC celebrates NAIDOC Week*. Retrieved 8 February 2024 from https://about.abc.net.au/press-releases/abc-celebrates-naidoc-week/

ABC. (2022b). *Annual Report 2022*. Retrieved 8 February 2024 from https://about.abc.net.au/wp-content/uploads/2023/06/2021-22-ABC-Annual-Report_updated.pdf

The ABC Act. (1983).

ABC News. (2014a). The Kettering Incident: *TV drama to employ hundreds of Tasmanians*. Retrieved 8 February 2024 from http://www.abc.net.au/news/2014-10-01/tv-kettering-incident-a-boon-for-tasmanian-screen-industry/5783026

ABC News. (2014b). *Tasmanian seaside town of Kettering to star in $15m TV series*. Retrieved 8 February 2024 from http://www.abc.net.au/news/2014-02-10/tas-seaside-town-to-star-in-new-tv-series/5248826

ABS. (2023a). *Crime Victimisation, Australia, 2021–22*. Retrieved 8 September 2023 from https://www.abs.gov.au/statistics/people/crime-and-justice/crime-victimisation-australia/latest-release

ABS. (2023b). *Recorded Crime–Victims, 2022*. Retrieved 8 September 2023 from https://www.abs.gov.au/statistics/people/crime-and-justice/recorded-crime-victims/latest-release

ACMA. (2020). *Trends in viewing and listening behaviour* (ACMA consumer survey, Issue). Retrieved 8 February 2024 from https://www.acma.gov.au/sites/default/

files/2020-11/Trends-in-viewing-and-listening-behaviour_ACMA-consumer-survey-2020.pdf

ACT Government. (2019). The city behind Secret City: Under the Eagle. *Our Canberra*. Retrieved 20 May 2019 from https://www.act.gov.au/our-canberra/latest-news/2019/march/the-city-behind-secret-city-under-the-eagle

ACT Government. (2023). *Visit Canberra*. Retrieved 6 September 2023 from https://visitcanberra.com.au/

Aird, C. (2022, 14 January). *Jane Millichip, Gabriel Silver, Nils Hartmann, Frank Jastfelder, Superna Kalle & Chris Aird* [Interview]. Retrieved 8 February 2024 from https://www.c21media.net/c21podcasts/jane-millichip-gabriel-silver-nils-hartmann-frank-jastfelder-superna-kalle-chris-aird/

Akyuz, G. (2012). All3Media's Miss Fisher wins admirers. *C21 Media*. Retrieved 12 February 2024 from https://www.c21media.net/news/all3medias-miss-fisher-wins-admirers/

Aldrich, J. (2019, 16 December). In *Shell Shock, Film Festivals, and Other Alliterations*. Retrieved 12 February 2024 from https://podcasters.spotify.com/pod/show/adventurespodcast/episodes/Shell-Shock--Film-Festivals--and-Other-Alliterations-e9hdbg

Allan, C., Grimes, A., & Kerr, S. (2013). *Value and culture: an economic framework* (Paper prepared for Manatū Taonga – Ministry for Culture and Heritage, Issue). Retrieved 12 February 2024 from https://www.motu.nz/our-research/wellbeing-and-macroeconomics/well-being-and-sustainability-measures/value-and-culture/

Allen & Unwin. (2022). *Kerry Greenwood*. Retrieved 24 August 2023 from http://phrynefisher.com/Kerrygreenwood.html

Allen, M. (Ed.). (2007). *Reading CSI: Crime Television Under the Microscope*. I.B. Taurus.

Amabile, T. M. (1983). *The Social Psychology of Creativity*. Springer.

Amabile, T. M., & Khaire, M. (2008). Creativity and the Role of the Leader. *Harvard Business Review*. Retrieved 8 February 2024 from https://hbr.org/2008/10/creativity-and-the-role-of-the-leader

Anderson, B. (2006). *Imagined Communities: Reflections on the origin and spread of nationalism* (revised editiion ed.). Verso.

Andreeva, N. (2016). CI lives on: Wins most watched drama series at Monte Carlo TV Festival. *Deadline*. Retrieved 14 August 2023 from https://deadline.com/2016/05/csi-cyber-canceled-2-seasons-cbs-1201754436/

Andy D. (2018, 23 September–7 October). *Review:* Mystery Road. Retrieved 8 February 2024 from https://thekillingtimestv.wordpress.com/2018/09/23/review-mystery-road-s1-e12-6/

Ang, L., Hawkins, G., & Dabboussy, L. (2008). *The SBS Story: The challenge of diversity*. UNSW Press.

Angelini, F., & Castellini, M. (2018). Cultural and economic value: A critical review. *Journal of Cultural Economics, 43*, 173–188. https://doi.org/10.1007/s10824-018-9334-4

Arts Law Centre of Australia. (2023). *Indigenous Cultural and Intellectual Property (ICIP)*. Retrieved 13 September 2023 from https://www.artslaw.com.au/information-sheet/indigenous-cultural-intellectual-property-icip-aitb/

Ausfilm. (2020). *Supporting Australian stories in our Screens Options Paper: Ausfilm submission*. Retrieved 8 February 2024 from https://www.infrastructure.gov.au/sites/default/files/submissions/sass-ausfilm.pdf

Australia Council for the Arts. (2020). *Domestic Arts Tourism: Connecting the country*. Retrieved 8 February 2024 from https://www.australiacouncil.gov.au/research/domestic-arts-tourism-connecting-the-country/?mc_cid=cc9ee176a9&mc_eid=079f92603d

Australian Bureau of Statistics. (2022). *Australia's Population by Country of Birth*. Retrieved 8 February 2024 from https://www.abs.gov.au/statistics/people/population/australias-population-country-birth/latest-release#country-of-birth-state-and-territory

Australian Broadcasting Corporation Act (1983). Retrieved 8 February 2024 from https://www.legislation.gov.au/Details/C2016C00300

Australian Government. (2023). *Tax rebates for film and television producers*. Department of Infrastructure, Transport, Regional Development, Communications and the Arts. Retrieved 16 August 2023 from https://www.arts.gov.au/funding-and-support/tax-rebates-film-and-television-producers

Australian Government. (2023). *Recognising Aboriginal and Torres Strait Islander peoples through a voice – Information Booklet*. Retrieved 8 February 2024 from https://voice.gov.au/sites/default/files/2023-06/voice-information-booklet-english.pdf

Australian Senate. (1963). *Select Committee on the Encouragement of Australian Productions for Television, 1962–63*. Retrieved 9 October 2023 from https://navigatesenatecommittees.senate.gov.au/events/select-committee-on-the-encouragement-of-australian-productions-for-television/11

Awad, A. (2018). Resilience, collaboration and inspiration in the writers' room. *Screen News*. Retrieved 8 February 2024 from https://www.screenaustralia.gov.au/sa/screen-news/2018/08-24-resilience-collaboration-writers-room

Bakhshi, H. (2012, 20 March). *Measuring Cultural Value*, Culture Count: Measuring Cultural Value Forum, Customs House, Sydney. Retrieved 8 February 2024 from https://media.nesta.org.uk/documents/measuring_cultural_value.pdf

Barraclough, L. (2016, 25 August). Amazon Prime Video takes U.S. rights to Australian drama 'The Kettering Incident'. *Variety*. Retrieved 8 February 2024 from http://variety.com/2016/digital/global/amazon-prime-video-u-s-rights-australian-drama-the-kettering-incident-1201844537/

Barrett, D. (2016). *Secret City* thrives on Scandi-noir ambition. *Mediaweek*. Retrieved 8 February 2024 from http://www.mediaweek.com.au/secret-city-thrives-on-scandi-noir-ambition/

Bastow, C. (2016, 10 June). *The Kettering Incident* review – Tasmanian gothic thriller par excellence. *The Guardian*. Retrieved 8 February 2024 from https://www.theguardian.com/tv-and-radio/2016/jun/10/the-kettering-incident-review-tasmanian-gothic-thriller-par-excellence

Batty, C., O'Meara, R., Taylor, S., & Dwyer, T. (Eds). (2021). *TV Transformations and Transgressive Women: From* Prisoner: Cell Block H *to* Wentworth. Peter Lang.

Baumol, W. J., & Bowen, W. G. (1966). *Performing Arts – The Economic Dilemma*. Twentieth Century Fund.

BBC Four acquires Australian drama *Mystery Road*. (2018). *Seenit*. Retrieved 8 February 2024 from http://www.seenit.co.uk/bbc-four-acquires-australian-drama-mystery-road/

BBC Worldwide. (2016a, 6 April). *BBC Worldwide licenses over 2000 hours of content across Central and Eastern Europe and the Middle East*. Retrieved 8 February 2024 from http://www.bbc.co.uk/mediacentre/worldwide/bbc-worldwide-licenses-over-2000-hours-of-content-across-central-and-eastern-europe-and-the-middle-east

BBC Worldwide. (2016b, 25 August). *BBC Worldwide North America Announces Amazon Prime Video as the Exclusive U.S. Premium Subscription Streaming Home of the New Australian Drama,* The Kettering Incident. Retrieved 8 February 2024 from http://www.bbcwpressroom.com/sales-and-co-productions/press/bbc-worldwide-north-america-announces-amazon-prime-video-exclusive-u-s-premium-subscription-streaming-home-new-australian-drama-kettering-incident/

Behrendt, L. (2018). *Mystery Road* review – TV spin-off unearths ambitious tale of small-town secrets. *The Guardian*. Retrieved 8 February 2024 from https://www.theguardian.com/tv-and-radio/2018/jun/03/mystery-road-review-tv-spin-off-unearths-ambitious-tale-of-small-town-secrets

Belfiore, E., Firth, C., & Holdaway, D. (2014). *How do we Value (and Undervalue) Culture?* (The Future of Cultural Value Commissioner Day 2 Brief, Issue). Retrieved 8 February 2024 from https://warwick.ac.uk/research/warwickcommission/futureculture/resources/commission/

Bertrand, I. (1990). A Bicentennial History: The Australian television miniseries. *Historical Journal of Film, Radio, and Television*, *10*(3), 293–303.

Bevan, J. (2016, 21 November). A Tasmanian home once lived in by actor Errol Flynn has hit the market. *The Mercury*. Retrieved 8 February 2024 from https://www.themercury.com.au/realestate/a-tasmanian-home-once-lived-in-by-actor-errol-flynn-has-hit-the-market/news-story/c2ff72fbb37af932e65a1b25b9f2bbb4

Bizzaca, C. (2016a, 1 June). Move over Washington, Westminster. *Screen News*. Retrieved 8 February 2024 from https://www.screenaustralia.gov.au/sa/screen-news/2016/06-01-move-over-washington-westminster

Bizzaca, C. (2016b, 29 June). Career-making moments: Vicki Madden. *The Screen Blog*. Retrieved 8 February 2024 from https://thescreenblog.com/2016/06/29/career-making-moments-vicki-madden/

Bizzaca, C. (2018). Bunya: *Sweet Country, Mystery Road* & more. *Screen Australia Screen News*. Retrieved 8 February 2024 from https://www.screenaustralia.gov.au/sa/screen-news/2018/01-17-bunya-sweet-country-mystery-road-and-more

Blatchford, E. (2015). Silver linings. *Inside Film* (164), 14–15.

Bloore, P. (2013). *The Screenplay Business: Managing creativity and script development in the film industry*. Routledge Taylor & Francis Group.

Blundell, G. (2012, 18 February). Catch of the day first watch. *The Australian*, 26.

Blundell, G. (2016, 27 August). Spreading the net. *The Australian*.

Blundell, G. (2018, 6 February). Outback noir. *The Australian*.

Blundell, G. (2022, 2 July). Off-road for a while but back to where it began. *The Australian*, 19.

Bowles, K. (1994). Soap opera: 'No end of story, ever'. In K. Bowles & S. Turnbull (Eds), *Tomorrow Never Knows: Soap on Australian television*. Australian Film Institute.

Buckingham-Jones, S. (2023, 2 May). Aussies added 189,000 streaming services despite cost-of-living crunch. *Australian Financial Review*. Retrieved 8 February 2024 from https://www.afr.com/companies/media-and-marketing/aussies-added-189-000-streaming-services-despite-cost-of-living-crunch-20230501-p5d4j2

Buckmaster, L. (2018, 13 August). Aaron Pedersen: is the *Mystery Road* star one of the greatest actors of his generation? *The Guardian*.

Buckmaster, L. (2019, 30 December 2019). *The Gloaming* Review – Shades of *Twin Peaks* in fog-swamped crime drama. *The Guardian*. Retrieved 8 February 2024 from https://www.theguardian.com/tv-and-radio/2019/dec/30/the-gloaming-review-shades-of-twin-peaks-in-fog-swamped-drama

Buckmaster, L. (2022, 5 July 2022). *True Colours* review – SBS detective drama plays it too by the book. *The Guardian*. Retrieved 8 February 2024 from https://www.theguardian.com/tv-and-radio/2022/jul/05/true-colours-review-sbs-detective-drama-plays-it-too-by-the-book

Bunya Productions. (2023). *About*. Retrieved 13 September 2023 from https://bunyaproductions.com.au/about/#bunya-productions

Buonanno, M. (2008). *The Age of Television: Experiences and theories* (J. Radice, Trans.). Intellect.

Bureau of Communications Arts and Regional Research. (2022, March). *Interactive dashboard: Subscription Video on Demand in Australia*. Retrieved 16 August 2023 from https://www.infrastructure.gov.au/research-data/bureau-communications-arts-and-regional-research/communications/subscription-video-demand-svod-dashboard

Burke, J. (2019, 4 March). Journos get the big picture, so the story goes. *The Australian*, 24.

Byrne, T. (2023, 31 January). Hugh Sheridan: 'I was Overwhelmed…'. *The Guardian*. Retrieved 8 February 2024 from http://www.theguardian.com/stage/2023/jan/31/hugh-sheridan-i-was-overwhelmed-with-grief-i-couldnt-believe-that-people-could-turn-so-quickly

Cameron, A., & Verhoeven, D. (2010). Above the bottom line: Analysing the culture of Australian screen content producers. *Lumina – Australian Journal of Screen Arts and Business*, 6, 40–61.

Caves, R. E. (2000). *Creative Industries: Contracts between arts and commerce*. Harvard University Press.

Chalaby, J. K. (2016). Television and globalization: The TV content global value chain. *Journal of Communication*, 66, 35–59.

Chalaby, J. K. (2019). Outsourcing in the U.K. television industry: A global value chain analysis. *Communication Theory*, 29, 169–190.

Chapman, P. (2019, 21 May). *Personal communication with Sue Turnbull and Marion McCutcheon* [Interview].

Clark, B. (2011). She Dunnit. *Herald Sun*, 2.

Clarke, S. (2018, 19 June). 'Mystery Road', Judy Davis and Aaron Pedersen drama series, heads to Acorn TV in the U.S. *Variety*. Retrieved 8 February 2024 from https://variety.com/2018/tv/news/mystery-road-to-acorn-in-the-us-1202850680/

Claydon, A. (2018, 8 March). *Jewelled Nights*: The surprising story of two Tasmanian women and their lost silent film. *State Library and Tasmanian Archives Blog*. Retrieved 8 February 2024 from https://archivesandheritageblog.libraries.tas.gov.au/jewelled-nights-the-surprising-story-of-two-tasmanian-women-and-their-lost-silent-film

Collins, F. (2016). After dispossession: Blackfella Films and the politics of radical hope. In Y. Tzioumakis & C. Molloy (Eds), *The Routledge Companion to Cinema and Politics* (1st Edition ed., pp. 11). Routledge. https://doi.org/10.4324/9781315678863

Collins, F., & Davis, T. (2004). *Australian Cinema after Mabo*. Cambridge University Press. https://doi.org/10.1017/CBO9780511802324

Collins, S. T. (2018). 'Secret City' on Netflix is an especially eerie instance of life imitating art. *Decider*. Retrieved 8 February 2024 from https://decider.com/2018/07/18/secret-city-on-netflix/

Commonwealth of Australia. (2023). *Revive: a place for every story, a story for every place – Australias cultural policy for the next five years*. Retrieved 8 February 2024 from https://www.arts.gov.au/publications/national-cultural-policy-revive-place-every-story-story-every-place

Corner, J., & Roscoe, J. (2016). Outside and inside television: a dialogue on 'value'. *Journal of Media Practice*, 17(2–3), 157–167.

Craven, P. (2022, 16 July). Gritty but gratifying journey on the road to revelation. *The Australian*, 21.

Crawley, P. (2017, 16 February). *The Kettering Incident* review: things get super-spooky on the far side of the world. *The Irish Times*. Retrieved 8 February 2024 from https://www.irishtimes.com/culture/tv-radio-web/the-kettering-incident-review-things-get-super-spooky-on-the-far-side-of-the-world-1.2977818

Crikey. (2022). A wet weekend lures viewers down ABC's *Mystery Road*. *Crikey*. Retrieved 4 July from https://www.crikey.com.au/2022/07/04/tv-ratings-wet-weekend-mystery-road/

Crossick, G., & Kaszynska, P. (2014). Under construction: Towards a framework for cultural value. *Cultural Trends*, 23(2), 120–131. https://doi.org/10.1080/09548963.2014.897453

Crowley, R., Pollitt, T., & Winn, P. (2017, 2 November). *Personal communication with Marion McCutcheon and Sue Turnbull* [Interview].

Csikszentmihalyi, M. (1990). *Flow: The psychology of optimal experience*. Harper & Row.

Cubis, S. (2017). *Jordskott* goes beyond the ususal. Retrieved 6 September 2023 from https://www.sbs.com.au/guide/article/2017/12/15/explore-creepiest-woods-scandinavia-jordskott

Cunningham, S., & Jacka, E. (1996). *Australian Television and International Mediascapes*. Cambridge University Press.

Curran, J. (2011). *Media and Democracy*. Routledge.

Curtin, M., & Sanson, K. (2016). Precarious creativity: Global media, local labor. In M. Curtin & K. Sanson (Eds), *Precarious Creativity: Global media, local labor*. University of Califormia Press.

Dams, T. (2020). Berlinale Series Market Unveils 2020 Selection. *Variety*. Retrieved 8 February 2024 from https://variety.com/2020/tv/news/berlinale-series-market-2020-selection-1203483991/#

Darling, C. (2018, 15 August). Aaron Pedersen: the latest Aussie actor everyone should know. *Houston Chronicle*. Retrieved 8 February 2024 from https://www.houstonchronicle.com/entertainment/tv/article/Aaron-Pedersen-the-latest-Aussie-actor-everyone-13157979.php

Davidson, D. (2016). Local drama a major driver of Foxtel's ratings growth in 2016. *The Australian*.

Davis, T. (2017). Australian indigenous screen in the 2000s: Crossing into the mainstream. In M. D. Ryan & B. Goldsmith (Eds), *Australian Screen in the 2000s*. Springer International Publishing AG. https://doi.org/10.1007/978-3-319-48299-6_11

Deloitte Access Economics. (2016). *What are our stories worth? Measuring the economic and cultural value of Australia's screen sector*. Retrieved 8 February 2024 from http://www.screenaustralia.gov.au/fact-finders/reports-and-key-issues/reports-and-discussion-papers/screen-currency

Dermody, S., & Jacka, E. (1988). *The screening of Australia* (Vol. 2). Currency Press.

Dibley, B., & Turner, G. (2018). Indigeneity, cosmopolitanism, and the nation: the project of NITV. In D. Rowe, G. Turner, & E. Waterton (Eds), *Making Culture: Commercialisation, transnationalism, and the state of 'Nationing' in contemporary Australia* (1st ed.). Routledge.

Disher, G. (2021). *The search for a true home: A novel and a critical review of recent Australian rural noir*. PhD thesis. Retrieved 8 February 2024 from https://opal.latrobe.edu.au/articles/thesis/The_Search_for_a_True_Home_a_Novel_and_a_Critical_Review_of_Recent_Australian_Rural_Noir/14226965

Donovan, C. (2013). *A holistic approach to valuing our culture: A report to the Department for Culture, Media and Sport*. Retrieved 8 February 2024 from https://www.gov.uk/government/uploads/system/uploads/attachment_data/file/197826/Holistic_Approach_10_May_2013finalforweb.pdf

Doyle, G. (2010). Why culture attracts and resists economic analysis. *Journal of Cultural Economics*, 34, 245–259.

Dubecki, L. (2020, 8 April). Sofia Helin swaps chilly Nordic noir for outback gothic Mystery Road. *The Sydney Morning Herald*. Retrieved 8 February 2024 from https://www.smh.com.au/culture/tv-and-radio/sofia-helin-swaps-chilly-nordic-noir-for-outback-gothic-mystery-road-20200403-p54gu0.html

Eagger, F. (2016). *Producer Fiona Eagger on* Miss Fisher's Murder Mysteries. Screen Australia.

Eckersley, J., & Ryan, A. (2022, 31 March–1 April). Meet the Buyers. Screen Forever, Gold Coast.

Eklund, O. (2022). Streaming platforms will soon be required to invest more in Australian TV and films, which could be good news for our screen sector. *The Conversation*. Retrieved 14 August 2023 from https://theconversation.com/streaming-platforms-will-soon-be-required-to-invest-more-in-australian-tv-and-films-which-could-be-good-news-for-our-screen-sector-198757

Enker, D. (2018, 24 May). The Judy factor: Davis returns to Australian TV on ABC's Mystery Road. *The Sydney Morning Herald*. Retrieved 8 February 2024 from https://www.smh.com.au/entertainment/tv-and-radio/the-judy-factor-davis-returns-to-australian-tv-on-abcs-mystery-road-20180516-h1059s.html

Bibliography

Every Cloud Productions. (2011). *Miss Fisher's Murder Mysteries, Series 1: Volume 1, 'Special features'*, Australian Broadcasting Corporation, Film Victoria and Screen Australia.

Every Cloud Productions. (2015). *About Us*. Retrieved 8 February 2024 from http://www.everycloudproductions.com.au/about-us/p/16

Every Cloud Productions. (2017). Miss Fisher Murder Mysteries *Branded Sales Information* (internal company report, Issue).

Every Cloud Productions. (2020a). Every Cloud *Statistics and Brand Information*. Internal company report.

Every Cloud Productions. (2020b). *Miss Fisher & the Crypt of Tears*. Press Kit.

Every Cloud Productions. (2020c). *Miss Fisher Brand – Economic Impact Victoria*. Internal company report.

Every Cloud Productions. (2022). Miss Fisher Murder Mysteries: *Brand and Economics Benefits Report*. Internal company report.

Fenton, A. (2015). *Miss Fisher's Murder Mysteries* to be a movie filmed in the UK. *News Corp Australia Network*. Retrieved 12 February 2024 from https://www.news.com.au/entertainment/tv/miss-fishers-murder-mysteries-to-be-a-movie-filmed-in-the-uk/news-story/be78fb3424f21b292ef2a24740845855

Fidgeon, R. (2001, 17 October). Halifax a cut above. *The Herald Sun*. Retrieved 8 February 2024 from http://www.australiantelevision.net/hfp/articles/cutabove.html

Film Victoria. (2011). *Annual Report 2010–11*. Retrieved 8 February 2024 from https://vicscreen.vic.gov.au/images/uploads/2010-11_Annual_Report.pdf

Film Victoria. (2012). *Annual Report 2011–12*. Retrieved 8 February 2024 from https://vicscreen.vic.gov.au/images/uploads/2011-12_Annual_Report.pdf

Film Victoria. (2019). *Annual Report Disclosure of Payments 2018–19*. Retrieved 8 February 2024 from https://vicscreen.vic.gov.au/images/uploads/FV_Payment_Listings_2018-19.pdf

Film Victoria. (2020). *Annual Report Disclosure of Payments 2019–20*. Retrieved 8 February 2024 from https://vicscreen.vic.gov.au/images/uploads/Film_Victoria_Disclosure_of_Payments_2019-20.pdf

Flew, T. (1995). Images of nation: Economic and cultural aspects of Australian content regulations for commercial television. In J. Craik, J. J. Bailey, & A. Moran (Eds), *Public voices, private interests : Australia's media policy*. Allen & Unwin.

Flew, T. (2019). Creative industries: Between cultural economics and cultural studies. In S. Cunningham & T. Flew (Eds), *A Research Agenda for the Creative Industries* (pp. 58–75). Edward Elgar.

Fowler, C. (2017). Remote Kimberley community welcomes horse trainer Jim Willougby and *Mystery Road* Film crew. *ABC News*. Retrieved 23 September 2023 from https://www.abc.net.au/news/rural/2017-10-16/horse-trainer-in-kimberley-abc-mystery-road-tv-series/9053178

Frater, P. (2017, 16 July). 'Mystery Road' Becomes TV Series With Aaron Pedersen, Judy Davis. *Variety*. Retrieved 8 February 2024 from https://variety.com/2017/tv/asia/mystery-road-becomes-tv-series-with-aaron-pedersen-judy-davis-1202496853/#

Frater, P. (2018). Australia's Stan, ABC Studios Launch Tasmania-set 'Gloaming'. *Variety*. Retrieved 6 September 2023 from https://variety.com/2018/tv/asia/australia-stan-abc-studio-gloaming-1202830477/

Frater, P. (2023). Australia raises location offset scheme to 30%, securing position as magnet for international film, TV production. *Variety*. Retrieved 16 August 2023 from https://variety.com/2023/film/news/australia-raises-location-offset-scheme-1235607296/

French, L. (2014). Gender then, gender now: Surveying women's participation in Australian film and television industries. *Continuum of Media & Cultural Studies*, 28(2), 188–200. https://doi.org/10.1080/10304312.2014.888040

Fry, A. (2018). Hot Picks: *Mystery Road*. *Broadcast*. Retrieved 8 February 2024 from https://www.broadcastnow.co.uk/international/mystery-road/5127895.article

George, S. (2022a). 'It's time to be very clear that Screen Australia is there for culture': Sandy George. *if.com.au*. Retrieved 14 August 2023 from https://if.com.au/its-time-to-be-very-clear-that-screen-australia-is-there-for-culture-sandy-george/

George, S. (2022b). Nobody talks about Australianness on our screens. Discussion Paper. *The New Platform Papers, No. 3*. Retrieved 8 February 2024 from https://currencyhouse.org.au/

George, S., & Tansley, R. (2018). *International TV Sales Snapshot for 2017*. Retrieved 8 February 2024 from https://www.screenaustralia.gov.au/sa/screen-news/2018/06-18-international-tv-sales-snapshot-for-2017

Giddings, L. (2014, 10 February). *$15 million televison series tipped to be Tasmania's Twin Peaks*. Retrieved 8 February 2024 from http://web.archive.org/web/20140220012915/http://www.premier.tas.gov.au/media_room/media_releases/$15_million_televison_series_tipped_to_be_tasmanias_twin_peaks

Gill, R. (2014, 13 February). Tasmania: Sex, death and apples. *Daily Review*. Retrieved 8 February 2024 from https://dailyreview.com.au/tasmania-sex-death-and-apples/3083/

Goddard, R., & Lehman, R. (2015, 30 March 2016). Dark Mofo festival: *The Kettering Incident* premiere sets scene for Tasmania's winter festival. *ABC News*. Retrieved 8 February 2024 from http://www.abc.net.au/news/2014-10-01/tv-kettering-incident-a-boon-for-tasmanian-screen-industry/5783026

Goldbart, M. (2022). 'A decimation of half the industry is not unrealistic': Danish producers urge Netflix, Viaplay & Create Denmark Union to return to negotiating table or risk $200M loss. *Deadline*. Retrieved 8 February 2024 from https://deadline.com/2022/09/netflix-viaplay-disney-denmark-commissioning-decimation-1235125461/

Goodall, J. (2018). Out there. *Inside Story*. Retrieved 8 February 2024 from https://insidestory.org.au/out-there/

Goodall, J. (2022). Casting *Mystery Road*. *Inside Story*. Retrieved 8 February 2024 from https://insidestory.org.au/casting-mystery-road/

Goodwin, V. (2016, 19 August). *Record audience for the final episode of* The Kettering Incident. Retrieved 12 February 2024 from https://www.premier.tas.gov.au/releases/record_audience_for_the_final_episode_of_the_kettering_incidentG

reenwood, K. (1989). *Cocaine Blues*. McPhee Gribble Publishers.

Groves, D. (2013). Rise of the showrunner. *InsideFilm, 156* (December–January).
Groves, D. (2015). Phryne Fisher and a curious case of sexism. *if.com.au*. Retrieved 1 July 2015 from http://if.com.au/2015/06/01/article/Phryne-Fisher-and-a-curious-case-of-sexism/DAWXFJFRKX.html
Groves, D. (2018a). 'The Kettering Incident' was Australia's top-selling drama overseas last year. *IF Magazine*. Retrieved 8 February 2024 from https://www.if.com.au/the-kettering-incident-was-australias-top-selling-drama-overseas-last-yeaar/
Groves, D. (2018b). 'Mystery Road' sets a new high for ABC's iView. *IF Magazine*. Retrieved from https://www.if.com.au/mystery-road-sets-a-new-high-for-abcs-iview/
Groves, D. (2019). Foxtel reaffirms Oz drama commitment. *C21 Media*. Retrieved 12 February 2024 from https://if.com.au/foxtel-reaffirms-its-commitment-to-austral ian-drama/
Hale, M. (2018). Review: In 'Mystery Road', Judy Davis Goes West. *The New York Times*. Retrieved 8 February 2024 from https://www.nytimes.com/2018/08/19/arts/television/mystery-road-review-judy-davis.html
Hansen, K. T., & Re, V. (2021). Producing peripheral locations: double marginality in Italian and Danish television crime narratives. *Cinéma & Cie, Film and Media Studies Journal, 21*(36/37), 57–81. https://doi.org/https://doi.org/10.13130/2036-461X/16388
Hansen, K. T., & Waade, A. M. (2017). *Locating Nordic Noir: From Beck to The Bridge*. Palgrave Macmillan.
Hardy, K. (2019, 4 March). A feminist edge to new *Secret City*. *The Canberra Times*, 2.
Harrington, S., & Eklund, O. (2024). Television. In B. Griffen-Foley & S. Turnbull (Eds), *The Media and Communications in Australia*. Routledge.
Hartley, J., & McKee, A. (2001). *The Indigenous Public Sphere*. Oxford Univeristy Press.
Hawkes, J. (2001). *The fourth pillar of sustainability: Culture's essential role in public planning*. Cultural Development Network of Victoria in association with Common Ground Publishing.
Hazelton, J. (2018). Acorn TV picks up Australian crime series 'Mystery Road'. *Screen Daily*. Retrieved 20 August 2018 from https://www.screendaily.com/news/acorn-tv-picks-up-australian-crime-series-mystery-road/5130242.article
Healy, C. (2008). *Forgetting Aborigines*. University of New South Wales Press.
Hernando, E., & Campo, S. (2017). An artist's perceived value: Development of a measurement scale. *International Journal of Arts Management, 19*, 33–47.
Hill, A. (2018). *Media Experiences: Engaging with drama and reality television*. Routledge.
Hill, A., & Kondo, K. (2022). Entertainment mobilisation: Nordic noir fans and screen tourism. In R. Trandafoiu (Ed.), *Border Crossings and Mobilities on Screen*. Routledge.
Hills, M. (2004). Defining Cult TV: Texts, inter-texts and fan audience. In R. C. Allen & A. Hill (Eds), *The Television Studies Reader*. Routledge.
Holden, J. (2004). *Capturing Cultural Value: How culture has become a tool of government policy*. Retrieved 8 February 2024 from https://www.demos.co.uk/files/CapturingCulturalValue.pdf
Holden, J. (2006). *Cultural Value and the Crisis of Legitimacy: Why culture needs a democratic mandate*. Retrieved 8 February 2024 from https://www.demos.co.uk/files/Culturalvalueweb.pdf

Hopewell, J. (2018). Series mania: Rachel Perkins, Greer Simpkin talk 'Mystery Road'. *Variety*. Retrieved 8 February 2024 from https://variety.com/2018/tv/festivals/series-mania-rachel-perkins-greer-simpkin-mystery-road-1202794296/#!

Hoskins, C., & McFadyen, S. (1993). Canadian participation in international coproductions and co-ventures in television programming. *Canadian Journal of Communication*, 18(2), 219–236. https://doi.org/10.22230/cjc.1993v18n2a745

Hoskins, C., McFadyen, S., & Finn, A. (1998). The effect of cultural differences on the international co-production of television programs and feature films. *Australian-Canadian Studies: An Interdisciplinary Social Science Review*, 16(2), 99–113.

Howell, A. (2017). Haunted Art House: The Babadook and international art cinema horror. In M. D. Ryan & B. Goldsmith (Eds), *Australian Screen in the 2000s* (pp. 119–139). Palgrave Macmillan.

Hulan, H. (2017). Bury Your Gays: History, usage, and context. *McNair Scholars Journal*, 21(1). Retrieved 8 February 2024 from https://scholarworks.gvsu.edu/mcnair/vol21/iss1/6

Hurst, D. (2022, 8 April). Caroline Kennedy praises Australia's bipartisan foreign policy despite PM's claims on Labor and China. *The Guardian*. Retrieved 8 February 2024 from https://www.theguardian.com/world/2022/apr/08/caroline-kennedy-praises-australias-bipartisan-foreign-policy-despite-pms-claims-on-labor-and-china

Hutter, M., & Frey, B. S. (2010). On the influence of cultural value on economic value. *Revue d'économie politique*, 120(1), 35–36.

Idato, M. (2016, 28 June). TV review: The Kettering Incident. *The Sydney Morning Herald*. Retrieved 8 February 2024 from http://www.smh.com.au/entertainment/tv-and-radio/tv-review-the-kettering-incident-20160628-gpth5h.html

IMDb. (2017). *Miss Fisher's Murder Mysteries*. Retrieved 8 February 2024 from http://www.imdb.com/title/tt1988386/

IMDbPro. (2023). *Secret City*. Retrieved 16 October 2023 from https://pro.imdb.com/title/tt4976512/companycredits

Inside Film. (2015). *ABC's iview takes top spot in free-to-air streaming for 2015*. Retrieved 8 February 2024 from https://if.com.au/abcs-iview-takes-top-spot-in-free-to-air-streaming-for-2015/#:~:text=ABC%20iview%20has%20maintained%20its,site%20and%20apps%20each%20month.

Ipsos Australia. (2013). *Hearts & Minds: How local screen stories capture the hearts & minds of Australians – a report for Screen Australia*. Retrieved 8 February 2024 from https://www.screenaustralia.gov.au/getmedia/b2dc80e7-ebb7-4341-9a20-8225b00064bb/Report-hearts-and-minds.pdf

Irons, G. (1995). *Feminism in Women's Detective Fiction*. Univeristy of Toronto.

Jacka, L. (1991). *The ABC of Drama 1975–1990*. Australian Film Television and Radio School.

Jensen, P. M., & Jacobsen, U. C. (2020). *The Global Audiences of Danish Television Drama*. Nordicom.

Jensen, P. M., & McCutcheon, M. (2020). 'Othering the Self and same-ing the Other': Australians watching Nordic noir. In P. M. Jensen & U. C. Jacobsen (Eds), *The Global Audiences of Danish Television Drama*. Nordicom.

Johnson, C. (2019). *Online TV*. Routledge.

Karp, P. (2023, 15 March). Paul Keating labels Aukus submarine pact 'worst deal in all history' in attack on Albanese government. *The Guardian*. Retrieved 8 February 2024 from https://www.theguardian.com/australia-news/2023/mar/15/paul-keating-labels-aukus-submarine-pact-worst-deal-in-all-history-in-attack-on-albanese-government

Klamer, A. (2004). Cultural goods are good for more than their economic value. In V. Rao & M. Walton (Eds), *Culture and public action* (pp. 138–162). Stanford Univeristy Press.

Klamer, A. (2008). The lives of cultural goods. In J. Amariglio, J. W. Childers, & S. E. Cullenberg (Eds), *Sublime Economy: On the intersection of art and economics* (pp. 250–272). Routledge.

Klamer, A. (2016a). *Doing the Right Thing: A value based economy*. Ubiquity Press. https://doi.org/https://doi.org/10.5334/bbb

Klamer, A. (2016b). The value-based approach to cultural economics. *Journal of Cultural Economics, 40,* 365–373.

Klinger, B. (2018). Gateway bodies: serial form, genre, and white femininity in imported crime TV. *Television & New Media, 19*(6), 515–534.

Knight, A. (2013). Now for the movie. *Australian Author, 45*(1), 26–29.

Knox, D. (2016a). *Kettering Incident* wins at Series Mania Festival. *TV Tonight*. Retrieved 8 February 2024 from http://www.tvtonight.com.au/2016/04/kettering-incident-wins-at-series-mania-festival.html

Knox, D. (2016b). *Secret City* deals in Canberra's house of cards. *TV Tonight*. Retrieved 8 February 2024 from https://tvtonight.com.au/2016/05/secret-city-deals-in-canberras-house-of-cards.html

Knox, D. (2016c). *Secret City* is top non-sports drawcard on Pay TV. *TV Tonight*. Retrieved 8 February 2024 from https://tvtonight.com.au/2016/06/secret-city-is-top-non-sports-drawcard-on-pay-tv.html

Knox, D. (2016d, 6 July). *Kettering Incident* launches to 115,000. *TV Tonight*. Retrieved 12 February 2024 from https://tvtonight.com.au/2016/07/kettering-incident-launches-to-115000.html

Knox, D. (2017). Foxtel dominates Drama wins. *TV Tonight*. https://tvtonight.com.au/2017/04/foxtel-dominates-drama-wins.html

Knox, D. (2018). *Mystery Road. TV Tonight*. Retrieved 1 August 2019 from https://tvtonight.com.au/2018/06/mystery-road.html

Langton, M. (1993). *Well I Heard It on the Radio and I Saw It on the Television*. Australian Film Commission.

Lattanzio, R. (2022). Lars von Trier's 'The Kingdom' and 6 more shows highlighted in TIFF's primetime program. *IndiWire*. Retrieved 13 September 2023 from https://www.indiewire.com/features/general/tiff-primetime-program-industry-2022-1234750120/

Lazarus, M. (2013). *MIPTV Report*. Retrieved 8 February 2024 from https://www.screenaustralia.gov.au/getmedia/5c4eb05a-c645-4f56-8aaa-1c56e5aa12eb/Travel-report-MIPTV2013.pdf

Ling, K. J. (2014). Deals for all3media's *Miss Fisher's Murder Mysteries*. *Asia OnScreen*. Retrieved 8 February 2024 from https://tva.onscreenasia.com/2014/02/deals-for-all3medias-aemiss-fishers-murder-mysteries/

Lobato, R., & Lotz, A. (2020). Imagining global video: the challenge of Netflix. *JCMS: Journal of Cinema and Media Studies, 59*(3), 132–136.

Lotz, A. D. (2017). Linking industrial and creative change in 21st century US television. *Media International Australia, 164*.

Lotz, A. D., & McCutcheon, M. (2023a). *Australian Screen Stories Viewing Report: Part 1: Watching series and movies in the 21st century.* Retrieved 8 February 2024 from https://eprints.qut.edu.au/238930/

Lotz, A. D., & McCutcheon, M. (2023b). *Australian Screen Stories Viewing Report: Part 4: Why we watch what we watch.* Retrieved 8 February 2024 from https://eprints.qut.edu.au/242476/

Lotz, A. D., & Potter, A. (2022). Effective cultural policy in the 21st century: Challenges and strategies from Australian television. *International Journal of Cultural Policy, 28*(6), 684–696. Retrieved 8 February 2024 from https://doi.org/10.1080/10286632.2021.2022652

Lotz, A. D., Potter, A., McCutcheon, M., Sanson, K., & Eklund, O. (2021). *Australian Television Drama Index, 1999–2019.* Retrieved 8 February 2024 from https://eprints.qut.edu.au/212330/

Lyons, M. (2018, 2 July). Three shows to watch this week. *The New York Times.* Retrieved 8 February 2024 from https://www.nytimes.com/2018/07/02/arts/television/three-shows-to-watch-this-week.html

Madden, V. (2016). *Interview* [Interview]. ABC. Retrieved 8 February 2024 from http://www.abc.net.au/radionational/programs/tvclub/tv-club-29-june-2016/7546342

Maier, R. (2021). *Drama Commissioners* [Interview].

Marcus, L. (2015). How *Miss Fisher's Murder Mysteries* conquered America. *The Guardian.* Retrieved 8 February 2024 from https://www.theguardian.com/tv-and-radio/2015/oct/13/how-miss-fishers-mysteries-conquered-america

Martain, T. (2016, 2 July). *Kettering Incident* creator Vicki Madden channels Tasmanian gothic. *The Mercery.* Retrieved 8 February 2024 from http://www.themercury.com.au/entertainment/tasweekend-kettering-incident-creator-vicki-madden-channels-tasmanian-gothic/news-story/4fefcf73654dabbc36db3130b319f2f8

Mathieson, C. (2017, 6 July). Foxtel has a dramatic plan to make HBO-quality shows. *Sydney Morning Herald.* Retrieved 8 February 2024 from http://www.smh.com.au/entertainment/tv-and-radio/foxtel-has-a-dramatic-plan-to-make-hboquality-shows-20170629-gx1nl5.html

Mathieson, C. (2018, 14 June). In the parlance of its outback setting, *Mystery Road* ends a long dry spell. *The Sydney Morning Herald.* Retrieved 8 February 2024 from https://www.smh.com.au/entertainment/tv-and-radio/in-the-parlance-of-its-outback-setting-mystery-road-ends-a-long-dry-spell-20180608-h115vp.html

Mathieson, C. (2022, 17 August). Long live Jay Swan: Here's why the ABS should keep this crime drama alive. *The Sydney Morning Herald.*

McCorry, P. (2015). 'The Phryneverse'. Sisters in Crime.

McCredie-Dando, A., & Karlovsky, B. (2016). Emma Freeman, Joanna Werner on starry Matchbox miniseries *Secret City*. *IF Magazine.* Retrieved 8 February 2024 from https://www.if.com.au/emma-freeman-joanna-werner-on-starry-matchbox-miniseries-secret-city/

McCulloch, R., & Proctor, W. (Eds). (2023). *The Scadinavian Invasion: Nordic Noir and beyond*. Peter Lang.

McCutcheon, M., & Cunningham, S. (2023). *Embedded Creative Employment and Creative Incomes* (The Creative Economy in Australia: What Census 2021 Tells Us, Issue). Retrieved 8 February 2024 from https://www.canberra.edu.au/research/faculty-research-centres/nmrc/major-projects/tabs/current-funded-projects/The-creative-economy-in-Australia-Briefing-paper-2.pdf

McCutcheon, M., & Lotz, A. D. (2022, 22–25 November). *21st Century Drama Trends: What's the story for Australia?* Australia and New Zealand Communications Association Conference, University of Wollongong.

McKee, A. (2017). *Fun! What Entertainment Tells us about Living a Good Life*. Palgrave Macmillan.

Meade, A. (2023, 9 May). ABC coverage of King Charles III coronation tops Australian ratings despite being attacked by monarchists. *The Guardian*. Retrieved 8 February 2024 from https://www.theguardian.com/uk-news/2023/may/09/abc-coverage-of-king-charles-iii-coronation-tops-australian-ratings-despite-being-attacked-by-monarchists

Meares, J. (2015). The Babadook actress Essie Davis opens up about Hollywood ambitions and motherhood. Australian actor Essie Davis is best known as lady detective Phryne Fisher, but she has her sights set far beyond. *The Sydney Morning Herald*. Retrieved 8 February 2024 from https://www.smh.com.au/entertainment/celebrity/the-babadook-actress-essie-davis-opens-up-about-hollywood-ambitions-and-motherhood-20150411-1mizvq.html

Mediaweek. (2016). Subscription TV week 28: *The Kettering Incident* the most-watched non-sports program. Retrieved 6 September 2023 from https://www.mediaweek.com.au/subscription-tv-week-28-the-kettering-incident-the-most-watched-non-sports-program/

Meyrick, J. (2016). Telling the story of culture's value ideal-type analysis and integrated reporting. *The Journal of Arts Management, Law, and Society*, 46(4), 141–152. https://doi.org/10.1080/10632921.2016.1225619

Millar, C. (2012). *Miss Fisher's Murder Mysteries*: Aunty tries her hand at lavish escapism. *Metro Magazine: Media & Education Magazine* (173), 42–47.

Moran, R. (2017). *Miss Fisher's Murder Mysteries* movie smashes Kickstarter goal in hours. *The Sydney Morning Herald*.

Morphet, J. (2019, 18 February). Foxtel and Netflix ink major deal. *The Daily Telegraph*.

National Museum of Australia. (2023, 4 May). *Defining Moments: World's first feature film*. Retrieved 16 August 2023 from https://www.nma.gov.au/defining-moments/resources/world-first-film

Neelands, J., Belfiore, E., Firth, C., Hart, N., Perrin, L., Brock, S., Holdaway, D., & Woddis, J. (2015). *Enriching Britain: Culture, creativity and growth – the 2015 report by the Warwick Commission on the future of cultural value*. University of Warwick. Retrieved 8 February 2024 from https://warwick.ac.uk/research/warwickcommission/futureculture/finalreport/warwick_commission_final_report.pdf

Neill, A. (2016). Down the laneways: *Miss Fisher's Murder Mysteries* and Melbourne history. *Metro Magazine*, 187, 44–49.

Neutze, B. (2014). Location, location, location – why Tasmania's BBC starring role is a coup. *Daily Review*. dailyreview.com.au

O'Brien, D. (2010). *Measuring the Value of Culture: A report to the Department for Culture, Media and Sport*. Retrieved 8 February 2024 from https://www.gov.uk/government/uploads/system/uploads/attachment_data/file/77933/measuring-the-value-culture-report.pdf

O'Meara, R., Dwyer, T., Taylor, S., & Batty, C. (Eds). (2022). *TV Transformations & Transgressive Women: From* Prisoner: Cell Block H *to* Wentworth. Peter Lang.

O'Regan, T. (1993). *Australian Television Culture*. Allen & Unwin.

Olafsson, D. O. (2019, 19 June). *Personal communication with Sue Turnbull* [Interview].

Olsberg.SPI. (2016). *Measuring the Cultural Value of Australia's Screen Sector*. Retrieved 8 February 2024 from http://www.screenaustralia.gov.au/fact-finders/reports-and-key-issues/reports-and-discussion-papers/screen-currency

Olsberg.SPI. (2023). *Study on the Impact of Film and Television Production Incentives in Australia: Report to the Australia and New Zealand Association*. Retrieved 8 February 2024 from https://anzsa.film/wp-content/uploads/2023/02/Study-on-the-Impact-of-Film-and-Television-Production-Incentives-in-Australia-Olsberg-SPI-Report-FEB-23-upload-mobile4.pdf

Papandrea, F. (1997). *Cultural Regulation of Australian Television Programs*. Australian Government Publishing Service.

Papandrea, F., & Albon, R. (2004). A model of employment in the arts. *Australian Economic Papers*, September.

Parrot Analytics. (2021). *Audience demand* [Commissioned dataset]. https://www.parrotanalytics.com/

Perry, K. (2023). FIFA Women's Cup 2023 Smashes Australian TV Records. *TV Blackbox*. Retrieved 8 February 2024 from https://tvblackbox.com.au/page/2023/08/21/fifa-womens-world-cup-2023-smashes-australian-tv-records/

Petski, D. (2020). Priyanka Chopra Jonas & Richard Madden to star in 'Citadel', Amazon's Russo Brothers international event series. *Deadline*. Retrieved 16 August 2023 from https://deadline.com/2020/01/priyanka-chopra-jonas-richard-madden-to-star-in-citadel-amazons-russo-brothers-international-event-series-1202830243/

Pragier, D. (2016). Behind the scenes: *The Kettering Incident* – Interview with Ari Wegner. Retrieved 12 February 2024 from https://acmag.com.au/2016/03/01/the-kettering-incident/

PricewaterhouseCoopers. (2013). *Game Changer: A new kind of value chain for entertainment and media companies*. Retrieved 12 February 2024 from http://www.strategic-tech.org/images/PwC_Value_Chain.pdf

Quinn, K. (2018, 14 June). A formidable package put to exceptional use. *The Sydney Morning Herald*. https://www.smh.com.au/entertainment/tv-and-radio/mystery-road-is-the-supergroup-of-indigenous-television-20180611-h118ig.html

Quinn, K. (2022, 24 May). What political thriller *Total Control* predicted about the election and what it missed. *The Sydney Morning Herald*. Retrieved 8 February 2024 from https://www.smh.com.au/culture/tv-and-radio/what-political-thriller-total-control-predicted-about-the-election-and-what-it-missed-20220523-p5ansi.html

Quinn, K. (2023a, 8 November). D-Day looms for Netflix, Disney as government firms new streaming rules. *The Sydney Morning Herald*. Retrieved 8 February 2024 from https://www.smh.com.au/culture/tv-and-radio/d-day-looms-for-netflix-disney-as-government-firms-new-streaming-rules-20231107-p5ei8h.html?btis=

Quinn, K. (2023b, 17 August). Fisk a global hit on Netflix as Aussie TV shows win over the world. *The Sydney Morning Herald*. Retrieved 8 February 2024 from https://www.smh.com.au/culture/tv-and-radio/fisk-a-global-hit-on-netflix-as-aussie-tv-shows-win-over-the-world-20230816-p5dwxd.html

Quinn, K. (2023c, 7 July). So hot right now: How Tasmania became TV's favourite place to be seen. *The Sydney Morning Herald*. Retrieved 8 February 2024 from https://www.smh.com.au/culture/tv-and-radio/so-hot-right-now-how-tasmania-became-tv-s-favourite-place-to-be-seen-20230706-p5dm9e.html

Raggatt, M. (2016, 5 June). It's no secret: ACT funds hope to emulate TV series success. *The Canberra Times*. Retrieved 8 February 2024 from http://www.canberratimes.com.au/act-news/act-funds-hope-to-emulate-secret-city-success-20160603-gpbac0.html

Ratings resurgence at Foxtel. (2016). *The Australian*.

Reijnders, S. (2009). Watching the detectives: Inside the guilty landscapes of Inspector Morse, Baantjer and Wallander. *European Journal of Communication*, 24(2), 165–181.

Reijnders, S. (2011). *Places of the Imagination: Media, tourism, culture*. Routledge.

Richards, G. (2018). Cultural tourism: A review of recent research and trends. *Journal of Hospitality and Tourism Management*, 36, 12–21. https://doi.org/10.1016/j.jhtm.2018.03.005

Riley, S. (2022, 28–30 March). *Meet the Buyers: Scripted screen forever*, Gold Coast.

Rose, R. (2013). Netflix reviewers think your lady detectives are slutty nuts. *Jezebel*. Retrieved 25 August 2023 from https://jezebel.com/netflix-reviewers-think-your-lady-detectives-are-slutty-1465924075

Ross, A. (2009). *Nice Work If You Can Get It: Life and labor in precarious times*. New York University Press.

Rotten Tomatoes. (2023). *Citadel (2023)*. Retrieved 16 August 2023 from https://www.rottentomatoes.com/tv/citadel/s01

Ryan, M. D. (2014). Film, cinema and streaming. In B. Griffen-Foley & S. Turnbull (Eds), *The Media and Communications in Australia*. Routledge.

Sacco, P. L. (2020). 'There are more things in heaven and earth…' A 'narrative turn' in economics? *Journal of Cultural Economics*, 44, 173–183. https://doi.org/10.1007/s10824-020-09377-1

Sanderson, C. (2023). *Eco-Anxiety, Ecological Thought and the Fabulative Turn in Nordic Noir TV: Investigating EcoNoir from the Arctic to the Antipodes*. University of New England.

Sangston, A., & McPhail, A. (2017, 14 August). Interview with Sue Turnbull and Marion McCutcheon. In S. Turnbull & M. McCutcheon [Interview].

Saunders, R. (2021). *Geopolitics, Northern Europe and Nordic Noir: What television tells us about world politics*. Routledge.

Schmidt, L. (2008). Profile: Kerry Greenwood. *The Sydney Morning Herald*. Retrieved 8 February 2024 from https://www.smh.com.au/business/profile-kerry-greenwood-20080625-gdsj93.html

Screen Australia. (2015a). *Annual Report 2014–15*. Retrieved 8 February 2024 from https://www.screenaustralia.gov.au/getmedia/85c10352-62eb-44fa-8d79-8a3423bf9ce1/SA-Annual-Report-2014-2015.pdf?ext=.pdf

Screen Australia. (2015b). *Gender matters: Women in the Australian screen industry*. Retrieved 8 February 2024 from http://www.screenaustralia.gov.au/getmedia/f20beab8-81cc-4499-92e9-02afba18c438/Gender-Matters-Women-in-the-Australian-Screen-Industry.pdf?ext=.pdf

Screen Australia. (2016). *Screen currency: Valuing our screen industry*. Retrieved 8 February 2024 from http://www.screenaustralia.gov.au/getmedia/1b1312e5-89ad-4f02-abad-daeee601b739/ScreenCurrency-SA-Report.pdf

Screen Australia. (2017). *Annual Report 2016–17*. Retrieved 8 February 2024 from https://www.screenaustralia.gov.au/getmedia/aeb0ff70-226e-4b35-929b-5a599db5ac3f/SA-Annual-Report-2016-2017.pdf?ext=.pdf

Screen Australia. (2019). *Annual Report 2018–19*. Retrieved 8 February 2024 from https://www.screenaustralia.gov.au/getmedia/98d29914-2704-4c9b-aab2-ae6fc9ee0b68/SA-Annual-Report-2018-2019.pdf?ext=.pdf

Screen Australia. (2022a). *Annual Report 2021–22*. Retrieved 8 February 2024 from https://www.screenaustralia.gov.au/getmedia/4af98de9-e06a-4269-aee3-98d7fd5c52ee/SA-Annual-Report-2021-2022.pdf?ext=.pdf

Screen Australia. (2022b). *Producer Offset Guidelines*. Retrieved 8 February 2024 from https://www.screenaustralia.gov.au/getmedia/70b2fae6-232c-4a48-be6d-e970aead20d9/Guidelines-producer-offset-2022.pdf

Screen Australia. (2023a). *Cinema Industry Trends: Box Office in Australia*. Retrieved 16 August 2023 from https://www.screenaustralia.gov.au/fact-finders/cinema/australian-films/feature-film-releases/box-office-share

Screen Australia. (2023b). *Seeing Ourselves 2: Diversity, equity and inclusion in Australian TV drama*. Retrieved 8 February 2024 from https://www.screenaustralia.gov.au/fact-finders/reports-and-key-issues/reports-and-discussion-papers/seeing-ourselves-2

Screen Illawarra. (2023). *Making the Illawarra a screen content region of global significance*. Retrieved 16 August 2023 from https://www.screenillawarra.com/

Screen Tasmania. (2017). *Strategic Plan*.

Screenwest. (2021, 12 October). Mystery Road: *Origin kicks off filming in Kalgoorlie-Boulder*. Retrieved 8 February 2024 from https://www.screenwest.com.au/news/latest-news/mystery-road-origin-kicks-off-filming-in-kalgoorlie-boulder/

Screenwest. (2022). *Western Australian Regional Screen Fund Guidelines*. Retrieved 8 February 2024 from https://www.screenwest.com.au/wp-content/uploads/2022/08/Western-Australian-Regional-Screen-Fund-Guidelines-August-2022-1.pdf

Sdraulig, S. (2014). The heightened world of the murder mystery. *Lumina – Australian Journal of Screen Arts and Business* (13), 46–54.

Shiller, R. J. (2017). Narrative economics. *Amercian Economic Review, 107*, 967–1004. https://doi.org/10.1257/aer.107.4.967

Smith, T. (2008). Creating value between cultures: Contemporary Australian aboriginal art. In M. Hutter & D. Throsby (Eds), *Beyond Price: Value in culture, economics and the arts* (23–40). Cambridge University Press.

Stadler, J. (2016). *Imagined Landscapes: Geovisualizing Australian spatial narratives.* Indiana University Press.

Stead, D. (1988, 16 August). Tony Hillerman's cross-cultural mystery novels. *New York Times.*

Steemers, J. (2004). *Selling Television: British television in the global marketplace.* British Film Institute.

Straubhaar, J. D. (2007). *World Television: From global to local.* Sage.

Sullivan, R., & McKee, A. (2015). *Pornography: Structures, agency and performance.* Polity.

Sundet, V. S. (2021). *Television Drama in the Age of Streaming.* Palgrave Macmillan.

Taddeo, J. A. (2016). Sex and the lady detective: Re-imagining the Golden Age in *Miss Fisher's Murder Mysteries. Journal of Popular Television, 4*(1), 49–67.

Throsby, D. (2003a). Determining the value of cultural goods: How much (or how little) does contingent valuation tell us? *Journal of Cultural Economics, 27*(3–4), 275–285.

Throsby, D. (2003b). Determining the value of cultural goods: How much (or little) does contingent valuation tell us? *Journal of Cultural Economics, 27*, 275–285.

Throsby, D., & Zednik, A. (2010). *Do you really expect to get paid? An economic study of professional artists in Australia.* Retrieved 8 February 2024 from http://www.australiacouncil.gov.au/workspace/uploads/files/research/do_you_really_expect_to_get_pa-54325a3748d81.pdf

Tiley, D. (2020). *How Phryne Fisher Took Her Revolver to Shanghai.* ArtsHub.

Tinic, S. A. (2005). *On Location: Canada's television industry in a local market.* University of Toronto Press.

Tonight, T. (2016). *Ratings.* Retrieved 19 October 2023 from https://tvtonight.com.au/category/ratings/

Torv is her own mistress. (2008, 4 May). *The Sydney Morning Herald.* Retrieved 8 February 2024 from https://www.smh.com.au/entertainment/celebrity/torv-is-her-own-mistress-20080504-gdsc5e.html

Turnbull, S. (2007). The Hook and the Look: CSI and the aesthetics of the television crime series. In M. Allen (Ed.), *Reading CSI: Crime television under the microscope* (pp. 15–32). I.B. Taurus.

Turnbull, S. (2014). *The TV Crime Drama.* Edinburgh University Press.

Turnbull, S. (2015). Trafficking in TV crime: Remaking *Broadchurch. Continuum, 29*(5), 706–717.

Turner, G. (2020). Dealing with diversity: Australian television, homogeneity and indigeneity. *Media International Australia, 174*(1), 20–28. https://doi.org/10.1177/1329878X19869481

TV Tropes. (2022, 18 November). *Water Rats.* Retrieved 8 February 2024 from https://tvtropes.org/pmwiki/article_history.php?article=Series.WaterRats

Royal Charter for the continuance of the British Broadcasting Corporation (2016). Retrieved 8 February 2024 from http://downloads.bbc.co.uk/bbctrust/assets/files/pdf/about/how_we_govern/2016/charter.pdf

Uluru Dialogue. (2023). *The Statement.* Retrieved 18 September 2023 from https://ulurustatement.org/the-statement/view-the-statement/

Velthuis, O. (2007). *Talking Prices: Symbolic meanings of prices on the market for contemporary art.* Princeton University Press.

Vinall, F. (2020). How *The Gloaming*'s Vicki Madden went from Brookes High to TV powerhouse. [Newspaper]. Retrieved 8 February 2024 from https://www.examiner.com.au/story/6527768/how-vicki-madden-went-from-brooks-high-to-tv-powerhouse/

Waade, A. M. (2016). Nordic Noir tourism and television landscapes: In the footsteps of Kurt Wallander and Saga Norén. *Scandinavia*, 55(1), 41–65.

Weissmann, E. (2012). *Transnational Television Drama: Special relations and mutual influence between the US and UK*. Palgrave Macmillan.

Whittingham, C. (2018a). Acorn navigates *Mystery Road*. *C21 Media*. Retrieved 12 February 2024 from https://www.c21media.net/news/acorn-navigates-mystery-road/

Whittingham, C. (2018b). BBC4 sets off down *Mystery Road*. *C21 Media*. Retrieved 13 September 2023 from https://www.c21media.net/news/bbc4-sets-off-down-mystery-road/

Whittock, J. (2013). BBC Worldwide, ITV Studios snag high end Oz dramas. *Television Business International*. Retrieved 8 February 2024 from http://tbivision.com/news/2013/12/bbc-worldwide-itv-studios-snag-high-end-oz-dramas/196021/

World Tourism Organization. (2018). *Tourism and Culture Synergies*. Retrieved 8 February 2024 from https://www.e-unwto.org/doi/book/10.18111/9789284418978

Zarkesh, A. (2022, 19 October). *Interview with Sue Turnbull* [Interview].

Index

Note: page references in *italics* indicate figures; **bold** indicates tables.

ABC (Australian Broadcasting Corporation), 12, 44, 50, 99, 104, 112, 119, 133–4, 136–7
   iView streaming service, 130, 137, 141
   see also Bay of Fires; Blackout; Cleverman; The Code; Fisk; The Gods of Wheat Street; Looking Black; Mabo; Message Stick; Miss Fisher's Murder Mysteries; Mystery Road; Redfern Now; Rosehaven; Total Control; Wakefield
Acorn TV (USA), 18, *19*, 128
aggregation, 39–41
   The Kettering Incident, 84–5
   Miss Fisher's Murder Mysteries, 54–6
   Mystery Road, 127–9
Aird, Chris, 8
All3Media, 54–5, 123, 127
Allen, Corey, 28–9, 32
Amazon Prime Video (USA), 18, *19*, 84, 87; *see also* Citadel; Deadloch; The Lost Flowers of Alice Hart
AMC (USA) *see Dark Winds*
Anderson, Benedict, 137
Andy D (blogger), 131
Angelini, F., 27
Aristotle, 22
ArtsATL[anta], 88
audiences, 1–2, 21, 42–6, 145–6, 148, 150
   The Kettering Incident, 86–8, **94**, *95*
   Miss Fisher's Murder Mysteries, 59–65, **74**, *74*
   Mystery Road, 129–31, **140**, *140*
   Secret City, 103–5, **115**, *116*
   see also consumption of television content; fans
Australian, The, 60, 65, 87, 132
Australian Broadcasting Corporation *see* ABC
Australian content, 9–13, 55, 96
   local quotas for, 10, 12, 16, 23, 45, 143
   shown internationally, 18–20, *19*, *20*
   The Vincent Report (1963), 143
Australian Financial Review, The, 142
Australian government policy, 9–14, 16, 22, 32, 83, 88, 102, 120
   tax incentives, 9, 13–15, 143, 144
Australian noir, 76, 80; *see also* outback noir
Australian screen production, 3–9, 12–16, *14*, 42, 81, 93, 101–3
   Canberra-based, 100–2, 107–8, 114, 151
   golden age, 144–5
   for the international marketplace, 3–9, 14–18, 39, 46, 143, 144, 146, 152; *see also* distribution
   Tasmanian-based, 78–80, 82–93, 141, 150–1
Australianness onscreen, 3–4, 6–8, 10–12, 14–15, 72, 101, 145–6; *see also* Indigenous representation onscreen; national identity
awards, 24
   The Kettering Incident, 75, 85–6, **94**
   Miss Fisher's Murder Mysteries, 53–4, 57, **73–4**
   Mystery Road, 126–7, 129, **138–9**

awards (*cont.*)
   Secret City, 105–7, **115**
Ayres, Tony, 99

Bakhshi, Hasan, 24
Barrett, Dan, 111
Bastow, Clem, 76, 81
Bay of Fires, 92, 93, 141
BBC (British Broadcasting Corporation), 44, 84, 85, 128; *see also The Tourist*; *The Valhalla Murders*
Behrendt, Larissa, 130
Belfiore, Eleonora, 27–8
Bertrand, Ina, 144
Birse, Shelley, 112
Bizzaca, Caris, 98
Blackfella Films, 103, 112, 113, 117, 119
Blackout, 133
Blair, Wayne, 121
Blak Wave, 120
Bloore, P., 34, 38
Blundell, Graeme, 52, 60, 69, 87, 130, 132
Bodey, Michael, 65
Bony, 5, 148
Borgen, 97, 108, 113–14, 123, 151
Bourchier, Dan, 133
Boyce, Marion, 53, 57, 61, 64, 65, 66
Bridge, The, 3, 5, 78, 89–90, 91, 97, 100, 117, 119, 125–6, 135, 147, 148
Bridie, David, 106
British Broadcasting Corporation *see* BBC
Buckmaster, Luke, 91–2, 127, 135
Bunyan Productions, 120, 121, 124, 129

Campo, Sara, 25
Canadian screen production, 15, 101
Castellini, M., 27
Caves, R. E., 33
Chalaby, J. K., 8, 34, 38
Channel 4 (UK), 3, 81
Chapman, Penny, 99–106, 111, 151
Christie, Agatha, 71–2
Citadel, 2
Clearing, The, 19
Cleverman, 119, 124
Code, The, 112–13
Collins, Felicity, 120

Collins, Sean T., 108
consumption of television content, 1, 10, 21, 142–3
COVID-19 pandemic, 8, 14, 15, 64, 89, 128
Cox, Deb, 49–52, 54, 55, 57–8, 62, 63, 65, 149
Craven, Peter, 132
Crawley, Peter, 88
Create NSW, 127
critical responses, 6, 42, 45
   The Kettering Incident, 87–8
   Miss Fisher's Murder Mysteries, 60–2
   Mystery Road, 129–31
   Secret City, 103–5
Crowley, Ross, 80, 96, 105
CSI (*Crime Scenes Investigations*), 2
cultural value and impact, 6, 9, 12, 24–32, 28, 36–7
   and economic value, 24–7, 47, 144
   and total value, 47, 149–50
   Miss Fisher's Murder Mysteries, 68–74, 150
   Mystery Road, 125, 126, 132–7
   Secret City, 107–14
   The Kettering Incident, 90–2
Cunningham, S., 2, 4, 104, 143, 145
Curran, James, 148

Daily Review, The, 87, 88–9
Dalton, Kim, 119
Danish screen production, 10, 89–90
Dark Winds, 147–8
Darling, Cary, 131
Davis, Essie, 57, 58–9, 60, 61
Davis, Therese, 120, 134–5
Deadloch, 6, 19, 86, 93–5, 141
Dear, Miranda, 50
Debicki, Elizabeth, 76, 84, 87
Decider (website), 108
Dermody, Susan, 144, 146
detective fiction, 71–2
development, 38–9
   The Kettering Incident, 81–4
   Miss Fisher's Murder Mysteries, 52–4
   Mystery Road, 121–9
   Secret City, 99–101
Dibley, B., 136–7

Disher, Garry, 118
Disney+ (USA), 18, *19*, 90; *see also The Clearing*; *The Gloaming*
distribution, 2, 21, 39–41, 142, 153
  The Kettering Incident, 84–5
  Miss Fisher's Murder Mysteries, 54–6
  Mystery Road, 127–9
  Secret City, 101, 103–5
diversity, 11, 15, 46, 47, 83, 136
Donovan, C., 27
Doyle, G., 22–3
DR/DR1 (Denmark) *see Borgen*; *Jordskott*; *The Killing*; *Unit 1*

Eagger, Fiona, 49–58, 63, 65–6, 149
Eagle, The, 3
EcoNoir, 77
Eklund, Oliver, 11
Enker, Debi, 118
environmental issues, 122–3
eudaimonia, 22
events/exhibitions, 53, 66–8, 150
Every Cloud Productions, 50, 54, 56, 63, 66, 67–8, 119, 149
externalities *see* flow-ons/externalities

fans, 62–5, 70, 71
female characters, 77, 106, 108–10, 119, 126, 131, 134, 151
female sexuality, 61–2, 69–70, 71–2
film festivals, 17, 120, 128–9
Film Victoria, 48, 52, 54
financing, 39–41, 101–2, 153
  crowdfunding, 48, 63, 64
  The Kettering Incident, 84–5
  Miss Fisher's Murder Mysteries, 54–6
  Mystery Road, 127–9
  Secret City, 101–3
Firth, Catriona, 27–8
Fisk, 19
Flew, Terry, 32, 145–6
flow-ons/externalities, 46–7
  The Kettering Incident, 88–92
  Miss Fisher's Murder Mysteries, 65–8
  Mystery Road, 131–7
Fortitude, 123
Forward, Nick, 90

Foxtel (Showcase) (USA), 75, 80, 81, 86, 96, 105, 106
Foxtel Now, 18, *19*
see also The Kettering Incident; *Secret City*; *Wentworth*
Frater, Patrick, 90
Freeman, Emma, 52, 106
French, Lisa, 68
Frey, B. S., 25

gender, 108–9, 113, 119, 149; *see also* female characters; female sexuality; transgender characters; women in the screen industry
geo-political issues *see* political issues
George, Sandy, 10–11, 56, 146
Gill, Raymond, 87
Gloaming, The, 90–2, 93, 151
global citizenship concept, 147–9
globalised screen production, 1–6, 32–8, 36, 40–1, 43, 73, 105, 145–9
Goalpost Pictures, 119
Gods of Wheat Street, The, 119, 124
Goldstone (film), 117, 126, 131
Goodall, Jane, 118, 125, 127
government policy *see* Australian government policy
Greagg, David, 64
greater good *see phronesis* and the greater good
Greenwood, Kerry, 49–52, 57, 63, 64, 69, 71, 149
Griffiths, Rachel, 113, 114
Grimes, Arthur, 28–9, 32
Groves, Don, 61–2, 81, 85
Guardian, The, 59–60, 76, 81, 91, 127, 130

Hale, Mike, 131
Halifax fp, 5, 79
Hansen, K. T., 90, 117
Harrington, Stephen, 11
Hartley, John, 120
Hawkes, Jon, 31
Hayu, 18, *19*
HBO, 56, 75, 76, 80, 86, 96; *see also The Tourist*
Healy, Chris, 120

Helin, Sofia, 125–6, 132
Hernando, Elisa, 25
Herriman, Damon, 7, 97, 106, 111–12
Hill, Annette, 89, 148
Hills, Matt, 64–5
Hillerman, Tony, 148
Holden, John, 25
Holiday, Dom, 27–8
Homicide, 4, 118
Horchner, Maarjtje, 54–5
Houston Chronicle, 131
Hulan, Haley, 110
Hutter, M., 25

Icelandic screen production, 17
Idato, Michael, 7, 78–9, 87
idea origins, 38
   The Kettering Incident, 78–80
   Miss Fisher's Murder Mysteries, 49–52
   Secret City, 98–9
If Magazine, 11, 62, 85
Indigenous cultural and political issues, 103, 122, 125, 126, 152
   Voice to Parliament initiative, 122, 132, 137, 141–2
Indigenous representation onscreen, 5, 45, 46, 47, 72, 112
   Indigenous characters, 119–20, 131, 136
   and *Mystery Road*, 117–21, 124–7, 129, 131–7, 152–3
   and *Total Control*, 103, 113–14
Irish Times, 88
Irons, Glenwood, 71

Jacka, Liz, 2, 4, 104, 143, 144, 145, 146
Jacobsen, U. C., 3
Jensen, P. M., 3
Jewelled Nights (film), 92
Jezebel (online magazine), 61
Jordskott, 76, 77, 88, 90, 91, 150
Jowsey, David, 117, 119, 121, 126

Kerr, Suzi, 28–9, 32
Kettering Incident, The, 5, 75–95, **94**, 95, 147
   audience response, 86–8, **94**, 95
   awards, 75, 85–6, **94**

critical response, 87–8
cultural value and impact, 90–2
development and production, 81–4
financing, distribution and aggregation, 84–5
flow-ons, 88–92
initial development/origins, 78–80
non-monetary benefits, 85–6
total value of, 92–5, 150–1
and tourism, 88–90
Killing, The, 2–3, 5, 78, 82, 91, 109, 119, 147, 148
Klamer, Arjo, 25–6, 31–2, 47
Klinger, Barbara, 109
Knox, David, 85, 130
Kondo, Koko, 89

Laboratory Adelaide project, 31
Langton, Marcia, 135
Lanser, Roger, 54, 57, 60
Larsson, Steig, 148
Le Nevez, Matthew, 77
Levy, Sandra, 144
Lewis, Steve, 98
Light, Alison, 72
Lilyhammer, 16–17
Looking Black, 133
Lost Flowers of Alice Hart, The, 19
Lotz, Amanda, 7–8, 11
Lovely, Louise, 92

Mabo, 119
McCarthy, Malarndirri, 133
McCorry, Paddy, 64, 65
McCulloch, R., 2
McCutcheon, M., 11
McIntyre, Paul, 92
McKee, Alan, 120
Madden, Vicki, 76, 78, 79, 80, 81, 82, 83, 85, 90, 91–2, 151
Maier, Rick, 8–9
Mailman, Deborah, 103, 113, 127, 129
Mankell, Henning, 148
Maslin, Sue, 68
Matchbox Pictures, 99–103, 151
Mathieson, Craig, 85–6, 129, 134
Meares, J., 58

merchandise, 65–6
Message Stick, 133
Metro magazine, 60–1, 66
Meyer, Jessica, 70
Meyrick, J., 33
Midnight Sun, 122, 147
Millar, Carly, 60–1, 71
Miss Fisher and the Crypt of Tears (film), 48, 58, 59, 62–4, 65, 74
Miss Fisher's Murder Mysteries, 5, 20, 48–73, **73–4**, 147
  audience response, 59–65, **74**, 74
  awards, 53–4, 57, **73–4**
  critical response, 60–2
  cultural value and impact, 68–74, 150
  development, production and post-production, 52–4
  fans, 62–5, 71
  financing, distribution and aggregation, 54–6
  flow-ons/externalities, 65–8
  idea origins/adaptation, 49–52
  non-monetary and intangible returns, 57–9
  total value of, 49, 73, 149–50
Miss S., 48, 56, 72, 149
Monkeys, The (advertising agency), 141
Murray, Steve, 88
music, 54, 106
Mystery Road, 5, 17, 117–37, **137**, 147
  audience and critical response, 129–31, **140**, 140
  awards, 126–7, 129, **138–9**
  cultural value and impact, 125, 126, 132–7
  development, production and post-production, 121–9
  financing, distribution and aggregation, 127–9
  flow-ons, 131–7
  Indigenous casting, 124–7, 152–3
  social value of, 126
  total value of, 152–3
Mystery Road (film), 117, 126, 131

national identity, 12, 15, 45, 119, 142, 144–5, 149; *see also* Australianness onscreen; Indigenous representation onscreen
National Indigenous Television Service *see* NITV
National Trust (Australia), 53, 66–8
Neill, A., 66
Netflix (USA), 17, 18, 19, 61; *see also* Lilyhammer; Secret City; Squidgame; *The Valhalla Murders*
Network Nine (Australia), 12; *see also* Halifax fp; Water Rats
Network Ten (Australia), 8, 12; *see also* Prisoner: Cell Block H
Neutze, Ben, 88–9
New York Post, The, 131
New York Times, The, 104
Nightingale, The (film), 92, 93
NITV (National Indigenous Television Service), 136; *see also* True Colours
Nixon, Henry, 77, 85
noir genre, 117; *see also* Australian noir; EcoNoir; Nordic Noir; outback noir
non-monetary benefits/returns, 41–2
  The Kettering Incident, 85–6
  Miss Fisher's Murder Mysteries, 57–9
Nordic Noir, 5–6, 15, 16, 147, 151
  and *The Kettering Incident*, 76–8, 80, 82, 86, 87, 89, 91–5, 150
  and *Mystery Road*, 117, 119, 122, 126, 130, 134, 135
  and *Secret City*, 96–7, 99–100, 101–3, 104, 107–14
Norwegian screen production, 16–17
NRK (Norway) *see Lilyhammer*

O'Brien, Dave, 28
Occupied, 98
Olafsson, David Oska, 17
Ólafsson, Ólafur Darri, 7, 17
O'Regan, Tom, 4, 12, 96
outback noir, 117, 118, 152

Page, Nathan, 62
Papandrea, Franco, 30–1
pay-per-view services *see* streaming platforms
Pedersen, Aaron, 126–7, 131, 133

Pedersen, Louise, 55
Penders, Monica, 102
Perkins, Rachel, 103, 117, 119, 120–1, 123, 131
Perkins, Robert, 53–4, 60
Perkins, Tyson, 121, 129
phronesis and the greater good, 22–3, 32, 37, 41, 47
Playmaker Media, 112
policy *see* Australian government policy
political issues, 100–1, 103, 107–8, 112–14, 117, 122–3, 134, 141; *see also* Indigenous cultural and political issues
Pollitt, Tony, 96
Porter, Michael, 32
post-production *see* production and post-production
Potter, Anna, 7–8
Prisoner: Cell Block H, 4, 96
Proctor, W., 2
production and post-production, 38–9
    The Kettering Incident, 81–4
    Miss Fisher's Murder Mysteries, 52–4
    Mystery Road, 121–9
    Secret City, 99–101
public service broadcasting, 2–3, 4, 5, 12, 15, 17, 40, 44, 119, 136
Purcell, Leah, 133

Quinn, Karl, 78, 92

Re, V., 117
Redfern Now, 119, 124, 125, 133–4
Reid, Daina, 52
Reijnders, Stijn, 90
Riley, Sally, 42, 119, 133–4
River, Dylan, 121, 129
Roscoe, Jane, 37
Rose, Rebecca, 61
Rosehaven, 83, 93
RÚV (Iceland) *see Trapped*; *The Valhalla Murders*
Ryan, Mark, 12

Sacco, P. L., 32
Samson and Delilah (film), 120

Sanderson, Coralie, 90
Sangston, Alex, 93
Saunders, Robert, 98
SBS (Special Broadcasting Service) (Australia), 3, 12, 17, 41, 45; *see also True Colours*
'Scandinavian Invasion', 2–3; *see also* Nordic Noir
Screen Australia, 10, 11, 23, 54, 55, 56, 68, 83, 84, 101, 127
    Indigenous TV Drama Production Fund, 128
    Seeing Ourselves 2 report (2023), 136
    Significant Australian Content (SAC) test, 13–14
Screen Canberra (ScreenACT), 102–3, 151
Screen Illawarra, 16
Screen NSW, 128
Screen Tasmania, 79, 83, 89, 93, 151
Screenwest, 127, 128
Sdraulig, Sandra, 57, 62
Secret City, 5, 75, 96–114, **115**, *116*, 147
    audience and critical response, 103–5, **115**, *116*
    awards, 105–7, **115**
    development and production, 99–101
    financing and screen industry, 101–3
    idea origins, 98–9
    politics and Nordic Noir, 112–14
    social and cultural value, 107–14
    total value of, 114, 151–2
    Under the Eagle, 103, 106–7
Sen, Ivan, 117, 121, 126, 127
Seven Network (Australia), 12
    7plus streaming service, 142
    see also Bony; *Homicide*
Sheehan, Vincent, 76, 79–80, 85, 86
Sheridan, Hugh, 111
Shiller, R. J., 32
Showcase *see* Foxtel (Showcase)
Simpkin, Greer, 119, 121, 124, 125–6, 127
Sky Atlantic *see Fortitude*
Smallacombe, Penny, 123
Smith, Terry, 25
Smit-McPhee, Siano, 76
soap operas, 4, 96, 144
social media, 62, 64, 86, 105

social value and impact, 25, 31, 44, 47, 141, 143, 148, 149, 150
    of *Miss Fisher's Murder Mysteries*, 49–50, 72
    of *Mystery Road*, 126
    of *Secret City*, 107–14
SoHo *see Wentworth*
South Australian Film Corporation, 8
Special Broadcasting Service *see* SBS
Spicer, Steve, 99, 100
sporting events, 142–3
Squid Game, 41
Stan (Australia), 6, 8, 18, *19*, 90; *see also The Gloaming*; *The Tourist*
Starz *see The Gloaming*
Steemers, Jeanette, 2
Story of the Kelly Gang, The (film), 4
streaming/subscription platforms, 1, 5, 10–11, 13, 16, 17, 18–20, *19*, *20*, 21, 40, 44, 142
    and *The Kettering Incident*, 75, 86, 90, 93
    and *Miss Fisher's Murder Mysteries*, 55–6, 59, 73
    and *Mystery Road*, 137
    and *Secret City*, 105
    see also ABC: iView; Acorn TV; Amazon Prime Video; Disney+; Foxtel Now; Hayu; Netflix; Seven Network: 7plus; Stan
Sun Herald, 92
Sundet, Vilde Schanke, 16
SVT (Sweden) *see The Bridge*; *Jordskott*; *Midnight Sun*
Swedish screen production, 89–90
Sweet Country (film), 120, 124
Swetman, David, 123
Sydney Morning Herald, The, 78, 87

Taddeo, Julie Ann, 61, 62, 68, 69, 70
Tansley, Rakel, 56
Tapsell, Miranda, 112
tax incentives, 9, 13–15, 143, 144
Tencent (China) *see Miss S.*
Thin Ice, 98, 108, 123, 147
Thornton, Warwick, 120, 142
Throsby, David, 25
Tiley, David, 56

Time magazine, 58
Tinic, Sara, 15, 101
Tonagh, Peter, 106
Torv, Anna, 97, 99, 105, 106, 108
Total Control, 103, 113–14
total value, 6, 21–47, 149–53
    accounting for, 36–7
    concept of, 21–32, *28*
    phronesis and the greater good, 22–3, 32, 37, 41, 47
    of television drama series, 32–47, *35*, *36*
    of *Miss Fisher's Murder Mysteries*, 49, 73, 149–50
    of *Mystery Road*, 152–3
    of *Secret City*, 114, 151–2
    of *The Kettering Incident*, 92–5, 149–50
tourism, 47, 63, 65, 78, 88–90, 102–3, 128
Tourist, The, 6–9, 14, 146
transgender characters, 109–12
Trapped, 17, 123
True Colours, 45, 118, 135
Turnbull, Sue, 63, 71
Turner, Graeme, 120, 136–7, 147
TV2 (Norway) *see Occupied*
TV4 (Denmark) *see Thin Ice*
24 (series), 97, 100
Twin Peaks, 78–9, 91, 109

Uhlmann, Chris, 98, 100
Uluru Dialogue, 141–2
Underbelly, 50
Unit 1, 3
Upfield, Arthur, 148

Valhalla Murders, The, 17
Van Zandt, Steven, 16
Variety magazine, 84, 90
Velthuis, O., 25
video on demand (VOD) *see* streaming platforms
viewers *see* audiences
violent crime, 110–11, 113, 122

WA Regional Film Fund, 128
Wade, A. M., 90
Wakefield, 42
Walker, Greg, 54

Walsh, Brian, 90
Wareham, Mark, 130
Water Rats, 5, 118
Watson, Reg, 4
Wegner, Ari, 82
Welland, Grant, 84
Wentworth, 96, 136
Werner, Joanna, 100
West Wing, The, 98
Western genre, 117, 118–19, 130, 134
Williams, Harry and Jack (Two Brothers), 8

Willoughby, Jim, 124
Wilson, Shaun, 83
Win, Penny, 75, 80, 81, 86, 96, 105, 106
women in the screen industry, 52, 68–9, 125; *see also* female characters
Wyllie, Dan, 107–8

Zarkesh, Anousha, 120, 124–6, 127, 142, 152–3
ZDF (Germany), 5; *see also The Killing*; *The Tourist*